Adolescence

Adulthood

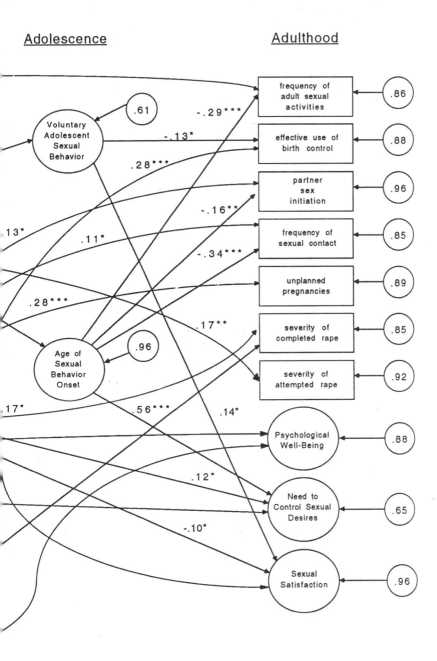

SEXUAL
ABUSE
AND
CONSENSUAL
SEX

This book is dedicated to my family: my mother, who taught me to be strong; my children, Lance and Lacey, who taught me to be gentle but firm; and Lewis, my husband and friend, who taught me that the best love that we could give each other was based in love for ourselves. God Bless You.

Gail Elizabeth Wyatt

I would like to thank Jamie Robertson for listening and rekindling the spark during times of frustration.

Monika H. Riederle

Sexual Abuse and Consensual Sex

Women's Developmental Patterns and Outcomes

Gail Elizabeth Wyatt

Michael D. Newcomb

Monika H. Riederle

SAGE Publications
International Educational and Professional Publisher
Newbury Park   London   New Delhi

Barnard

For information address:

 SAGE Publications, Inc.
2455 Teller Road
Newbury Park, California 91320

SAGE Publications Ltd.
6 Bonhill Street
London EC2A 4PU
United Kingdom

SAGE Publications India Pvt. Ltd.
M-32 Market
Greater Kailash I
New Delhi 110 048 India

Printed in the United States of America

Library of Congress Cataloging-in-Publication Data

Wyatt, Gail Elizabeth.
    Sexual abuse and consensual sex : women's developmental patterns
and outcomes / Gail Elizabeth Wyatt, Michael D. Newcomb, Monika H.
Riederle.
        p.   cm.
    Includes bibliographical references and index.
    ISBN 0-8039-4733-X (cloth)
    1. Women—Sexual behavior. 2. Adult child sexual abuse victims.
I. Newcomb, Michael D. II. Riederle, Monika H. III. Title.
HQ29.W853 1993
306.7'O82 1993   93-20712
                                                                CIP

93 94 95 96 10 9 8 7 6 5 4 3 2 1

Sage Production Editor: Megan M. McCue

Contents

Preface

This book includes some of the results that emerged from my life's work: 10 years of research on women's sexual and psychological functioning. The design of the study and its approach to data analysis were developed in an effort to gain a more comprehensive understanding of various dimensions of women's sexual experience that are rarely examined together in one study, while being sensitive to the manner in which these data should be collected. This work is being completed in an era of increasing concern about how to define sexual abuse, especially of children and adolescents, and whether survivors can accurately recall such incidents, many of which occurred many years earlier.

My experience as a professor at a medical school and as a psychologist who also has a private practice has convinced me that, although the effects of trauma do influence memory, we know very little about how to ask about potentially traumatic experiences and help people recall them in a research context. It will only be possible to obtain consistent information about sex-related experiences if we continue to refine the process of asking pertinent questions by conducting the kind of work that is presented here. Indeed, one of the main purposes of this research was to develop a methodology for asking sensitive questions in multiethnic samples of women who range in literacy and life experience. The methods used to collect these data and the questions asked are as important to the study as the findings. Far too often, professionals have not understood that not all sexual experiences are consensual and that what individuals learn about sex early in life is communicated in a variety of ways and experiences.

Data on sexual socialization and sexual experiences in childhood and adolescence were collected retrospectively from adult women. We must be aware of the fact that most of the sexual abuse incidents were not disclosed at the time they occurred and that many consensual sexual experiences are also considered to be a private matter. Retrospective methods are useful to identify some of the issues that we need to address to prevent the occurrence of sexual abuse and to understand consensual sex as much as possible. We refined the research design in an attempt to put our respondents at ease and to stimulate recall during the interviews, which were conducted at locations of their choice. Even with our efforts to facilitate memory without influencing what women remembered, it remains likely that experiences of abuse were under- rather than overreported. Respondents simply do not organize their life experiences as consensual or abusive. Only with careful questioning can they recall and discuss abusive incidents. Depending on the level of trauma and self-blame experienced, such questions may be extremely difficult for a survivor.

This study attempted to identify characteristics of women who range in their vulnerability to risky sexual decision making. Unfortunately, women who take sexual risks are often overlooked or misunderstood in our current legal, health, and mental health systems because we know so little about the factors that contribute to their behaviors. To shed more light on sexual abuse and consensual sexual experiences, as well as the predictors, correlates, and outcomes of women's sexual patterns, I conducted this study in 1983 through grants awarded by the National Institute of Mental Health. My colleagues Michael Newcomb, Ph.D., and Monika Riederle, M.A., worked tirelessly with me for the last five years to complete this book. Cindy Notgrass, M.A., and Jennifer Lawrence, M.D., provided valuable assistance with specific review chapters. We thoroughly investigated and reported the sexual development of women, both with and without sexual abuse histories, and the effects on sexual and psychological functioning over the life course in a multiethnic community sample of adult women. One of my personal goals is ensuring that research on one specific group of women is not used as a standard by which others will be gauged without examining the diversity of subjects' life experiences and incorporating them into research.

We used a developmental approach that allowed us to determine the impact of both voluntary and involuntary sexual experiences in childhood on adolescent sexual activities, as well the consequences of childhood and adolescent sexual experiences on women's sexual behavior in adulthood and the influence of adult sexual abuse. Important factors contributing to sexual socialization, such as the quality of life in the family of origin, the closeness of individual family members, parental messages about sex and sexuality, and sexual attitudes and beliefs conveyed by other sources of sexual socialization, along with parental demographic characteristics, were also included. This information created the context in which women learn about sexuality. There was once a time when being sexually active was assumed to have no consequences. This study, however, included several outcome variables, such as women's attitudes toward sex and sexuality in adulthood, including general well-being, sex guilt, and sexual satisfaction. A thorough review of the relevant literature that places these variables into the perspective of state-of-the-art research on female sexual functioning over the life course precedes the results. It is important to assess our current level of knowledge before challenging the reader with new and often contradictory findings.

To analyze our data, we used linear structural model equations that allowed us to investigate associations between many variables simultaneously. As a result, our study is unique in its scope and combination. It includes a developmental approach to sexual experience over the life course in a multiethnic community sample of women; in-depth, face-to-face data collection; and sophisticated statistical analyses.

Information is presented at several levels of detail and complexity to allow our readers to easily locate the findings that are of most interest to them. At the beginning of Chapters 13 and 15, the major findings are presented in overview form. As a whole, this book provides sound information about sexual development and sexual patterns, as well as suggestions for therapeutic interventions for women with and without histories of sexual abuse. It is a highly useful tool for a variety of clinicians who treat women with a wide range of sexual experiences, clinicians who conduct research and testify in court cases about sexual abuse, researchers who wish to study and use statistical models that allow for the examination of associations between a range of variables in one study, and lawyers who prosecute or defend sexual abuse cases. Most important, the book will give new scholars and clinicians a broader, more comprehensive view of sexuality. Others who will find this book of interest include professionals in training from various mental health-related fields who are seeking to acquire research skills, particularly in the area of sex research, as well as clinical expertise in developing appropriate treatment modalities for sexual and psychological problems, and those who wish to develop policy regarding assessment and treatment of survivors and their families.

We hope this book will stimulate more sophisticated and appropriately conducted research, treatment, and policy efforts in the area of sexual abuse and consensual sex. It certainly illustrates the importance of understanding how women's learning about sex influences their own sexual experiences, their feelings about themselves, and the decisions they make about their sexual and psychological health. Sex has a context. To view sexual behaviors without comprehending the factors that influence these actions is to exploit sex for its shock value rather than to understand it for its power to shape our lives.

■ Acknowledgments

The context in which I have conducted research has greatly influenced my ability to complete this book. There are many people who have been and continue to be supportive on many levels and make this work worthwhile.

Research of this scope and magnitude is expensive, time-consuming, and extremely difficult. In 1980, when I first obtained funds to conduct sex research within a multicultural perspective, there were many who did not think that my focus was important or necessary. However, that was not the case with the National Center for the Prevention and Control of Rape, headed by Mary Lystad at the National Institute of Mental Health (NIMH). I appreciate the input from the many project directors who guided and encouraged me for more than eight years. My NIMH Research Scientist Career Development Award provided me with the much-needed time to concentrate on this work. I deeply appreciate Leonard Lash, Ph.D., and Stan Schneider, Ph.D., from whom I gained the courage to pursue the award. They have also provided invaluable insights into my research and the direction of my career and still continue to do so. My support from the University of California at Los Angeles began with L. J. West, M.D. and chair of psychiatry, and Jim Simmons, M.D., chief of the child division; the support currently is provided by Gary Tischler, M.D., executive chair of psychiatry, and Marv Karno, M.D., chair of social psychiatry. Their endorsement of the research that I pursue makes it possible to devote myself to demanding projects such as this one.

My collaboration with Michael Newcomb, Ph.D., is long-standing. I sat on his dissertation committee years ago and recognized immediately that he was an exceptional person with an enormous ability to conceptualize the issues around sexual functioning. He is extremely sensitive to gender, ethnic concerns, and clinical issues in research, and we managed to get things done in a timely fashion in spite of almost impossible schedules. I have learned a great deal from him and value our friendship.

I have known Monika Riederle for five years, before she began her graduate studies at the California School of Professional Psychology. Now she is about to embark on her own career. We have worked on some difficult assignments together, and I have never seen her waver. She is committed to research and to sensitive clinical issues regarding abuse survivors.

Two other women worked on sections of this project. One is Jennifer Lawrence, M.D., and the other is Cindy M. Notgrass, M.A. Both of these colleagues conducted extensive reviews of certain portions of the literature, and Ms. Notgrass provided able assistance on Table 11.2. Their input was invaluable. Of course, this book would not have been completed without the very able secretarial support provided by Sarah Lowery. She is an integral part of our team that made the editorial process a little easier.

A data set as complicated as this one was made easily accessible by the excellent statistical consultation, guidance, and programming support offered by Don Guthrie, Ph.D., and Gwen Gordon, respectively. I appreciate their patience and willingness to always be of help.

We appreciate the editorial guidance of Terry Hendrix at Sage Publications. Terry has been a source of constant support and encouragement throughout this entire process. We also want to thank the reviewers and staff, who helped to get the manuscript into published form. We hope that you are as proud of the finished product as we are.

Finally, we are deeply indebted to the 248 women who had the courage to speak openly, face-to-face, about a topic that deserves more attention in our society. We wish them safe passage in life and the right to decide how to express their sexuality.

Gail Elizabeth Wyatt, Ph.D.

With assistance from

Monika H. Riederle, M.A.

PART I

Introduction

1

The Effects of Sexual Abuse on Women's Sexual and Psychological Functioning

There are many dimensions of women's sexual health we have yet to understand. Sexual health includes all aspects of psychosexual functioning: knowledge of one's anatomy and physiology; sex-related information, attitudes, and beliefs about acceptable sexual practices; and the variety, circumstances, and effects of consensual and nonconsensual sexual experiences encountered over the life course. Sexual health ranges from unhealthy to healthy and can influence subsequent sexual decision making, reproductive choices, and psychological well-being. Both the recognition and acceptance of oneself as a sexual being and a positive self-image facilitate the development and maintenance of sexual health.

One major reason why we have failed to teach women how to improve their sexual health is that we do not have a clear understanding of women's sexuality. Although research has partially examined some dimensions of sexual health, we have neglected to distinguish between consensual or voluntary sexual experiences in which a woman willingly participates and those that are abusive or nonconsensual and occur against her will or without her ability to give consent. The important difference between consensual and abusive experiences is that the former allow women to develop sexually, integrate their experiences psychologically, and explore their sexual desires and preferences according to their own level of readiness and comfort, whereas the latter do not.

Unfortunately, sexual activity frequently occurs without a woman's full knowledge of or consent to what is about to happen. Regardless of age, a child or woman may have no knowledge about what she is being asked to do, be unaware of the intent behind an invitation to sexual activity, and may have declined if she had completely understood what the initiator intended. Sexual activity may also be forced on a child or woman against her will, independent of her level of sexual experience. Furthermore, the perpetrator may be someone close to her, such as a family member, a long-term partner, a husband, or a friend. Factors such as an imbalance of power, an inability to understand the implications of activities that lie outside of one's range of cognitive development or experience, a need to maintain a relationship with a previously trusted perpetrator, feeling guilt or shame about experiencing sexual pleasure, and fearing retribution or harm to oneself or others may make it very difficult to refuse to participate in sexual acts proposed or instigated by the abuser.

Why is it important to separate consensual and abusive experiences? We need to examine how one type of experience influences the other and their impact on sexual functioning, self-perceptions, and psychological well-being. There is some evidence to suggest that early sexual experiences along with what we learn as children and teenagers about sex may adversely affect later psychological functioning (Greenwald & Leitenberg, 1990) and thus impair sexual functioning and decision making. Accordingly, sexually abusive experiences may be associated with subsequent consensual sexual patterns that increase women's risk of contracting sexually transmitted diseases (STDs) (Wyatt, 1988a). Women with histories of nonconsensual encounters are less likely to use barrier methods of contraception and tend to have multiple sexual partners and shorter sexual relationships (Wyatt, 1988a; Wyatt, Guthrie, & Notgrass, 1992), factors that may compromise sexual health and increase the risk of unintended and aborted pregnancies, as well as STDs. These women may also avoid inquiring about their partners' sexual histories, which could provide important information about potential sexual health risks (Wyatt & Lyons-Rowe, 1990). On the other hand, women who have the opportunity to develop and experiment with sex at their own pace may be better equipped to base decisions about sexual behaviors on some understanding of what is important, meaningful, and pleasurable to themselves as well as their partners. To date, few studies have examined the differential impact of abusive versus nonabusive sexual experiences over the life course on later sexual and psychological functioning (Wyatt, 1988b, 1992). One study of a volunteer sample of female incest survivors provided specific detail about the sexual experiences and problems that these women encounter (Westerlund, 1992). It did not examine, however, the effects of sexual abuse from a developmental perspective; it focused exclusively on effects of abuse in adulthood. On the whole, a comprehensive picture of the effects of various aspects of sexual socialization and their relationship to abusive versus nonabusive sexual experiences has yet to be developed.

The literature on human sexuality also lacks a thorough and clear description of a range of women's sexual experiences. There is a growing acknowledgement that we need far more information about women's general physical health, including variables such as age, education, income, ethnicity, culture, and past health risks. In comparison, we have been insufficiently concerned with women's sex-related health in spite of alarming current developments.

We know that women are at high risk for STDs. A disproportionate number of women suffer from serious long-term health consequences of gonorrhea and chlamydia, including pelvic inflammatory disease (PID), infertility, ectopic pregnancy, and postpartum infection [Centers for Disease Control (CDC), 1991]. Primary and secondary syphilis rates have also increased for women in ethnic minority groups (CDC, 1990). Furthermore, the percentage of women who have contracted HIV (human immunodeficiency virus) and AIDS (acquired immune deficiency symdrome) through heterosexual contact has increased by 20% since 1982 (Guinan & Hardy, 1987). Between April 1991 and March 1993, 15,679 women were reported to have contracted AIDS (CDC, 1993). Today, women are the fastest growing subgroup of AIDS victims (Ehrhardt, Yingling, & Wayne, 1991), and African-Americans and Latinas are at disproportionately high risk for AIDS infection (Cimons, 1990).

When women are infected with STDs, their unborn children are also at risk (Taylor, 1992). Indeed, many women do not know they are infected with STDs because they have no symptoms. Syphilis, for example, can be transmitted congenitally or may lead to stillbirths (CDC, 1991). Other bacterial and viral STDs can also affect infants in utero or at the time of birth (CDC, 1991). Herpes infection is estimated to occur in 1 out of 3,000 to 1 out of 20,000 newborn infants (Guinan, Wolinsky, & Reichman, 1985). Finally, the reported AIDS cases in U.S. children under 13 years of age totaled 4,249 by the end of March 1993, many of whom are African-American (CDC, 1993).

In addition to exposing women and their children to health- and life-threatening STDs, women's sexual practices and decision making may also result in unintended pregnancies and subsequent abortions. More than half of the approximately 6 million annual pregnancies are unintended, and approximately 1.6 million of them end in abortion (Silverman, Torres, & Forrest, 1987).

Sexual activity is the major channel of transmission for all of the above-mentioned STDs, and it also often leads to other unwanted outcomes. Naturally, prevention of high-risk sexual behavior is the best available means of reducing the incidence of HIV infection (Flora & Thorensen, 1988; National Academy of Science, 1986), other STDs, and unintended pregnancies.

Clearly, we need to understand the circumstances under which women's sexual activities take place and the decision-making processes that produce unplanned outcomes so that we can develop strategies that effectively prevent sexual risk taking as early in life as possible.

Understanding normal sexual functioning can help us identify those groups of women most likely to suffer from sex-related health problems at present and those most at risk of incurring them in the future. In addition, we may obtain useful information about potentially risky sexual practices that fall under the rubric of normal sexual functioning, thus allowing us to design interventions directed at minimizing these risks. Finally, beginning to understand normal sexual functioning over the life course can offer valuable clues about the nature of sexual experiences earlier in life, such as in childhood, that may contribute to the development of healthy sexual practices in adolescence and adulthood. Sex research, however, has developed as a field of research quite separate from child sexual abuse or adult rape (Wyatt, 1991b). It is time to integrate the research by providing a model to examine consensual and abusive experiences within one study and their interaction with one another.

Within the context of establishing a clear and comprehensive picture of sexual health, it is also important to examine the relationship between sexual and psychological functioning. As previously mentioned, early sexual experiences can have an adverse impact on later psychological functioning. This is very obvious for women who were sexually victimized as children or adults and have subsequently suffered from a range of psychological problems, including depression, anxiety, and social withdrawal, that are frequently found repercussions among sexual abuse survivors (Browne & Finkelhor, 1986; Finkelhor, 1988). Naturally, a woman may be depressed and anxious without ever having been sexually abused, which is also likely to affect her sexual functioning. The point relevant to this study, however, is that sexual and psychological functioning do not exist in a vacuum, and clearly affect each other.

■ The Impact of Sexual Experiences on Sexual and Psychological Functioning: Theoretical Underpinnings

A synthesis of conceptual and theoretical formulations that help explain some of the effects that both consensual and nonconsensual sexual experiences may have on sexual and psychological functioning is presented here. None of these theories of behavior fully consider the factors that influence both normal sexual development and that which occurs as a result of sexual abuse. Thus, we include several different conceptualizations that can account for both types of sexual experiences.

According to social learning theory, we learn a great deal about ourselves through social interactions with others (Goffman, 1967; Murphy, 1947). As children, we learn through direct instruction—which is usually provided by parents, peers, and religious or social institutions—as well as through the incidental learning in our social interactions (Powell, 1975). Thus we learn not only through direct social contact but also by simply observing others, modeling their behavior, and by learning vicariously from their mistakes or successes (Bandura, 1969).

The process of social learning continues throughout life and extends to a wide spectrum of life experiences. What we learn about sex, whether consensual or nonconsensual, is no exception. Many sexual experiences involve interpersonal contact and thus direct learning through social interaction. Not all social learning experiences that involve sex are appropriate or consensual, however. This is particularly true when sexual abuse occurs in childhood or adulthood. Abusive sexual experiences usually occur in the context of some form of interaction with another person. The length of time and the frequency with which the victim is in contact with the perpetrator vary from interaction to interaction.

We have adopted a developmental approach to traumatic experiences that separates incidents that occur early in life from those that take place in adulthood. Several conceptual frameworks describe the traumatic effects of child sexual abuse on the survivor, whereas others focus on the repercussions of rape in adulthood. The type of social learning that occurs when an individual is sexually abused is described in some of these models.

■ Conceptualizing Childhood Sexual Abuse

A few conceptualizations of childhood sexual abuse outcomes are consistent with social learning theory (i.e., Finkelhor & Browne, 1985; Summit, 1983). The effects associated with the trauma of child sexual abuse may be viewed as a result of the child's social learning in the context of inappropriate interactions with the offender and others in the child's environment.

The child's emotional and cognitive reactions as well as behaviors are sometimes developed in the course of her efforts to find a way to accommodate or avoid the abuse. Through the secrecy surrounding sexual abuse, as well as the often unsympathetic response from adults if disclosure is attempted, the young girl learns that she has done something shameful for which she deserves to be blamed (Finkelhor & Browne, 1985; Finkelhor, 1988). Furthermore, she learns that she cannot trust other people or exert control over them. She is often powerless to resist another's sexual suggestions or advances, especially if compliance results in acceptance and approval (Finkelhor & Browne, 1985). In her attempts to understand how and why she was selected to be involved in the abuse, the survivor frequently begins to feel stigmatized and develops negatively distorted perceptions and feelings about herself (Finkelhor & Browne, 1985; Summit, 1983, 1988). The experience of being powerless to control an aversive event can result in fear and anxiety, an impaired sense of self-efficacy, and an inability to cope with the world (Finkelhor, 1988; Finkelhor & Browne, 1985; Wyatt & Newcomb, 1990). In addition, the survivor learns developmentally inappropriate sexual behaviors, including misconceptions about certain body parts and sexual behaviors, as well as distorted sexual morals and values (Finkelhor, 1988; Finkelhor & Browne, 1985). She learns different arousal patterns and often associates frightening memories and even painful events with sexual activities. Furthermore, she may initiate and engage in sexual behaviors and arousal patterns with a frequency and intensity far beyond those of her peers.

Child sexual victimization, particularly incest, in effect can be considered a stressor early in life (see, for example, Lindberg & Distad, 1985). Its repercussions may not emerge full-blown until years later when survivors present with posttraumatic stress disorder symptomatology in addition to other effects (Finkelhor, 1988). Stressful experiences are mediated by two major psychological processes: appraisal and coping (Holroyd & Lazarus, 1982). *Appraisal* refers to the personal meaning the individual attributes to the stressful circumstances and involves a sense that something of value is jeopardized. *Coping* refers to the efforts made to control and overcome the stressful circumstances. When a child is sexually abused, she is likely to experience the demands imposed on her by the perpetrator, as well as any internal demands, as taxing or exceeding her resources for their management. In Holroyd and Lazarus's (1982) stress theory, the manner in which an individual copes is not necessarily rational and is influenced by "previous experiences in similar situations, generalized beliefs about the self and the environment, and the availability of personal and environmental resources" (p. 23). Having been inappropriately sexualized and traumatized, a child— who is likely to perceive herself as powerless and as damaged goods (Finkelhor & Browne, 1985)—may attempt to cope with the stressful experience of sexual abuse by spending excessive amounts of time focusing on or manipulating her own or others' genitalia (Finkelhor & Browne, 1985; Friedrich, 1988; Wheeler & Berliner, 1988), becoming depressed, or dissociating from memories of the event to the extent of developing multiple personality disorder (Putnam, 1989). Later in life, she may experience sexual problems, such as an aversion to sex, flashbacks during sex, and difficulty with arousal and orgasm (Briere, 1984a,b; Courtois, 1979; Finkelhor, 1988; Langmade, 1983; Tsai & Wagner, 1978). She may also continue to repress her own sexual urges and try to become as asexual as possible. Although sexually abusive experiences may result in immediate attempts to avoid the perpetrator and sex in general, survivors may develop accelerated sexual patterns later in life (Friedrich, 1988). Furthermore, survivors may experience other difficulties, such as drug abuse and uncertainty about their sexual orientation. If they are sexually active, their selection of sexual partners and sexual practices may be influenced by early abuse experiences and attributions to those incidents.

The social learning that occurs when a child is sexually abused, including the negative effects on the child's psyche, is reinforced when, implicitly or explicitly, the child is given the message that the consequences of noncompliance will be more devastating than all the negative effects associated with the abuse. This idea is continuously strengthened in the typical abuse situation and becomes more powerful as the molestation continues over a prolonged period of time. Furthermore, being in a sexually abusive relationship may provide the only kind of "love," attention, and approval the child receives and, for that matter, the only relationship in which the child is involved. Consequently, sex with a perpetrator becomes secondary to gaining approval and affection that may not be available elsewhere.

Finally, abuse that occurs within the context of a dysfunctional family system is likely to confirm basic assumptions the child makes, such as assuming herself worthless and powerless, as well as other conclusions she may reach about herself and people in her environment. Her family may be estranged and lack close interpersonal relationships between and among family members. Other dimensions of family dysfunction, including physical battering, drug and alcohol abuse, and antisocial behavior, may also be present (Cicchetti & Howes, 1991). In this type of family environment, the role of being "special," or being able to expect and demand special treatment, may sometimes outweigh, or at least seemingly mediate, the negative aspects of being victimized.

■ Conceptual Frameworks of the Effects of Rape

Posttraumatic stress disorder (PTSD) has been associated not only with child sexual abuse but also with rape. Burgess (1983) and Putnam (1985, 1989), among others, have significantly contributed to our understanding of the rape trauma syndrome and its relationship to PTSD. This syndrome is also considered to be a stress reaction to a life-threatening situation. It consists of somatic, cognitive, psychological, and behavioral symptoms, including fear, anxiety, depression, guilt, memory impairment, an inability to concentrate, intrusive imagery, nightmares, other disturbances in sleep patterns, an exaggerated startle response, hyperalertness, numbing of responsiveness to and decreased involvement with the environment, and avoidance of activities that might trigger recollections of the rape incident (Burgess, 1983).

Much of the work in the area of rape trauma has been based on a behavioral conditioning model (Kilpatrick, Veronen, & Resick, 1982; Koss & Burkhart,

1989) that explains rape-related symptoms as the result of classical and higher-order conditioning (Koss & Burkhart, 1989). Thus, the initial rape experience is considered to be an unconditioned stimulus with life-threatening aspects that evokes unconditioned responses of extreme fear and anxiety. Other stimuli present during the rape, such as objects, persons, or events, often become associated with this unconditioned stimulus and also subsequently acquire the capacity to evoke fear and anxiety. As a result, stimuli conditioned in this manner are capable of producing conditioned responses of fear and anxiety through their association with rape-induced terror. In addition, these fear and anxiety responses may be further generalized to stimuli similar to the conditioned stimuli present during the rape (Kilpatrick et al., 1982). Although this model takes into account behavioral processes, it frequently does not pay sufficient attention to the complex cognitive and emotional processes that the survivor faces in the aftermath of rape (Koss & Burkhart, 1989; Wyatt, Newcomb, & Notgrass, 1990).

According to Koss and Burkhart (1989), three major factors influence the cognitive appraisals and coping of rape survivors. First, the survivor must cope with the shattered beliefs about her sense of safety and invulnerability in a world that was presumed not to harm her. Second, her positive perception of self is called into question. And third, society's response to victimization is often less than understanding and far from sympathetic.

This is especially true for African-American women, who frequently doubt their own ability to defy the odds that they, as black women, will be victimized (Wyatt, 1992). A survivor may find herself in a "cognitive-emotional paralysis" (Koss & Burkhart, 1989, p. 32) that arises from conflict between her subjective experience of having been intimately violated and victimized and the response of her external social environment. The most common solution to this conflict is the denial of the reality of the rape experience, including a failure to anticipate or recognize sexual needs. Self-blame is another harmful strategy that survivors often use to cope with the rape and its aftereffects (Koss & Burkhart, 1989; Wyatt, Newcomb, & Notgrass, 1990; Wyatt, Notgrass, & Gordon, in press).

Similar to childhood sexual abuse, rape also involves social learning. Implicit in the rape situation is the threat of being harmed or killed, an almost certain element of assault likely to trigger extreme fear in most women. The manner in which a woman behaves under such life-threatening circumstances may reinforce negative cognitions she may have about herself and her behavior in other situations. These cognitions may simply be strengthened by what the survivor perceives to be the consequence of her behavior—and that is to survive the rape, rather than succumb to it. As a result of such cognitions about repeated acts of abuse, survivors may be unable to develop alternative coping strategies that prevent revictimization with the same or other perpetrators (Koss & Burkhart, 1989; Wyatt, Guthrie, & Notgrass, 1992).

Obviously, we need to go beyond understanding how women who report the effects of these experiences differ from women who do not report non-consensual sexual experiences. If we examine the effects of sexual experiences across the life course, we must recognize that the developmental period in which a certain experience occurs can have differential lasting effects. Perhaps with more empirical documentation we can begin to broaden our understanding of how sexual experiences recalled as early as in childhood and adolescence can reinforce sexual experiences and psychological adjustment later in life.

■ Summary of the Current Study

This study develops a model for examining the relationships among a range of psychosexual factors, including early sexual socialization and sexual experiences, and women's subsequent sexual functioning during the life course, including sexual satisfaction and psychological well-being. The sample consists of women who have mostly been involved in heterosexual relationships. Some of the sexual behaviors in which these women have engaged compromised their sexual health and thus increased their risk of STD transmission, including AIDS, as well as unintended and aborted pregnancies.

To obtain a complete and thorough description of women—ranging from those who function well sexually and psychologically and engage in relatively safe sexual practices to those whose sexual and psychological functioning increase health risks and endanger their lives—community samples are most appropriate and will yield more generalized results. Community samples not only capture the variety of women and sexual experiences found in a large-scale epidemiological survey, but also include women who are unwilling or unable to seek professional services. Given that community samples of women are most likely to be representative of the population of women in general, findings gleaned from such groups have the potential to provide clear guidelines for broad-based interventions directed at changing high-risk sexual practices, as well as identify some of the psychological sequelae for women who engage in risky sexual behaviors.

The sample-selection process was also influenced by the ethnic diversity of Los Angeles County and the United States. It is essential to avoid establishing the sexual practices of only one ethnic group as the norm by which to identify healthy or unhealthy sexual and psychological functioning. To clarify potential differences between ethnic groups and design methods of intervention that incorporate sociocultural and ethnic issues, two ethnic groups were included in this study: African-American and white women. The study is limited to only two ethnic group community samples in order to develop a methodology appropriate for these groups, as well as to provide a basis for suitable research with other ethnic groups. This approach has a distinct advantage over research that does not attempt to identify ethnic or sociocultural group similarities or differences.

Finally, by choosing to study only women, we stand to gain much-needed information not only about women's sexual and psychological functioning, but also about their perspectives on relationships with men, as well as information about factors that may affect women's sexual health and decision-making processes. We are ever mindful of the fact that many women in heterosexual relationships are not the powerful breadwinner, or decision maker, in matters of family life and functioning. As a result, women are often in a precarious position, needing to learn how to advocate for themselves and their children, while accommodating in their relationships with others on whom they are dependent.

The women who participated in this study were at least 18 years of age. Therefore, data about their childhood and adolescent sexual experiences were obtained retrospectively. We are aware of the potential disadvantages of this type of data collection, such as incomplete or vague memory (Wyatt, 1985, 1990a). We believe, however, that data gathered retrospectively also have clear advantages. First, the bias of obtaining parental consent from minors who may have been abused by their parents was eliminated. Second, it is not uncommon that the passage of time permits more emotional distance from various life experiences and allows for greater clarity of both child and adolescent experiences. Retrospection may also enable respondents to provide more comprehensive accounts of events that occurred earlier in life. Furthermore, we were interested above all in women's own perceptions of their sexual socialization and sexual experiences. Their accounts allow us to understand what was important to them personally and what they felt influenced their sexual health.

We believe that the best method of obtaining information that is as accurate as possible and allows for a clarification and definition of sexual terms, anatomy, and physiology is the face-to-face interview. This method allows for rapport between interviewer and respondent to be established that, if successful, is likely to generate greater and more personal disclosure than a questionnaire self-report or telephone survey (Wyatt, 1990a; Wyatt, Lawrence, Vodounon, & Mickey, 1992).

Hopefully, this approach to research with the models and results presented will provide (a) direction for educational and therapeutic intervention and future research by identifying some of the most important correlates and predictors of abusive and nonabusive sexual experiences; (b) information about the consequences of sexual behaviors associated with a higher risk of contracting STDs and with effective rather than ineffective contraceptive use; and (c) assistance in minimizing unintended and aborted pregnancies. To develop our model, a nonexhaustive review of the most rigorous research findings, primarily of the last 20 to 30 years, will place into context what is currently understood about sexual socialization as well as consensual and nonconsensual sexual experiences and some of the psychological variables related to health and the development of coping strategies. Much of this research was reviewed for its inclusion of multiethnic samples and the relevance of such findings for those groups. Unfortunately, information specifying the national origin of the groups classified as "black" or "white" was rarely given. Therefore, we use these classification terms loosely in our review of the literature and consider African-descended people to have been included as blacks and European-descended people as whites. It is important to remember, however, that other ethnic groups may also have been represented in the samples of the research that will be reviewed under the broad classification terms of black and white.

PART II

What We Know About Sexual Behavior

2

Voluntary or Consensual
Childhood Sexual Behavior

With Cindy M. Notgrass

In the next three chapters, we review some of the empirical research on female sexual development over the life course. Such a review is important because it provides a backdrop to some of the sexual behavior patterns that emerge from sexual and socialization experiences during the course of development from childhood to adulthood. This information gives us an idea about some of the sexual practices that are typical or normative for women as they develop sexually. Throughout our review, we focus on the specific variables we investigated in the study. Each review section is concluded by a description of ethnic differences, a critique of the literature, and a brief chapter summary for the reader who prefers more general to detailed information. The information in the review may be of particular interest to clinicians or researchers who wish to develop an expertise in female sexual functioning.

This chapter presents a nonexhaustive overview of what we know about the sexual behavior of children during the early and middle childhood period. Because these descriptions may reflect a process of normal sexual development and functioning in children, we anticipate finding similar patterns in this study. Sexual behavior in adolescence and adulthood will be discussed separately in the two subsequent chapters.

■ Sexual Arousal, Self-Exploration, Masturbation, and Orgasm

The myth that children are nonsexual beings has long been dispelled. Today we know that children of all ages, even newborn infants, respond to a great variety of sensations that they experience as sexually stimulating (Kinsey, Pomeroy, Martin, & Gebhard, 1953; Martinson, 1977, 1980; Rutter, 1971).

Newborn female babies experience vaginal lubrication, and a male may have an erection when he is still in his mother's womb (Kinsey et al., 1953; Langfeldt, 1981; Martinson, 1980). Indeed, sexual arousal in infants may occur as often as 10 to 20 times a day (Langfeldt, 1981).

Naturally curious about their bodies (Kleeman, 1975; Langfeldt, 1981), young children begin to touch or rub their genitals once they have developed the necessary motor coordination (Masters, Johnson, & Kolodny, 1992). Usually, they start to explore their genitals between 7 and 18 months of age (Kleeman, 1975) and may continue to engage in genital play and masturbation during early and middle childhood (Bakwin, 1974; Friedrich, Grambsch, Broughton, Kuiper, & Beilke, 1991; Martinson, 1977; Rutter, 1971). Provided that retrospective data from adult women are reliable, it appears that not all girls explore their bodies and sexual responses in childhood. In one study, 77% of women had engaged in self-touch by age 10 (Kinsey et al., 1953), whereas in another study only 35% to 40% of women under age 13 reported having done so (Wyatt, Peters, & Guthrie, 1988a, 1988b).

In addition to sexual arousal and masturbation, children are also capable of experiencing orgasm, although it remains uncertain at which age they develop this ability. Some studies found that infant girls are able to masturbate to orgasm before one year of age (Kinsey et al., 1953; Martinson, 1980) and suggest that the infants' orgasms do not differ in any aspect from those of adult women (Kinsey et al., 1953). Yet other research documents that the genital play of babies in the first two years of life does not lead to a climax and that children do not intentionally masturbate to orgasm before two-and-a-half to three years of age (Kleeman, 1975).

Once the behavior is discovered, young girls use a variety of methods to masturbate. Most commonly, they manipulate their genitalia, usually the clitoris, with their fingers. Some girls also masturbate with objects that they have found to stimulate them to orgasm by coincidence, such as a bedpost (Langfeldt, 1981). The second most common technique involves rhythmically moving the pelvis while lying face down on the bed, often rubbing against a toy, a blanket, or another object (Kinsey et al., 1953).

As children's interest in their genitals continues to increase between two and five years of age (Rutter, 1971), they engage in sexual behaviors such as self-stimulation and exhibitionism more and more frequently. At some point during the years three to five, sexual activity reaches a peak and then appears to decrease until age 12 (Friedrich et al., 1991). This does not mean, however, that children's sexual interest actually diminishes during this period of sexual behavior latency (e.g., Masters et al., 1992). Children may even remain sexually active, although not overtly so. A gradual increase in mas-

turbatory activity as well as opposite- and same-gender play prior to adolescence has also been described (Kinsey et al., 1953). These seemingly contradictory findings may be explained by the process of socialization children
undergo as they progress from infancy to childhood and as their world
expands beyond the family. It is likely that children learn that public displays
of sexual interest and activity are not condoned and therefore conceal them
more effectively during the prepubertal period (Rutter, 1971). Thus, sexual
exploration before adolescence may become associated with both secrecy and
the notion of privacy that extend into adolescence.

■ Childhood Sexual Play With Opposite and Same Gender

Beginning with self-exploration, children move on to explore others. They
become curious about their parents' and playmates' bodies (Kinsey et al., 1953)
and start to engage in sex play with other children. Much of sex play consists
of "Mom and Dad" and "Doctor" games (Gundersen, Melas, & Skar, 1981;
Kinsey et al., 1953; Newson & Newson, 1968) and involves undressing, showing
one's genitals to another, and exploring one anothers' bodies and sexual
organs (Gundersen et al., 1981; Kinsey et al., 1953; Masters et al., 1992).
Young children also imitate adult sexual practices in their play (Kinsey et al.,
1953). They may mount each other or present their genitalia as early as age
two (Langfeldt, 1981). It is much rarer that they engage in sexual activities
that are more aggressive, such as oral exploration of others' genitals or insert-
ing objects into the vagina or anus (Friedrich et al., 1991; Kinsey et al., 1953).
Nevertheless, a significant number of children appear to experience some
form of incomplete coitus (Kinsey et al., 1953; Masters et al., 1992).

Sex play often begins around age four (Newson & Newson, 1968) and may
continue during preadolescence and early adolescence (Leitenberg, Greenwald,
& Tarran, 1989). One in five (Wyatt et al., 1988a, 1988b) to one in three
women report having engaged in preadolescent sex play with children of the
opposite and same gender (Kinsey et al., 1953). Although they are common,
heterosexual play experiences tend to occur infrequently and rarely develop
into steady patterns (Kinsey et al., 1953). During the early school years,
children become gradually and increasingly interested in sexual activity with
the opposite sex. In contrast, interest in same-sex play appears to occur as a
transient phase or as an isolated event during early adolescence in approximately one in four female children (Rutter, 1971).

■ Ethnic Differences in
Voluntary Childhood Sexual Behavior

Orgasmic experience may differ slightly for black and white children. Gebhard and Johnson (1979) analyzed the Kinsey data on bisexual behavior from ages 3 to 12 for different ethnic and educational groups. They found that slightly more than 90% of white college and white noncollege women had their first orgasm through masturbation, whereas 100% of black college women experienced their first orgasm by masturbating at these same ages. It is difficult, however, to generalize these findings to larger and current populations. Given the sampling limitations found with the Kinsey data (Wyatt et al., 1988a, 1988b), we do not have adequate information about ethnic differences in childhood sexual practices.

■ Critique of the Literature
on Childhood Sexual Behavior

Very little empirical, prospective research has examined some of the developmental stages of sexual behavior (Money & Ehrhardt, 1972). In the area of voluntary childhood sexual experiences, the dearth of information is particularly conspicuous. Childhood has been referred to as "the last frontier in sex research" (Money, 1976) because few reliable data exist about sexual behavior during this important period of development and findings are often subject to guesswork and inference (Masters et al., 1992). The available data are primarily based on relatively unstructured clinical observations of children (Kleeman, 1975; Langfeldt, 1981) or on adults' retrospective self-reports (Gebhard & Johnson, 1979; Kinsey et al., 1953; Langfeldt, 1981; Leitenberg et al., 1989). Both of these data-collection methods have distinct disadvantages when we consider the need for valid research on typical childhood sexual experiences and development. Often the criteria used for direct clinical observations of children's sexual behavior are not clearly specified, which compromises the objectivity of findings. Assessments of adults' recollections, on the other hand, are clearly biased by memory performance error, yielding limited and possibly distorted information. Most people do not readily recall details of early life events unless they were unique for them (Bradburn & Davis, 1984; Cash & Moss, 1972) or unless they are prompted to recall them with specific interview techniques. Adults may also give distorted reports when they exaggerate or omit certain information out of embarrassment or a desire to seem "normal" (Masters et al., 1992).

Sample selection is another shortcoming of this research. Based on Rutter's (1971) review of the literature, Friedrich et al. (1991) point out that many findings on normal sexual development and behavior are anecdotal or based on small samples. This description of the research is characteristic of studies on childhood sexual behavior (see, for example, Kleeman, 1975; Langfeldt, 1979, 1981).

Furthermore, analyses of data obtained in studies of childhood sexual behavior are largely descriptive and do not examine correlates of behavior. Finally, environmental factors—such as ethnic, cultural, religious, economic, and regional differences in childhood sexual behaviors—have rarely been examined in this area of research.

■ Summary: What We Know About Voluntary Childhood Sexual Behavior

A pattern of children's sexuality that changes in accordance with physiological development and socialization processes emerges from our limited fund of knowledge on childhood sexual behavior. Apparently, many children progress from exploring their own bodies and stimulating their own genitalia in infancy to exploring their playmates' bodies and sex organs in early childhood. Thus, learning about their sexual responses partially gives way to a growing interest in other children of the same or opposite gender. Following a peak of sexual activity by age five, children tend to become increasingly more secretive or private about their sexual behaviors and interests as they approach adolescence and learn that society tends to disapprove of overt sexual practices.

3

Adolescent Consensual Sexual Behavior

With Jennifer Lawrence

In this chapter, we will review some of the currently available information on voluntary sexual behavior during the next stage of development: adolescence. We have intentionally omitted studies describing sexual practices of runaway and homeless adolescents, emancipated minors living away from home, and teenage prostitutes or gang members. Most of the women in our study lived at home in childhood and adolescence, unlike these specific groups of teenagers noted above. Therefore, the literature on normative sexual behavior in adolescents is more likely to reflect what we may expect in terms of the sexual practices of this sample.

■ Age of Onset

Masturbation, Necking, Petting, and Orgasm in Adolescent Women

As children mature, their bodies go through age-appropriate physiological and hormonal changes that propel them into adolescence, a period of heightened sexual interest in others. It is well documented that adolescents engage in a variety of sexual behaviors that range from self-touching (Kinsey, Pomeroy, Martin, & Gebhard, 1953) and masturbation (Kinsey et al., 1953; Sorensen, 1973; Wyatt, 1989) to necking and petting (Kinsey et al., 1953; Wyatt, 1989), and from achieving orgasm (Kinsey et al., 1953; Wyatt, 1989) to all forms of intercourse. Naturally, not all adolescents participate equally in all sexual activities. Approximately 33% to 40% of women report ever having masturbated by age 17 or 19 (Kinsey et al., 1953; Sorensen, 1973; Wyatt, 1989), approximately 20% to 40% of 15- and 16-year-olds have been involved in petting (Kinsey et al., 1953; Wyatt, 1989), and 10% to 25% of women appear to have experienced orgasm by age 15 (Kinsey et al., 1953; Wyatt, 1989). In one study, 40% of women reported that they had climaxed during petting (Kolodny, 1980). Some research suggests that more sexually advanced petting begins for most female adolescents just before age 17 (Darling & Davidson, 1986).

Age of Onset of Intercourse

Necking and petting in adolescence often lead to first intercourse. Today, approximately one in two adolescent women has experienced sexual intercourse by either age 17 (Planned Parenthood, 1986; Reinisch, Sanders, & Ziemba-Davis, in press; Rubenstein & Tavris, 1987; Wyatt, 1989) or age 19 (Bachrach & Horn, 1988; Ehrhardt, Yingling, & Warne, 1991; Hofferth, Kahn, & Baldwin, 1987; Ostrov, Offer, Howard, Kaufman, & Meyer, 1985; Thornton & Camburn, 1987; Zelnik & Kantner, 1980), regardless of ethnicity when other demographic sample characteristics are controlled (Wyatt, 1989). Adolescents who grow up in low socioeconomic status and single-parent homes tend to engage in sexual activity early (Wyatt, 1989). For example, in a sample of inner-city adolescent women, the mean age of first intercourse was 14.8 years (Jaffe, Seehaus, Wagner, & Leadbeater, 1988).

Apparently, many young women continue to have intercourse after their first experience (Hofferth, 1990), even though they may do so infrequently and often without using contraceptives. Adolescents are notorious for their nonuse of birth control (see, for example, Morrison, 1985). As a consequence, they are at risk for unwanted pregnancies (see, for example, Panzarine & Santelli, 1987) and may experience social repercussions, such as school failure and dropout, economic dependency, unwed motherhood, and failed teenage marriage if pregnancy does result (McCarthy, 1981). In addition, adolescents are a high-risk group for HIV infection (DiClemente, 1990); in fact, the virus has already spread within that group to an alarming degree. Although we do not know exactly how many teenagers are HIV-positive, the number of 13- to 24-year-olds diagnosed with AIDS increased 77% since 1989 (Kantrowitz et al., 1992). As a result of their longer-term exposure to sexual activity, adolescent women who begin to engage in intercourse at younger ages than their peers who delay sex may face a higher risk of becoming pregnant and contracting STDs, including AIDS. An early onset of intercourse in preadolescence or early adolescence has also been associated with a higher number of intercourse partners in young adulthood and longer relationships involving intercourse (Leitenberg et al., 1989).

■ Number of Sex Partners

Having sex with multiple partners, however, may further increase young women's risk for unwanted pregnancies and STDs (Hofferth, 1990). Approximately half of girls up to age 19 have had one sexual partner (Thornton & Camburn, 1987; Zelnik & Kantner, 1980), whereas the other half of adolescent women report two or more partners. Only a relatively small minority of adolescent women have had four and more sexual partners (Zelnik, 1983). Adolescents who come from lower socioeconomic status (SES) backgrounds tend to have more sexual partners (Wyatt, 1989).

■ Ethnic Differences in Voluntary Adolescent Sexual Behavior

Some ethnic differences have emerged with respect to adolescent sexual activity. Black adolescents are less likely to engage in self-touch, masturbation, necking, and petting than their white peers (Wyatt, 1989). On the other hand, blacks have historically been more likely to experience first intercourse at younger ages (Bachrach & Horn, 1988; Hofferth et al., 1987; Planned Parenthood, 1986; Zelnik & Kantner, 1980). This difference, however, appears to be more a function of family income and structure (single-parent homes) than of ethnicity per se (Wyatt, 1989). Few studies control for the demographic characteristics of adolescents in studies of first coitus. When these variables are controlled, significant differences in age at onset of coitus by ethnicity diminish (Wyatt, 1989).

Ethnic differences are also found in the number of partners and extent of sexual activity during adolescence, but the research is contradictory. In some studies, white teenagers report more frequently that they have had only one partner compared to their black cohorts. In 1979, approximately half of 15- to 19-year-old white women had one partner only, as opposed to two-fifths of black teenage women (Zelnik, 1983). Similarly, white adolescents were twice as likely as black teens to report intercourse only once in 1982 (Hofferth, 1990). These findings are consistent with a study that found black unmarried women at age 14 and 15 to be approximately twice as likely to ever have been sexually active than their white peers and approximately 1.5 times as likely at ages 16 and 17 (Alan Guttmacher Institute, 1981). Other evidence also exists. Wyatt (1989) found that when demographic characteristics such as education and income were controlled, white adolescent women had more sexual partners than their black cohorts. In another study, black teens engaged in intercourse less frequently compared to their white peers, even though they were more likely to have had intercourse than white women (Zelnik, 1983).

A final difference between the two ethnic groups concerns the relationship between age and number of sexual partners during adolescence. White teenage women tend to have a slightly higher number of sex partners as they become older than do black adolescent women (Zelnik & Kanter, 1972). Such conclusions are, however, problematic because they are often based on a very narrow range of ages. For example, when greater differences in ages of adolescents were compared in a sample of white men and women, a steady increase in sexual activity with age emerged overall, as would be expected (Newcomb, Huba, & Bentler, 1983). It is obvious that we need more research on the sexual experiences of adolescents from diverse ethnic groups and economic backgrounds if we are to gain a clear understanding of how ethnicity contributes to sexual behavior differences in adolescence.

■ Critique of the Literature on Adolescent Sexual Development

The bulk of research on the sexual experiences of adolescents focuses on first intercourse, unintended pregnancies, and other related health outcomes. Other aspects of adolescent sexual activity, such as masturbation, orgasm, and courtship behaviors involving necking and petting have received little attention (Kinsey et al., 1953; Newcomb, Huba, & Bentler, 1986; Sorensen, 1973; Wyatt, 1989). Such gaps in our knowledge naturally limit our understanding of adolescents as sexual beings (Diepold & Young, 1979).

We also know little about how often adolescents engage in various sexual behaviors (Barrett, 1980; Zelnik & Kantner, 1980), in spite of the fact that such information may be essential to nationwide efforts to identify those patterns that lead to high rates of pregnancy among teenagers and infection with STDs. One of the only studies that examined average frequencies of a number of adolescent sexual activities, including masturbation, was conducted in Sweden (Lewin, 1982). We did not include data from this study in our review, however, because these findings cannot be generalized to American adolescents.

In addition to lacking information about important aspects of adolescent sexual behavior, the existing research suffers from other limitations. Unfortunately, respondents' ethnicities have not been specified in various studies (Aldous, 1983; Barrett, 1980; Libby, Gray, & White, 1978; McNab, 1976; Mirande, 1968; Murstein & Holden, 1979), which limits findings to describing overall patterns that may, in actuality, be influenced by ethnic and cultural differences. Studies that have examined different ethnic groups often focus on age at first intercourse and the number of adolescent sexual partners (see, for example, Kaats & Davis, 1970; Ostrov et al., 1985), but neglect to control for confounding variables, such as socioeconomic status, and the voluntary or involuntary nature of adolescents' sexual experiences (Wyatt, 1989; Zelnik & Kantner, 1980). Furthermore, age at first intercourse is frequently used to identify adolescents who are sexually active. Although most young women who have intercourse once continue to be sexually active (Hofferth, 1990), first coitus may be a relatively isolated event for some adolescent girls and not necessarily set the stage for increased sexual activity until years later (Masters et al., 1992). In a statewide survey in Minnesota, for example, most teenagers engaged in intercourse relatively infrequently (a few times a year or less) after their first experience (Blum, 1989). Teenagers in steady, long-term relationships may have sex more often, depending on whether they can secure privacy for themselves. Without adequate follow-up studies, however, it is impossible to determine how many adolescents continue to have sex after their first intercourse experience and how many remain sexually inactive for prolonged periods of time.

The sampling and data-collection methods most commonly used in research on adolescent sexual behavior further limit our existing fund of knowledge. Many studies are conducted with college students (Barrett, 1980; Kaats & Davis, 1970; Murstein & Holden, 1979), who do not represent the general population. In fact, only one in three Americans obtains an education beyond high school graduation (Bureau of Census, 1990). Some studies have used high school students, often with the intent of evaluating a pregnancy prevention program (Ostrov et al., 1985; Zabin, Hirsch, Smith, Streett, & Hardy, 1986), and only a few studies have been conducted with community samples stratified by ethnicity (Newcomb et al., 1986; Thornton & Camburn, 1987; Wyatt, 1989; Zelnik & Kantner, 1980). The latter are likely to yield more representative data on adolescent sexual behavior. These studies would also be more likely to include teenagers who drop out of school, are gay, are homeless, or grow up away from their families and may be at highest risk for unintended pregnancies and thus most in need of pregnancy and HIV prevention. Naturally, longitudinal studies of sexual development would be optimal, but they have yet to be conducted.

In terms of data collection, the most popular method for studying adolescent sexual behavior is the self-report questionnaire (for example, see Barrett, 1980; Kaats & Davis, 1970; Murstein & Holden, 1979; Newcomb et al., 1986; Thornton & Camburn, 1987). Self-report measures, however, presuppose literacy in the English language, unless translations are provided, as well as familiarity with sexual terminology (Wyatt, Lawrence, Vodounon, & Mickey, 1992). Furthermore, self-report questionnaires do not allow the respondent and the interviewer to establish rapport, which is important when sensitive questions, such as those about sexual behavior, are asked. If respondents' discomfort is not monitored and addressed, they may give incomplete or inaccurate answers (Wyatt, Lawrence, Vodounon, & Mickey, 1992). With adolescent women who may feel uneasy discussing their sexual behaviors and may know little about sex and sexuality, face-to-face interviews that allow them to build trust and receive clarification of terms are essential.

■ Summary: What We Know About Voluntary Adolescent Sexual Behavior

Adolescence is a phase of life when most teenagers continue sexual experimentation and begin intercourse, although they appear to do so less often and with fewer sexual partners than do adults. An early age at onset of intercourse and the probability of multiple partners are influenced by growing up in single-parent homes and in families of low socioeconomic status, as well as by other problems that are not included in this study, such as poor school achievement, substance abuse, or other psychological issues. First intercourse in preadolescent years or in early adolescence is also associated with having multiple partners in young adulthood, whereas ethnic minority status is not clearly related to an early onset of intercourse when demographic variables are controlled. Research on adolescent samples needs to be conducted with face-to-face interviews that allow teenagers to build a rapport with their interviewers and to have questions about sexual terminology answered if we are to obtain accurate and useful information about adolescent sexuality.

4

Adulthood Consensual Sexual Behavior

As adolescent women make the transition to adulthood, some patterns of sexual behavior may change, while others stay the same. In this chapter, we present an overview of a variety of adult women's voluntary sexual experiences. We also discuss sexual initiation and birth control use, as well as unintended and aborted pregnancies. These variables are affected by the decisions women make in the context of their sexual activities. Examining them along a continuum of women's sexual experiences and sexual socialization from childhood through adulthood may help us gain more clarity about the nature of women's sexual decision making and sexual health.

■ Frequency of Masturbation

Similar to children and adolescents, many adult women stimulate themselves sexually. Masturbation is a safe, although not universally sanctioned, alternative to both heterosexual and homosexual contact in this era of AIDS, as well as a sexual outlet for people who do not have partners (Masters et al., 1992). The most common form of masturbation among women involves stimulation of the clitoris, mons, or vaginal lips by stroking, rubbing, or applying pressure by hand (Fisher, 1973; Masters & Johnson, 1966, 1979). More than 70% of females have masturbated at one time or another (Masters et al., 1992), and Kinsey and his colleagues (1953) found that single women between the ages of 18 and 24 masturbated an average of 21 times a year.

■ Frequency of Heterosexual Contact

Many adult women are more interested in heterosexual contact than masturbation, however. Especially young women who have experienced intercourse engage in an array of sexual practices among which masturbation occurs least frequently (Darling & Davidson, 1986). Approximately 15% (Blumstein & Schwartz, 1983) to 40% (Rubenstein & Tavris, 1987) of adult women are involved in various sexual behaviors with partners once a week or less, and between 25% (Rubenstein & Tavris, 1987) and 40% (Blumstein & Schwartz, 1983) of women do so three or more times a week.

■ Frequency of Intercourse, Oral Sex, and Anal Sex

Intercourse is probably the most common sexual experience of adulthood. On the average, adult women typically have intercourse two to four times per week (Fisher, 1980; Gebhard & Johnson, 1979) and less frequently with increasing age (Brecher, 1984). When young women have had sexual intercourse, they also tend to engage in oral-genital stimulation (Darling & Davidson, 1986). Approximately 50% of women reportedly participate in oral sex, both cunnilingus and fellatio, sometimes or even frequently (Athanasiou, Shaver, & Tavris, 1970; Blumstein & Schwartz, 1983; Rubenstein & Tavris, 1987). Not all of these sexual behaviors occur during the same lovemaking session, however. Apparently, heterosexual couples who usually have oral sex do not always have intercourse; those who rarely have oral sex may always have intercourse (Blumstein & Schwartz, 1983).

Some adult women also engage in anal sex with their partners. Anal intercourse among heterosexuals, a behavior long neglected by research, has finally received more attention in recent years after it was identified as a high-risk behavior for HIV transmission and infection. Statistics for its prevalence vary considerably. Between approximately 20% (MacDonald et al., 1990; Reinisch, Hill, Sanders, & Ziemba-Davis, 1990; Wyatt & Lyons-Rowe, 1990) and almost 50% of women have ever had anal sex (Rubenstein & Tavris, 1987). Among female sexual partners of men infected with HIV, approximately one third participate in anal sex (Padian et al., 1987). A total of 39% of American women are estimated to have engaged in anal intercourse at least once (Reinisch, Sanders, & Ziemba-Davis, 1988).

Percentages of women who have anal sex on a more regular basis also fluctuate. In two clinical convenience samples, 8% and 23% of women, respectively, reported that they engaged in anal sex regularly (Bolling, 1977, 1987). According to a recent review of the literature, as many as 10%, if not more, of sexually active American women participate in anal intercourse relatively regularly (Voeller, 1991). Some speculate that women engage in anal sex for pleasure and use it as a method of contraception (Bolling, 1977). Although receptive anal intercourse does not lead to pregnancy, it is the sexual behavior associated with the highest risk of infection with an HIV virus (Hicks, Voeller, Resnick, Silva, Weeks, & Cassity, 1990; Voeller, 1991). Thus, women who have anal sex without using a barrier method of contraception face a high risk of contracting the deadly disease.

■ Sexual Initiation

It is obvious that adult women may engage in a variety of sexual behaviors, including intercourse and oral and anal sex, with their partners, but we know far less about if and how often women decide to initiate these sexual activities. Initiation may be a key factor in the decision-making processes that lead women to engage in sexual behaviors that promote or compromise their sexual health. Traditionally, men have been the initiators of sexual contact, and women have controlled whether sex would take place or not (Brownmiller, 1975; McCormick, 1979), unless an incident involved sexual assault. This traditional pattern may reinforce women's passivity vis-à-vis men. When women do not initiate or initiate rarely they also acquiesce to participating in sexual behaviors they themselves would not have chosen.

Women who describe themselves as happily married (Brecher, 1984) and those who have satisfactory sexual relationships with their primary partners (Wyatt & Lyons-Rowe, 1990) report higher rates of initiation. In couples who feel sexually satisfied in their marriages, both women and their partners tend to initiate or refuse sex equally as often (Blumstein & Schwartz, 1983).

■ Contraceptive Use and Consequences of Unplanned Pregnancies

Examining patterns of birth control use is another way of learning about decision-making processes that involve women's sexual health. Indeed, whether to use a contraceptive and what kind to use are vital decisions that can prevent unintended pregnancies and the transmission of STDs.

Decisions to use effective means of birth control have been associated with more frequent intercourse (Athanasiou et al., 1970). This relationship may be based on the fact that the more frequently a woman has sex, the more likely she is to become pregnant. Naturally, engaging in intercourse without the effective use of contraception may result in pregnancy. More than half of the approximately 6 million pregnancies that occur each year are unintended, and approximately 1.6 million end in abortion (Silverman, Torres, & Forrest, 1987). Currently, abortion is still a legal option for many American women. Approximately 15% (Athanasiou et al., 1970) to 30% (Forrest, 1987;

Tietze, Forrest, & Henshaw, 1988) of women of childbearing age end their pregnancies by abortion. Those who are most likely to have abortions are 18- to 19-year-old women, although women of all ages under 30 are likely to do so (Adler, David, Major, Roth, Russo, & Wyatt, 1991; Henshaw & Silverman, 1988).

Evidence suggests that women who terminate pregnancies become pregnant as a result of non- or inconsistent use of contraceptives (Henshaw & Silverman, 1988). In 1987, 8% of all women of reproductive age who were involved in a sexual relationship and thus at risk for pregnancy were not using any contraceptive method (Forrest & Fordyce, 1989). Yet nonuse or inconsistent use of contraception does not necessarily imply the desire to become pregnant. The fact that women often use contraceptives inconsistently indicates that they intend to prevent pregnancies but frequently do not succeed in protecting themselves effectively. Being insufficiently informed about contraceptives, specific sexual activities, and how a woman's body works may at least partially account for such inconsistent and ineffective birth control use.

Just as effective use of contraceptives is likely to prevent unintended pregnancies, barrier methods of birth control, such as the condom used in conjunction with a spermicide, may prevent STD infection, including HIV. Women are not all equally willing to explore different methods of birth control, but many young adults are obviously unwilling to abstain from sex out of fear of disease (Murstein, Chalpin, Heard, & Vyse, 1989). In a 1986 study of sexually experienced female and male students, 60% reported ever having used a condom as a method of contraception (Murstein et al., 1989). This indicates that a significant percentage of sexually active college students do not adequately protect themselves from the risk of contracting an STD, including AIDS. These findings are corroborated by research at the Kinsey Institute (Reinisch et al., 1990).

As part of our efforts to facilitate women's sexual health, it is important to understand exactly why some women who do not want to become pregnant do not use contraceptives consistently or effectively. By the same token, it is critical to investigate the range of circumstances that influence women's decisions not to use barrier contraceptives or even contraceptives at all despite potential health risks and pregnancies.

■ Ethnic Differences

Patterns of sexual activity and contraceptive use in adulthood appear to vary for different ethnic groups. White women tend to report more frequent sexual activity (Aral & Cates, 1989; Wyatt, 1991a) and a greater number of sexual partners than their black cohorts (Aral & Cates, 1989). Apparently, African-American women also engage in cunnilingus and fellatio much less often than do their white peers (Aral & Cates, 1989; Wyatt, 1991a; Wyatt & Lyons-Rowe, 1990).

Ethnic differences in frequency of vaginal and anal intercourse, however, are inconsistent. In one study, black college women had a slightly higher overall frequency of vaginal intercourse than did white college women (Gebhard & Johnson, 1979), but other studies report no ethnic differences for these behaviors (Fisher, 1980; Wyatt, 1991a). Conversely, some research suggests that nearly twice as many white than black women have ever had anal intercourse (Aral & Cates, 1989; Gebhard & Johnson, 1979; Wyatt, 1991a), whereas another study reports identical results for both ethnic groups for this behavior (Bolling, 1977). More similarity in reports of sexual practices in black and white women emerges when demographic characteristics are controlled (Aral & Cates, 1989; Wyatt, 1991a; Wyatt & Lyons-Rowe, 1990).

Research involving black women's fertility patterns and contraceptive use has also often generated contradictory findings. One study reported that black females used effective methods of contraception less often than did white women (Gebhard & Johnson, 1979), but other studies found that black women were more likely than white women and others to use the pill and less likely to use the condom or the diaphragm (Adler et al., 1991; Henshaw & Silverman, 1988). Overall, black women tend to use barrier methods of contraception and disease transmission less frequently than their white peers (Wyatt, 1991a) and are less likely to use them today than in Kinsey and colleagues' (1953) study 40 years ago (Wyatt et al., 1988a, 1988b).

■ Critique of the Literature on Adult Sexual Behavior

Clearly, the research on adult women's sexual behavior is limited in several respects. Little information is available on anal intercourse and sexual initiation patterns among heterosexual women in general and on frequencies of sexual behaviors such as oral-genital sex and anal intercourse in particular.

Data on anal intercourse often specify simply the percentage of heterosexual women who have engaged in this activity at least once in their lives (MacDonald et al., 1990; Reinisch et al., 1990; Wyatt & Lyons-Rowe, 1990). Even when studies have attempted to measure frequencies of anal intercourse and oral-genital sex, going beyond whether the respondent has ever engaged in such activities, response categories are often vague, imprecise, and incompatible, rendering cross-study comparisons difficult, if not impossible. For example, frequencies of sexual behaviors have been examined in categories such as "regularly" (Bolling, 1977), "frequently," "several times," "usually," or "sometimes" (Athanasiou et al., 1970). An average number of times women engage in anal or oral sex behavior within a certain period of time would be more helpful.

Furthermore, research findings on the frequency of anal intercourse have been inconsistent, most likely because convenience samples were often used and respondents may have been reluctant to disclose these activities (Bolling, 1977). Consequently, estimates that at least 10% of sexually active American women engage in anal intercourse with some regularity (Voeller, 1988, 1991) may be based on highly stratified samples and therefore less than valid.

Similar to data on anal intercourse, information about women's patterns of sexual initiation is sorely lacking. We need far more information on the circumstances under which couples make decisions about who initiates sex, who decides which behaviors are included in sexual encounters, and which, if any, contraceptives are to be used. Determining the factors involved in decisions to engage in sex generally and in risky sexual behaviors more specifically is desperately needed at a time when the percentage of women infected with HIV has been steadily increasing (CDC, 1992; Guinan & Hardy, 1987).

■ Summary: What We Know About Adult Women's Consensual Sexual Behavior

Many adult women engage primarily in vaginal intercourse with their partners and less often in oral and anal sex. They appear to be generally more interested in heterosexual contact than in self-stimulation and masturbation. The frequency of sexual initiation increases with happiness and sexual satisfaction in relationships. Having intercourse often is associated with more effective birth control use. Yet many women do not use birth control at all or do so inconsistently and thus ineffectively, which leads to millions of unintended pregnancies and abortions each year.

It also appears that some adult women do not use barrier methods of contraceptives to protect themselves adequately from infection with STDs. Yet contraceptive use is one of the most crucial aspects of sexual health today. Hopefully, decisions about contraceptive use will receive greater research attention in the context of sociocultural health and relationship factors.

5

Sexual Socialization of Children and Adolescents and Other Family Variables

With Cindy M. Notgrass

Having reviewed important aspects of voluntary sexual behavior in childhood, adolescence, and adulthood, we continue in this chapter with an overview of some of the factors that influence women's sexual practices and sexual decision making. Again we focus on variables that are critical to this study. Beginning with a description of children's and adolescents' early sexual socialization by the family and other sources of socialization, we proceed with various family variables, including socioeconomic status and the quality of family life.

■ Agents of Sexual Socialization

What children learn about sex and sexuality from the men and women in their environment is likely to have some influence on their later sexual functioning. Thus, it is not surprising that the family of origin, particularly the mother (Barrett, 1980; Elias, 1978; Gebhard, 1977; Weinstein & Thornton, 1989; Woody, 1973; Yarber & Greer, 1986), peers (Dickinson, 1978; Wyatt, 1989), religious affiliations (Barrett, 1980; Libby et al., 1978; Murstein & Holden, 1979; Wyatt & Lyons-Rowe, 1990), and sex education taught in school (Dawson, 1986; Furstenberg, Moore, & Peterson, 1985) appear to affect young girls' sexual attitudes and behavior. This is not to suggest that the media should not be considered as major sources of sexual socialization, but research on their impact is not covered here.

■ Parental Sexual Attitudes

Parents exert influence directly through conversations (Lewis, 1973; Planned Parenthood, 1986; Spanier, 1977) or indirectly by serving as role models (Inazu

& Fox, 1980; Shelley, 1981; Yarber & Greer, 1986). Some of the earliest sexual learning may take place when infants incorporate their parents' responses to sexual reflexes that occur during nursing, bathing, diaper changing, and play (Masters et al., 1992). When a parent reacts with shock or discomfort, disapproval is likely to be conveyed to the child, whereas a calm reaction conveys acceptance of sexuality (Masters et al., 1992). At around age three, children tend to become aware of whether their parents approve or disapprove of genital play. Confusion is likely to arise when parents encourage their children to be aware of their bodies in general, but not of their genitals (Masters et al., 1992). Parental expressions of disapproval, verbal or nonverbal, of all forms of sexual experimentation in which a child engages may contribute to later sexual difficulties (Calderone, 1978; Masters & Johnson, 1970).

Parents' attitudes and practices with regard to nudity in the home certainly affect children's self-consciousness (Masters et al., 1992) and may continue to do so in subsequent stages of development, including adulthood. Thus, exposure to family nudity has been associated with increased sexual behavior for children of all ages (Friedrich et al., 1991). Adolescents whose parents had a permissive stance toward nudity in the home exhibited more liberal attitudes toward sex and sexuality (Shelley, 1981). In addition, women who recall their parents' sexual attitudes and influence in childhood and adolescence report older ages at onset of sexual intercourse (Wyatt, 1989), fewer premarital sexual partners (Lewis, 1973; Planned Parenthood, 1986; Spanier, 1977), and sexual similar attitudes to their parents' (Libby et al., 1978; McNab, 1976; Thornton & Camburn, 1987; Weinstein & Thornton, 1989; Yarber & Greer, 1986). Although research suggests that parents overall have little or no influence on sexual socialization among young adults (Kaats & Davis, 1970; Mirande, 1968), there is some evidence that parental impact on sexual attitudes may be lasting. Adult women who were exposed to parental nudity as young children were found to engage in sexual activity more frequently than their nonexposed peers and did not seem to have any sexual difficulties (Lewis & Janda, 1988). Insufficient and negative parental messages about sex also seem to persist. Thus, adult women in cohabiting relationships who had received less accurate sexual information during childhood and experienced more negative attitudes toward sex from their parents than a noncohabiting comparison group reported more sexual experience and younger ages at first sex (Newcomb, 1986). These findings lend support to the idea that parents who do not inform their children about sex and do not endorse sex and sexuality may unwittingly contribute to a greater interest in sex and more liberal sexual attitudes in their adult cohabiting offspring.

Also noted are findings that reveal that parental influence in adulthood may be less direct. In one study of adult women, parents' sexual attitudes were unrelated to women's ages at onset of sexual behaviors such as masturbation, noncoital sex, and intercourse (Newcomb, 1984). Parental sexual attitudes did, however, affect dating competence and assertiveness, which in turn influenced women's sexual behaviors (Newcomb, 1984).

■ Peers

The discrepancies in reported findings indicate that parental influence on sexual attitudes and behavior may vary and is not necessarily continuous throughout life. Indeed, parents' influence is often mediated by other important forces. Thus, as young girls grow older, peers become instrumental in determining sexual attitudes and behavior (Dickinson, 1978; Mirande, 1968), as well as sexual knowledge (Masters et al., 1992). Although parents who are perceived as more influential than peers can contribute to a delay in age at first coitus (Wyatt, 1989), most female teenagers who are already sexually active tend to have a peer reference group that is similarly active or at least condones sexual behavior (Mirande, 1968). Parents' attitudes toward birth control also have only a limited impact on adolescents' contraceptive use (Morrison, 1985). Nevertheless, when parents have a positive attitude toward sex, they may promote in their children a tolerance of genital manipulation, which may lead the latter to consider using contraceptives such as the intrauterine device (IUD) and the diaphragm and ultimately contribute to a positive view of these methods of birth control (Kelley, 1979).

■ Parents' Socioeconomic Status

In addition to being influenced by direct and indirect parental messages about sex and sexuality, sexual socialization may also be affected by other family variables, such as socioeconomic status (SES). Some evidence suggests that parents' economic resources, as well as their level of education, may help to create a family environment in which young women's knowledge of sex-related information is enhanced. Adolescents whose parents fall into higher SES groups are more likely to be informed about periods of heightened risk for pregnancy when compared to lower SES adolescents (Zelnik & Kantner, 1979).

■ Other Sources of Sexual Socialization

Factors such as religiousness and sex education also contribute to sexual socialization. Young girls' religious involvement has been associated negatively with sexual permissiveness (Libby et al., 1978), coital involvement, sexual experiences (Barrett, 1980; Murstein & Holden, 1979), and sexual responsiveness in adulthood (Wyatt & Lyons-Rowe, 1990). These findings have not been entirely consistent, however. Religiousness in adolescents has also been found to be unrelated to their sexual and contraceptive experiences (McCormick, Izzo, & Folcik, 1985). Such contradictory results may at least be explained partly by differences in the definition of religious involvement or religiousness across studies.

The effect of school-based sex education on adolescent sexual behavior has been similarly inconclusive. One third of U.S. junior high schools and one half of senior high schools offer sex education courses (Kenney, Guardad, & Brown, 1989; Orr, 1982). In some studies, a lack of sex education has been linked to a greater likelihood of sexual intercourse (Furstenberg et al., 1985) or earlier age at first intercourse (Zabin et al., 1986). Yet other research has found that exposure to sex education was related to a slight increase in the probability of adolescent intercourse (Marsiglio & Mott, 1986), as well as greater contraceptive knowledge and use (Dawson, 1986), and to a decrease in teenage pregnancy (Zelnik & Kim, 1982). Finally, there are studies that suggest that sex education is associated with neither the likelihood of intercourse (Dawson, 1986) nor greater knowledge of sex-related information (Morrison, 1985).

Masters and associates (1992) point out that much of preadolescent school or parental sex education consists of lecturing solely about elementary facts of anatomy and reproduction and ignores other vital aspects of sex education. Indeed, very few parents provide their children with sufficient and accurate meaningful sex education. As a result, children are likely to obtain a substantial amount of information about sex through media and various other sources that often present distorted views of sex and sexuality (Masters et al., 1992).

■ The Quality of Family Life

Up to this point, we have described parents, peers, religiousness, and school sex education as potentially influential sources of sexual socialization. We have also briefly touched on the impact a family's socioeconomic status may have on children's sexuality and sexual attitudes. A final variable we would like to consider now is the quality of family life. Defined as the overall degree of closeness within the family and the level of happiness prevalent in the parents' relationship with each other, the quality of family life is likely to play a major part in influencing children's sexual attitudes and behavior (Holmbeck & Hill, 1986).

Indeed, family stability and close parental ties, particularly to mothers, tend to delay premarital sex including intercourse (Inazu & Fox, 1980; Mott, 1984; Murstein et al., 1989; Murstein & Holden, 1979; Simon, Berger, & Gagnon, 1972; Strasburger, 1985; Zelnik, Kantner, & Ford, 1981). Furthermore, adolescents who feel comfortable confiding in their parents report a greater sense of happiness (Gordon, Scales, & Everly, 1979) and fewer sexual relations (Fox, 1979; Gordon et al., 1979). In contrast, teenagers who are unhappy at home, do not feel close to their mothers, and experience conflict with parental values tend to have more than two sexual partners in adolescence (Fox, 1979).

The nature of the parental relationship also makes a difference. Women whose mothers displayed affection for their husbands report more positive attitudes toward assertive behavior in sexual relationships in adulthood (Koblinsky & Palmeter, 1984). On the other hand, parental conflict, estrangement, and divorce are often associated with difficulties in adolescence, such as lower self-esteem, poorer academic performance, more "nervous" feelings (Saucier & Ambert, 1986), drug use (Newcomb & Bentler, 1988a), a history of childhood sexual abuse (Edwards & Alexander, 1992), increased teenage sexual activity (Gordon et al., 1979; Ostrov et al., 1985), and less sexual satisfaction in adulthood (Heiman, Gladue, Roberts, & LoPiccolo, 1986; Jobes, 1986).

■ Ethnic Differences

There are few known differences between African-American and white adolescent women in the area of sexual socialization. One study conducted with both ethnic groups indicated that the relationship between perceptions of parental influence on adolescent sexual behavior and delaying intercourse was slightly stronger for white adult women than for their African-American cohorts, but both groups delayed intercourse until later adolescence (Wyatt, 1989). Another study of teenage women found information sources about sex to be different in their effectiveness for the two groups (Zelnik, 1979). For African-Americans, sex education classes were the most effective source of information about the greatest monthly risk period of pregnancy, whereas friends and parents were poor sources. For whites, on the other hand, home was the best source of information and sex education at school a relatively poor source (Zelnik, 1979). Overall, however, the information obtained from all sources did not adequately address the range and depth of knowledge that young women need in adolescence and adulthood.

■ Critique of the Literature on Sexual Socialization

Shortcomings of the research on sexual socialization are similar to those in other areas of the literature we have reviewed so far. Although many studies used large samples (Athanasiou et al., 1970; Inazu & Fox, 1980; Libby et al., 1978; Thornton & Camburn, 1987; Wyatt, 1985), numerous studies have been conducted with small samples (Barrett, 1980; Holmbeck & Hill, 1986; Mirande, 1968; Shelley, 1981; Yarber & Greer, 1986). As in other areas of research, many investigators have also relied on self-report measures (Holmbeck & Hill, 1986; Murstein & Holden, 1979; Ostrov et al., 1985; Saucier & Ambert, 1986; Shelley, 1981; Yarber & Greer, 1986), a point already made in previous chapters. Furthermore, limited information about ethnic differences in sexual socialization is available from research using samples stratified by ethnic group (Dickinson, 1978; Inazu & Fox, 1980; Wyatt, 1985; Zelnik, 1979). Finally, comprehensive studies of the effects of sexual socialization on sexual behavior have yet to be conducted. Apparently, few researchers consider sexual knowledge and influences on perceptions of sex and sexuality to be important aspects of sexual health that need to be taken into account when strategies aimed at sexual behavior change are developed.

■ Summary of Sexual Socialization Variables

Various sources of sexual socialization can have considerable influence on children's emerging sexual attitudes and behaviors. Parents convey direct and indirect messages about sex, sexuality, and nudity in the home that are subsequently incorporated by their children. Although parental influences may persist into adulthood, most adolescents begin to look to their peers instead to determine the nature and extent of their own sexual activities. Religiousness and sex education at school may inhibit or delay sexual activity for some adolescents but have no effect on others. Parental influence, however, sometimes continues into adulthood. Insufficient information from parents and negative parental messages about sex may have the unwanted effect of increasing some aspects of adult sexual activity.

In general, parents may be relatively poor and inaccurate sources of sexual information, but perhaps more so in lower SES families. Adolescents who feel close to their families—in particular, their mothers—also tend to feel happier, delay sexual intercourse, and engage in less sexual activity. When the parental relationship is estranged, teenage sexual activity may increase and happiness decrease. The combination of increased sexuality and unhappiness may heighten teenagers' sexual health risks.

6

Abusive Sexual Experiences in Childhood

We now turn from consensual sexual experiences and sexual socialization processes to sexual abuse. In this chapter, we focus on nonconsensual sexual experiences in childhood; in the following, we continue with sexual abuse in adulthood.

As sexual abuse has received more attention by researchers as well as the media, it has become abundantly clear that not all sexual behaviors are voluntary and consensual. In fact, many are involuntary and abusive and can begin very early in life. Perpetrators who compel children to engage in sexual activities to which they are psychologically and developmentally unprepared to consent and with which they cannot cope come from all walks of life and include family members, family friends, acquaintances, and strangers. Unfortunately, child sexual abuse is an all too common occurrence.

■ Prevalence

Prevalence rates for child sexual abuse range from a low of 5.3% (Siegel, Sorenson, Golding, Burnam, & Stein, 1987) to a high of 38% (Russell, 1986) and even 45% (Wyatt, 1985) in community samples. Overall, as many as 20% of adults may have been sexually abused by the time they reach their midteens (Briere, 1991). The majority of survivors are traumatized by their experiences in various ways, and sexual adjustment is often jeopardized.

■ Effects Associated With Child Sexual Abuse

The psychologically and sexually traumatizing impact of sexual abuse on children and adolescents has been studied primarily over the last 10 to 15 years. Research evidence suggests that survivors of child sexual abuse may experience a host of initial and long-term repercussions. Among the effects found are depression, anxiety, suicidal ideation, self-destructive behavior, sexual maladjustment, sexually inappropriate behavior, anger, hostility, aggression, hyperactivity, concentration and memory problems, learning difficulties, sleep problems, withdrawal, feelings of isolation and stigma, poor self-esteem, difficulty trusting others, problems with interpersonal—particularly male-female—relationships, a tendency toward being revictimized, substance abuse, delinquency, somatic complaints, phobias, eating disorders, dissociative disorders, posttraumatic stress disorder, and multiple personality and borderline syndromes (for example, see Alter-Reid, Gibbs, Lachenmeyer, Sigal, & Massoth, 1986; Bagley & Ramsay, 1985, 1986; Briere, 1984a,b; Briere & Runtz, 1988a,b; Briere & Zaidi, 1989; Browne & Finkelhor, 1986; Burgess, Groth, & McCausland, 1981; Burgess, Hartman, McCausland, & Powers, 1984; Burgess, Hartman, McCormick, 1987; Conte & Schuerman, 1988; Courtois, 1979; Finkelhor, 1990; Friedrich, Urquiza, & Beilke, 1986; Greenwald & Leitenberg, 1990; Herman, 1981; Kluft, 1984; Lindberg & Distad, 1985; Lusk & Waterman, 1986; Mackey, Hacker, Weissfeld, Ambrose, Fisher, & Zobel, 1991; Meiselman, 1978; Oppenheimer, Howells, Palmer, & Chaloner, 1985; Putnam, Guroff, Silberman, Barban, & Post, 1986; Rew, 1989; Westerlund, 1992; Wyatt, 1988b; Wyatt & Mickey, 1988; Wyatt & Newcomb, 1990).

Other effects have been specifically linked to intrafamilial abuse and include repressed anger and hostility, impaired ability to trust, blurred role boundaries, role confusion, pseudomaturity, failure to accomplish developmental tasks, and difficulty with self-mastery and control (Porter, Blick, & Sgroi, 1982). Adult incest survivors also tend to experience less satisfaction in their sexual relationships (Jackson, Calhoun, Amick, Maddever, & Habif, 1990; Langmade, 1983) and greater sex guilt (Langmade, 1983) compared to their nonabused cohorts.

These damaging effects are mediated by the nature and circumstances of the abuse, such as the victim-perpetrator relationship, type of sexual act, use and amount of physical force, the victim's age at onset of abuse, response to disclosure, resources that are available, and the duration and frequency of abuse (Browne & Finkelhor, 1986). Certain aspects of the abuse experience, such as the nature of the victim-perpetrator relationship and the type of sexual contact, have received a fair amount of attention by researchers. The most salient and traumatizing aspects appear to be abuse by father figures (Browne & Finkelhor, 1986; Greenwald & Leitenberg, 1990) and abuse involving genital contact and force (Browne & Finkelhor, 1986). Other important mediating variables of sexual abuse experiences, such as their duration and frequency and the number of perpetrators (Tharinger, 1990), have been examined less extensively. Actual duration and frequency of early abuse experiences vary considerably, however. Thus, a child may be subjected to a single incident of abuse or to molestation that continues over a period of 10 or more years (Edwards & Alexander, 1992; Fromuth, 1983); 31 weeks may be an average period of time for girls to be sexually victimized (Finkelhor, 1979). Similar to duration, the frequency of abuse may also range from one time to so many incidents that survivors cannot recall the exact number of times they were victimized (Wyatt, 1990b).

■ Effects Associated With Duration and Frequency of Child Sexual Abuse

Duration is certainly one indicator of sexual abuse severity (Bjork & Yutrzenka, 1991). Child and adult survivors who have been exposed to longer durations of abuse exhibit increased psychological problems (Adams-Tucker, 1982; Briere & Runtz, 1988a,b; Rimsza, Berg, & Locke, 1988; Wyatt, 1988b; Wyatt, 1990b; Wyatt & Newcomb, 1990). They report depression and chronic somatization, along with acute and chronic dissociation (Briere & Runtz, 1988a); decreased well-being, manifested in fewer positive expressions, fewer cheerful moods, and less emotional stability (Wyatt, 1985); and a higher frequency of reported somatic symptoms (Rimsza et al., 1988). More severe emotional disturbances are also linked to increased duration and younger age at onset of abuse (Adams-Tucker, 1982).

Children who are intrafamilially abused tend to be subjected to a longer duration of abuse (Dube & Hebert, 1988; Fromuth, 1983; Wyatt & Newcomb, 1990) and greater negative consequences. Perceptions of lasting harm (Herman, Russell, & Trocki, 1986), poor self-esteem, hopelessness, depersonalization, and psychological numbness, variously combined with guilt and chronic depression (Bagley & McDonald, 1984), greater internalizing as well as externalizing behaviors (Friedrich et al., 1986), a higher probability of sexual revictimization later in life (Russell, 1986), and problems with intimacy in male-female relationships (Wyatt & Newcomb, 1990) have all been found in incest survivors whose abuse experiences were longer-lasting.

Frequency of abuse also affects the survivor's degree of trauma. Increased sexualized behavior has been related to a higher frequency of abuse incidents by more than one perpetrator (Friedrich et al., 1986). Furthermore, survivors of abuse by multiple perpetrators in childhood are more likely to have experienced intrafamilial abuse at first victimization, compared to those abused by one perpetrator (Long & Jackson, 1991).

Although longer duration and higher frequency of child sexual abuse have been associated with more negative effects (Adams-Tucker, 1982; Bagley & Ramsay, 1985; Briere & Runtz, 1988a,b; Browne & Finkelhor, 1986; Friedrich et al., 1986; Herman et al., 1986; Kilpatrick, 1987; Peters, 1988; Rimza et al.,

1988; Russell, 1986; Sedney & Brooks, 1984; Tsai, Feldman-Summers, & Edgar, 1979; Wyatt, 1988b; Wyatt, 1990b; Wyatt & Newcomb, 1990), not all findings have been consistent (Cohen & Mannarino, 1988; Courtois, 1979; Finkelhor, 1979; Langmade, 1983; Seidner & Calhoun, 1984; Tufts New England Medical Center, 1984). One study indicated that higher frequency of abuse incidents was associated with less social maturity but more self-acceptance (Seidner & Calhoun, 1984), whereas other studies did not find any significant relationships between longer duration (Courtois, 1979; Finkelhor, 1979; Langmade, 1983; Tufts, 1984) or higher frequency (Cohen & Mannarino, 1988) of abuse and negative effects. Nevertheless, most studies that used a measure specific to sexual abuse, or combined such a measure with more general mental health instruments, found that longer duration of abuse correlated with greater trauma (Briere & Runtz, 1988a; Fromuth, 1983; Herman et al., 1986; Peters, 1988; Wyatt, 1990b; Wyatt & Newcomb, 1990).

■ Ethnic Differences

Very little is known about ethnic differences in the effects of child sexual abuse. The existing research has investigated some differences in sexual abuse among ethnic subgroups of white American (Finkelhor, 1979) and African-American women (Wyatt, 1985, 1990b, 1990c; Wyatt, Guthrie, & Notgrass, 1992). In terms of prevalence, sexual abuse seems to be of equal concern for both white and African-American women before age 18. Reporting patterns differ markedly, however (Wyatt, 1985). African-American women are most likely not to involve police in child sexual abuse and tend to attribute occurrences of abuse more to something about the perpetrator (Wyatt, 1985). Subtle differences in the characteristics and circumstances of child sexual abuse exist between black and white women. Young African-American preteens are most likely to experience contact abuse in their homes, mostly by black male perpetrators who may be members of the nuclear or extended family. White women, however, are at risk of being abused mostly by white perpetrators who may involve them in contact abuse incidents indoors and no-contact abuse incidents outdoors during early childhood and the preschool years (Wyatt, 1985).

■ Critique of the Literature
on Childhood Sexual Abuse

Research on childhood sexual abuse and its effects is riddled with several methodological flaws. Although more empirical studies have been conducted on involuntary than on voluntary childhood sexual experiences, particularly within the last decade, the samples used have been primarily clinical (Adams-Tucker, 1982; Bagley & McDonald, 1984; Cohen & Mannarino, 1988; DeJong, Emmett, & Hervada, 1982; DeJong, Hervada, & Emmett, 1983; Dube & Hebert, 1988; Friedrich et al., 1986; Rimsza et al., 1988). Thus, many subjects are in treatment and highly self-selected (Browne & Finkelhor, 1986). Few empirical studies have included control and comparison groups (Bjork & Yutrzenka, 1991). College students have been another preferred population (Lusk & Waterman, 1986), which naturally limits the applicability of findings to other populations (Wyatt & Peters, 1986a).

Furthermore, there is a lack of standardized outcome measures that assess the effects of abuse (Bjork & Yutrzenka, 1991; Lusk & Waterman, 1986). As a result, cross-study comparisons are less than meaningful. General mental health measures are often administered, but may not be sufficiently sensitive to abuse-specific effects. Finally, differential definitions of childhood sexual abuse further complicate cross-study comparisons of findings (Lusk & Waterman, 1986).

Moving from research on sexual abuse in general to the literature on effects linked to duration and frequency in particular, it is obvious that empirical studies of the consequences of different durations in both intra- and extrafamilial childhood sexual abuse are needed (Alter-Reid et al., 1986). Because only a few studies have examined and differentiated between frequency of abuse and the total number of abuse contacts with all perpetrators (Dube & Herbert, 1988; Peters, 1988; Wyatt, 1988b; Wyatt & Newcomb, 1990), it has been virtually impossible to determine and consistently document the frequency of sexual contacts in victim-perpetrator relationships of different durations and to evaluate the effects of different frequencies in intra- and extrafamilial victim-perpetrator relationships.

■ Summary: Sexual Abuse in Childhood

Childhood sexual abuse is a widespread phenomenon in the United States. It has a variety of initial and long-term psychological, cognitive, and behavioral effects on survivors. Duration and frequency are two abuse characteristics that mediate the effects of sexual victimization experiences. Child sexual abuse of longer duration that occurs more frequently has been associated with greater trauma. Incest tends to continue for years and is particularly damaging when perpetrated by father figures. Still in its infancy as an area of research, childhood sexual abuse lacks methodologically sound studies conducted with community samples that are stratified by ethnicity.

7

Sexual Abuse in Adulthood

With Cindy M. Notgrass

Naturally, sexual abuse also leaves its imprint on women when they are sexually violated in adulthood. This chapter provides a brief overview of the prevalence and effects of sexual assault on adult women, specifically incidents of attempted and completed rape. In addition, we examine several other aspects of the rape experience that influence how severely a survivor can be traumatized.

■ Prevalence

Like childhood sexual abuse, sexual assault in adulthood is a relatively common occurrence. A recent study of a large community sample reports a 13.5% prevalence rate for completed rape of women (Sorenson, Stein, Siegel, Golding, & Burnam, 1987). The prevalence of incidents of both completed and attempted rape in a lifetime is somewhat higher, ranging from 15% to 20%. Yet even this figure is most likely underestimated because women often do not view themselves as rape victims or survivors (Burt & Estep, 1981; Koss & Burkhart, 1989; Koss, Dinero, Seibel, & Cox, 1988), particularly when the perpetrator is known or even considered to be a friend.

■ Traumatic Effects of Rape and Sexual Assault Characteristics

Rape in adulthood is likely to affect at least three areas of a woman's life: mood and psychological functioning, attitude toward intimate relationships, and sexual functioning (Becker & Kaplan, 1991). Indeed, negative effects on women's psychological adjustment (Cohen & Roth, 1987; George, Winfield, & Blazer, 1992; Holmes & St. Lawrence, 1983; Kilpatrick et al., 1989; Kilpatrick, Best, Veronen, Amick, Villeponteaux, & Ruff, 1985; Kilpatrick, Veronen, & Resick, 1982; Kramer & Green, 1991; Marhoefer-Dvorak, Resick, Hutter, & Girelli, 1988; Meyer & Taylor, 1986; Ruch & Chandler, 1983; Sales, Baum, & Shore, 1984; Siegel, Golding, Stein, Burnam, & Sorenson, 1990), intimate relationships (Becker, Skinner, & Abel, 1983; Cohen, 1988; Cohen & Roth, 1987; Mackey et al., 1991; Meyer & Taylor, 1986; Resick, 1983; Wyatt, Newcomb, & Notgrass, 1990), and sexual functioning (Becker, 1989; Becker, Skinner, Abel, Axelrod, & Cichon, 1984; Becker, Skinner, Abel, & Cichon, 1986; Burgess & Holmstrom, 1979; Cohen & Roth, 1987; Ellis, Calhoun, & Atkeson, 1980; Feldman-Summers, Gordon, & Meagher, 1979; George et al., 1992; Mackey et al., 1991; McCahill, Meyer, & Fischman, 1979; Siegel et al., 1990; Veronen & Kilpatrick, 1980) have been found in many studies. The severity of survivors' postassault trauma is determined to some extent by various characteristics of a rape incident such as whether the rape was completed or attempted, the number of rape incidents, the number of perpetrators, and the amount of coercion used by the perpetrator (Wyatt et al., 1990). Postrape psychological and sexual functioning depend partially on these variables.

■ Severity of Trauma in Completed and Attempted Rapes

Obviously, incidents of completed rape differ in some respects from incidents of attempted rape. Thus it is likely that survivors of these two types of sexual assault manifest some differences in postrape trauma. Unfortunately, these two types of incidents have often been combined in research, and potential differential effects have been examined in few studies (Becker, Skinner, Abel, Howell, & Bruce, 1982). Both groups of assault victims experienced predominantly fear and anger in the acute postassault stage but did not differ with respect to long-term effects in one study (Becker et al., 1982; Koss, 1985). Other research found, however, that survivors of completed rapes face increased sexual problems (Becker, Abel, Bruce, & Howell, 1978) and take protective measures to prevent future assaults less frequently than do survivors of attempted rapes (Becker et al., 1982). It is likely that, during completed rapes, women experience a greater sense of violation and powerlessness than during attempted rape incidents. As a result, they may feel incapable of protecting themselves adequately and may neglect to take the necessary measures to do so (Wyatt et al., 1990).

■ Severity of Trauma and Number of Perpetrators

Repeated incidents of attempted and completed rape by one or several perpetrators may further reinforce a victim mentality and thus impair postassault adjustment. The available research on repeat trauma in incidents of attempted and completed rape has yielded inconsistent results. Wyatt and associates (1990) report that a greater number of rapes by one perpetrator per incident predicted more negative initial and lasting attitudes toward sex and intimacy in survivors. Similarly, a study that examined the impact of multiple assailants per incident revealed a statistically nonsignificant trend that indicated that a higher number of assailants was associated with heightened trauma (Ruch & Chandler, 1983). These findings differ from those of other studies that have examined the effects of multiple incidents or assailants. For instance, Kramer and Green (1991) found no relationship between the number of assailants per incident and the severity of trauma, as expressed by PTSD symptoms, or between the number of assailants and the development of assault-related sexual problems.

■ Severity of Trauma and Number of Rape Incidents

The number of attempted and completed rape incidents also affects the severity of postassault trauma. Survivors of multiple rape incidents report more and greater psychological problems (Cohen & Roth, 1987; Ellis, Atkeson, & Calhoun, 1982; Kramer & Green, 1991; Murphy et al., 1988), greater disruption in social functioning (Ellis et al., 1982; Frank, Turner, & Stewart, 1980), a higher rate of victimization in violent crimes other than rape, a history of many more suicide attempts (Ellis et al., 1982), increased sex-related problems (Becker et al., 1984), greater difficulty recovering from the trauma (Burgess & Holmstrom, 1979), and a greater delay in trauma response (Ruch & Leon, 1983) when compared with survivors of single rape incidents. These results have not been consistently obtained, however (Marhoefer-Dvorak et al., 1988). One study found that repeated sexual victimization had only a minimal effect on the long-term functioning of survivors (Marhoefer-Dvorak et al., 1988).

■ Degree of Coercion as a Determinant of Severity of Trauma

The use of coercion is a common characteristic of sexual assault. It may include verbal pressure, threats of harm, use of weapons, physical restraint, and physical harm (Sorenson et al., 1987). Coercion in rape and its effects have been examined in several studies (Becker et al., 1984; Frank et al., 1980). Greater physical force has been associated with impaired sexual and social relations and lower self-esteem (Queen's Bench Foundation, 1975), higher overall symptoms of psychological distress (Cohen & Roth, 1987; Girelli, Resick, Marhoefer-Dvorak, & Hutter, 1986), stronger fears and increased avoidance behaviors (McCahill et al., 1979), and more difficulty in recovery (Bard & Sangrey, 1980; Peters, 1977). Sexual distress is also related to greater physical threat during sexual assault (Siegel et al., 1990). Inconsistent with such findings are a few reports suggesting that the degree of coercion did not significantly affect survivors' psychological distress levels (Frank et al., 1980) or the development of rape-related sexual problems (Becker et al., 1984).

■ Ethnic Differences

Wyatt (1992) proposes that African-American women who are subjected to attempted or completed rapes experience an increased level of trauma and stress. Racial discrimination is a daily stressor in their lives to begin with, and public reaction to the rape of African-American women has often been less than sympathetic. Yet little information is available about potential differences in the effects of rape for different ethnic groups. One large community study found lower rates of sexual assault in Hispanic than non-Hispanic white women (Sorenson et al., 1987), but the study did not include African-Americans per se. Although other studies have included black women (see, for example, Becker et al., 1984; Ellis et al., 1982), they have not investigated the potential differences in adjustment between black and white rape survivors. Similarly, few studies have examined ethnic differences in terms of specific characteristics of sexual assault (Wyatt, 1992).

■ Critique of the Literature on Adulthood Sexual Abuse

Several of the sexual assault characteristics, such as the effects of multiple assailants per incident and repeated sexual assault incidents, have received scanty attention from researchers. Furthermore, few studies have differentiated between incidents of completed and attempted rape; most have combined both types of abuse into one rape category (Becker et al., 1982). We also need more information on ethnic differences in reporting rape, self-blame, response of police and other authority figures, and effects of assault experiences on survivors' psychological and physical well-being (Wyatt, 1992).

Many studies examining the effects of rape are limited by their designs. Including only clinical samples (Becker et al., 1984; Burgess & Holmstrom, 1979; Burnett, Templer, & Barker, 1985; Ellis et al., 1982; Frank et al., 1980; Girelli et al., 1986; Kramer & Green, 1991; Ruch & Leon, 1983; Sales et al., 1984) prevents generalizability of findings to larger populations. There are only a few exceptions (Murphy et al., 1988; Sorenson et al., 1987; Wyatt et al., 1990; Wyatt, 1992). Consequently, there is a great need for research that addresses rape-related issues in samples representing a broader range of women.

■ Summary: Sexual Abuse in Adulthood

Sexual assault of women is alarmingly prevalent in our society, yet it often goes unreported. Similar to child sexual abuse, rape has been associated with a variety of negative effects on survivors' psychological and sexual functioning, as well as on their attitudes toward intimate relationships. The severity of postassault trauma may be influenced by the number of perpetrators, the degree of coercion, multiple incidents, and whether a rape was completed or attempted. Of these assault characteristics, repeated rape incidents and greater physical force have been most consistently linked to greater trauma. African-American survivors may experience an increased level of stress and trauma compared to their white peers because they have to cope not only with the sexual assault trauma per se, but also with racial discrimination and unsympathetic societal responses to the rape of minority women.

PART III

The Effects of Sexual Experiences on Psychological and Sexual Functioning

In the two previous chapters, we considered some of the negative effects linked to sexual abuse. We now describe the psychological constructs that will be examined in relation to nonconsensual and consensual sexual experiences. We begin with psychological well-being and its dimensions of general well-being and self-esteem, and then we continue with a discussion of women's need to control their sexual desires and their experience of sexual satisfaction.

8

Psychological Well-Being

Consensual as well as nonconsensual sexual encounters during the life course not only influence a variety of women's sexual attitudes and practices but also psychological well-being. For our purpose, psychological well-being is defined as a concept that includes both general well-being and self-esteem.

General well-being involves women's perceptions of themselves and their environment, their comfort with the roles they assume in life, and their ability to make decisions and cope with problems. An interest in life, enjoyment of work, life satisfaction, and overall health have been associated with positive well-being (Scheier & Newcomb, in press; Ware, Davies-Avery, Brook, & Johnston, 1978). Unfortunately, little information is available about the relationship between sexual behaviors, including those that compromise one's sexual health, and psychological well-being. The many and diverse aspects of psychological well-being also need to be examined more extensively (Scheier & Newcomb, in press; Ware et al., 1978).

One component of psychological well-being that has received greater attention is self-esteem (Newcomb, 1985; Rosenberg & Simmons, 1971; Wyatt, 1988b). According to Rosenberg and Simmons (1971), individuals with high self-esteem have feelings of worth and self-respect, appreciate their own merits, and may be less resistant to recognizing their shortcomings. Low self-esteem, on the other hand, implies a lack of respect for oneself and feeling unworthy, inadequate, or otherwise deficient as a person.

Among the many aspects associated with psychological well-being and self-esteem are the quality of family life (Harlow & Newcomb, 1990), a history of child or adult sexual abuse, and ethnic background. Young adult women who perceive their parents as happy together report higher self-esteem than those who consider their parents to be unhappy (Long, 1986). Furthermore, maternal acceptance predicts young women's self-esteem (Holmbeck & Hill, 1986). In contrast, impaired psychological well-being (Wyatt, 1988b), low self-esteem (see, for example, Bagley & Ramsay, 1985; Browne & Finkelhor,

1986; Finkelhor, 1990; Kilpatrick, 1986), depression (see, for example, Bagley & Ramsay, 1985; Browne & Finkelhor, 1986; Finkelhor, 1990; Kilpatrick, 1986), and poor mental health (Bagley & Ramsay, 1985) are correlates of child sexual abuse. Greater severity of abuse per se has been linked to lower psychological well-being in adult survivors, including negative expressions, low energy, emotional instability, depressed mood, tension, and worries about health, especially among survivors who report sexual abuse involving more severe body intrusion and a longer duration of incidents (Wyatt, 1988b). They also tend to experience diminished self-esteem and less general well-being in adulthood (Wyatt, 1988b). Among incest survivors, difficulties with self-esteem appear to be especially prevalent (Browne & Finkelhor, 1986; Herman, 1981). Finally, abusive sexual experiences in adulthood, such as rape, are linked to depressive symptomatology, as well as low self-esteem and feelings of worthlessness (see, for example, Frank, Turner, & Duffy, 1979).

■ Ethnic Differences

The association between ethnicity and psychological well-being, including self-esteem, has yet to be consistently confirmed in research. Studies that did not control for confounding variables, such as social class, report lower self-esteem for blacks than for whites (Dregar & Miller, 1960, 1968). There is evidence, however, from other studies that controlled for SES that self-esteem among the black population is comparable to (Cole, 1978; Couchman, 1970; Housley, Martin, McCoy, Greenhouse, Stigger, & Chopin, 1987) or exceeds the self-esteem of whites (Cole, 1978; Jacques, 1976; Kohn, 1969; Rosenberg & Simmons, 1971; Stein, 1988; Yancey, Rigsby, & McCarthy, 1972). No ethnic differences in psychological well-being have been reported (Husaini & Neff, 1980).

■ Critique of the Literature on Psychological Well-Being and Self-Esteem

Comprehensive studies of variables that make up psychological well-being have yet to be conducted both to clarify the concept and to shed some light on its association with women's sexual practices and experiences. In our research, we need to use measures that not only identify psychological problems and unhealthy coping strategies but also help us understand psychological health and a sense of positive well-being. By including measures of psychological well-being, we will hopefully be able to identify a range of psychological and life quality effects associated with abusive sexual experiences. Potential relationships between self-esteem and sexual behaviors also need to be clarified to determine how self-esteem exerts its influence on the nature of women's sexual decision making, including sexual risk taking.

Finally, empirical research that controls for confounding variables and uses stratified community samples, including multiethnic samples, is needed to obtain a thorough picture of ethnic group differences and correlations between sexual behavior and psychological well-being, including self-esteem.

■ Summary

Psychological well-being—including women's assessment of their roles in life, their perceptions of the environment, their ability to cope with problems, and their self-esteem—is a concept that has yet to be examined extensively in relation to sexual health. Women who have healthy sexual self-images and engage in sexual decision making that is in their own best interest are likely to report adequate psychological well-being.

9

Sex Guilt: The Need to Control One's Sexual Desires

We know that sexually abusive experiences are associated with poor psychological well-being and self-esteem. Sex guilt or the degree to which women feel they need to control their sexual desires is also likely to affect their sexual attitudes and behavior. Women's perceptions of a range of socially desirable behaviors and the personal guidelines they use to label and select sexual practices are best understood by reviewing the concept of sex guilt.

Sex guilt is defined as a general tendency to punish oneself by means of anxiety whenever internal sexual standards are violated in thought or in deed (Mosher, 1968). This need or tendency is likely to vary, depending on the individual's sexual socialization and sexual experiences, and it manifests itself as resistance to sexual temptation, inhibited sexual behavior, or disruption of cognitive processes in sex-related situations (Gerrard, 1987).

Generally, it appears that women who report high sex guilt engage in less sexual activity and have fewer sexual experiences (Gerrard, 1982, 1987; Gerrard & Gibbons, 1982; Kutner, 1971; Langston, 1973; Love, Sloan, & Schmidt, 1976; Mosher, 1973, 1979; Mosher & Cross, 1971; Sack, Keller, & Hinkle, 1984). Specifically, high sex guilt has been associated with less accurate knowledge of sexual terms and reproduction (Mendelsohn & Mosher, 1979), less interest in heterosexual contact (Abramson, Mosher, Abramson, & Woychowski, 1977), less sexual activity before marriage (Dunn, 1986; Mendelsohn & Mosher, 1979; Mosher & Cross, 1971), less intimate forms of sexual experience (D'Augelli & Cross, 1975; Mosher, 1973; Mosher & Cross, 1971), and less sexual satisfaction but more sexual dysfunction (Cado & Leitenberg, 1990).

Another important factor associated with sex guilt is the use of contraceptives. Several studies have demonstrated an inverse relationship between these two variables (Gerrard, 1982, 1987; Mosher, 1973; Mosher & Vonderheide, 1985; Upchurch, 1978). Women high in sex guilt apparently use less reliable methods of birth control, or do not use contraception at all, as opposed to women who score low on sex guilt (Gerrard, 1982, 1987; Mosher & Vonderheide, 1985). Although sex guilt has some positive and negative aspects, it is one of few concepts in sex research that attempts to assess the control that individuals may have over sexual practices they may perceive to be unacceptable. Given that women are encountering a variety of health problems as a result of their sexual attitudes and practices, it is important to identify how exerting control over sexual desires might influence sexual behaviors in women who do and do not have a history of abusive sexual experiences.

In this study, we have renamed sex guilt "need to control one's sexual desires" because we deem the latter to be less judgmental with regard to the internal controls women exercise over their sexual behaviors. The use of internalized controls over sexual practices that may compromise sexual health has yet to be studied in samples whose sexual abuse experiences are separated from consensual practices. In this study, the need to control one's sexual desires is examined along a continuum rather than as a categorically less desirable trait.

■ Ethnic Differences

The associations between sex guilt—or the need to control one's sexual desires—and different ethnic groups have been largely overlooked (Dunn, 1986), and the available findings are inconsistent. Wyatt and Dunn (1991) examined differences in sex guilt and sexual permissiveness among comparable community samples of African-American and white women. Contrary to previous reports, they found that African-American women generally had higher sex guilt and lower levels of sexual permissiveness than their white cohorts. African-American women of lower socioeconomic status scored significantly higher on sex guilt than did white women of all SES levels (Wyatt & Dunn, 1991). An earlier study, however, did not find any ethnic differences with regard to sex guilt among women of different ethnicities (Slane & Morrow, 1981).

■ Critique of the Literature

Similar to other areas of the sex research literature, the majority of studies on sex guilt have examined samples of undergraduate college women (D'Augelli & Cross, 1975; Gerrard, 1982, 1987; Gerrard & Gibbons, 1982; Langston, 1973; Mendelsohn & Mosher, 1979; Morokoff, 1986; Mosher, 1979; Mosher & Vonderheide, 1985; Sack et al., 1984; Slane & Morrow, 1981;

Upchurch, 1978). These college students are likely to differ substantially from the general population in their sexual attitudes and behaviors. We need studies of community samples stratified by age, ethnicity, and SES to ascertain any potential differences that may exist between African-Americans' and whites' college and community samples. Finally, more research needs to examine sex guilt as a correlate of sexual abuse among women.

■ Summary

Overall, women who reportedly experience a greater need to control their sexual desires are less interested in sex than their peers, less familiar with sexual terminology, and less sexually active and experienced, and they report less sexual satisfaction and more sexual dysfunction. They also tend to be poor users of contraception.

Certain aspects of the construct "need to control sexual desires" may be associated with both reduced and increased risks to sexual health. In this study, we hope to gain a better understanding of the sexual and psychological experiences that are linked to this concept.

10

Sexual Satisfaction

A final dimension related to women's sexual health is sexual satisfaction. Research definitions of this concept have focused on certain aspects of satisfaction, including the reported amount of sexual satisfaction, frequency of intercourse, number of orgasms, ability to satisfy one's partner, partner's enjoyment, and freedom from sexual dysfunction (Blumstein & Schwartz, 1983; Jobes, 1986; Newcomb & Bentler, 1983; Pinney, Gerrard, & Denney, 1987; Wyatt & Lyons-Rowe, 1990). Greater sexual satisfaction has been linked to satisfaction with and commitment to one's sexual partner (Pinney et al., 1987); higher frequencies of sexual contact (Rubenstein & Tavris, 1987), including intercourse (Pinney et al., 1987; Wyatt & Lyons-Rowe, 1990); verbal and nonverbal communication of sexual needs (Wyatt & Lyons-Rowe, 1990); positive feelings about first intercourse (Gebhard & Johnson, 1979; Heiman et al., 1986; Weis, 1983); and positive childhood sexual experiences (Leitenberg et al., 1989). In contrast, feelings of guilt, less sexual responsiveness, and a lower frequency of orgasm (Newcomb & Bentler, 1983; Wyatt & Lyons-Rowe, 1990), as well as negative childhood (Leitenberg et al., 1989) and adulthood sexual experiences (Orlando & Koss, 1983) have been associated with diminished sexual satisfaction in adulthood. Specifically, Leitenberg and associates (1989) report that overall sexual satisfaction in adulthood, sexual satisfaction in the most current relationship, and sexual dysfunction are affected by whether women had positive or negative childhood sexual experiences.

Sexual satisfaction may also be affected by other variables such as being able to depend on one's relationship with one's partner and not solely on one's ability to satisfy oneself (Pinney et al., 1987; Wyatt & Lyons-Rowe, 1990). Other research reports that women felt a greater degree of sexual satisfaction when they felt responsible for their own sexual arousal and pleasure (Rubenstein & Tavris, 1987). Finally, although greater dating competence and general assertiveness have been associated with high orgasmic responsiveness (Newcomb, 1984), women's traditional or nontraditional role expectations appear to be independent of their experience of sexual satisfaction (Jobes, 1986).

■ Ethnic Differences

Few ethnic differences have been noted in the research on sexual satisfaction. One study found that fewer black than white women enjoyed first coitus (Gebhard & Johnson, 1979). Another study of African-American women who reported less sexual responsiveness revealed that they also experienced dissatisfaction in their sexual relations with their primary partner, experienced greater feelings of guilt, and were less likely to be orgasmic (Wyatt & Lyons-Rowe, 1990). On the other hand, black women who were sexually satisfied engaged in a variety of sexual activities, had a high frequency of intercourse, and expressed their sexual needs both verbally and nonverbally (Wyatt & Lyons-Rowe, 1990). It is not known, however, whether these patterns are different or similar for women of other ethnic backgrounds.

■ Critique of the Literature

It is difficult to compare outcomes across studies because sexual satisfaction has been defined in many different ways. If we want to understand better how cultural values influence attitudes about sexual behavior and sexual satisfaction, we need to conduct community studies using multiethnic samples and sound, comprehensive definitions that include the major components of sexual satisfaction.

■ Summary

Women's sexual satisfaction appears to increase when sex takes place more frequently and sexual needs are openly communicated in committed sexual relationships. Sexual socialization experiences, such as positive feelings about first intercourse and positive childhood sexual experiences, also enhance sexual satisfaction. On the other hand, negative sexual experiences in childhood, guilt feelings, diminished sexual responsiveness, and infrequent orgasms decrease adult women's experience of sexual satisfaction.

11

Description of the Study and Methodology

This study was designed to identify and assess several domains of important influences, behaviors, events, and outcomes related to the sexual development, consensual sexual experiences, and sexual abuse of women from infancy to adulthood. More specifically, domains were selected to reflect areas of women's lives that may be most strongly predictive of, associated with, or affected by child or adult sexual abuse experiences.

In all, 12 distinct domains were chosen based on the theoretical and empirical literatures reviewed in the previous chapters. These 12 domains generally covered four broad areas of life. One area was a critical source of early influence and reflected features of the family (of origin) context. The other three areas represent aspects of three developmental periods: childhood, adolescence, and adulthood. These four areas of life and the associated 12 domains are depicted in Figure 11.1.

Family context was represented by socialization influences of the parents in addition to peers, religious affiliation, and school-based sex education, parent education, and the quality of family life. The childhood period included assessments of voluntary childhood sexual behavior. Similarly, measures of voluntary adolescent sexual behavior reflected adolescence. Assessments of the ages of onset for types of sexual activity spanned both childhood and adolescence (because they may have occurred anytime during these periods of life). Finally, four domains were represented in the measures from adulthood: (a) sexual activity, (b) standards of sexual conduct, (c) sexual satisfaction, and (d) psychological well-being, including general well-being and self-esteem.

The last two domains included several measures of sexual abuse during these three life stages. Childhood sexual abuse was reflected in two scales of severity that covered the first 18 years of each woman's life. These measures spanned both childhood and adolescence to conform with many legal and

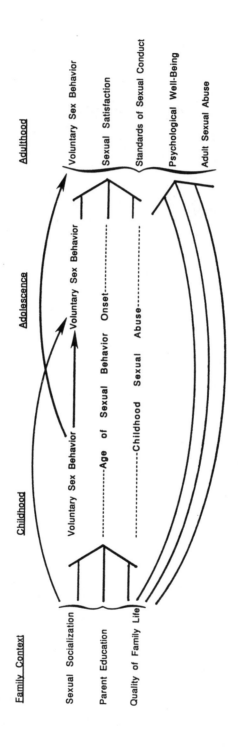

Figure 11.1.

operational definitions of child sexual abuse. These two scales include intra-familial and extrafamilial sexual abuse incidents. Two scales represented experiences of sexual abuse in adulthood: (a) severity of completed rape and (b) severity of attempted rape.

Misleading and spurious conclusions may be reached in studies where (a) critical variables are not assessed and only a restricted and limited segment of a complex and multifaceted process can be analyzed, and (b) statistical methods reduce multidetermined and multiple outcomes of experiences to a series of separate analyses that ignore and cannot express the interdependent nature of complex, real-world phenomena. We hope to minimize these pit-falls by (a) carefully selecting and assessing a wide range of possible pre-dictors, correlates, and consequences of sexual abuse over the entire period of each woman's life; and (b) using structural equation models to examine all of these variables in one simultaneous, comprehensive analysis.

■ Methodology

Sample Selection

Multistage, stratified probability sampling with quotas (for education, marital status, and number of children) was used to recruit comparable groups of African-American and European-American women 18 to 36 years of age in Los Angeles County. "African-American women" were defined as women of African descent whose parentage included a variety of other ethnic and racial groups, as well. The terms European-American and white American are used interchangeably. They refer to women of Caucasian descent and include women of Jewish heritage. Women in both ethnic groups spent at least 6 of the first 12 years of their childhood in the United States. The subjects were located via random-digit telephone-dialing procedures (see Wyatt, 1985, for complete details). Of the 1,348 households identified in which a woman resided, 975 women met the demographic criteria, and 709 agreed to participate. Thus, 266 of the eligible women were not willing to be interviewed, yielding a 27% refusal rate. The first 248 eligible women—126 African-American women and 122 European-American women out of the 709 who agreed to participate—were selected and completed the interview. These figures do not include 335 women who terminated telephone contact before their eligibility could be assessed. When these women are included among the decliners, the conservative refusal rate increases to 45%.

To identify possible biases in the sample, several comparisons were made. The 248 women interviewed were compared with Los Angeles County women (using 1980 Bureau of Census data) on age, ethnicity, marital status,

Table 11.1 Demographic Characteristics of Probability Sample of African-American and European-American Women (*N* = 248)

	African-American Women (126)		European-American Women (122)	
	Number	*Percent*[a]	*Number*	*Percent*[a]
Age Range				
18-26	58	46	47	39
27-36	68	54	75	61
Education				
11th grade or less	19	15	20	16
High school graduate	43	34	37	30
Partial college	47	37	43	35
College graduate	10	8	10	8
Graduate education	7	6	12	10
Children				
None	38	30	53	43
1 child or more	88	70	69	58
Marital Status				
Married	35	28	57	47
Separated	5	4	8	7
Divorced	24	19	21	17
Widowed	1	1	0	0
Single	53	42	32	26
Not with husband	8	6	4	3

[a]Percentages may not total 100% because of rounding.

and the presence of children (see Table 11.1 for demographic characteristics). The African-American sample was representative of the Los Angeles County population, whereas moderate distortions were found in the comparisons of European-American women. As in other studies (Yamaguchi & Kandel, 1985), a minimal loss of efficiency in estimating population averages was noted on the basis of the quotas for European-American women when differential weighing was used (for more detail, see Wyatt, 1985).

We were unable to match the two groups on income level, a demographic characteristic that differs from one ethnic group to the other (Bureau of the Census, 1980). According to the Los Angeles County census, the median income of European-American families exceeds that of African-American families by more than $9,000. In our sample, income levels ranged from $5,000 to $50,000 per year. With the exception of the lowest income levels, however, income was comparable for the two groups. Of those women reporting less than $5,000 per year, 80% were African-American and 20% were white American. Discrepancies between groups were also found in Los Angeles County statistics for income by ethnicity (Wyatt, 1985). These rates

are consistent with Los Angeles County and national demographic characteristics (Bureau of the Census, 1980).

Furthermore, no differences were seen with respect to women's education,
marital status, and the presence of children when the 248 subjects were
compared with the 266 women who refused to participate and the 727 women
who met the criteria, agreed to participate, but were not interviewed. We can
assume, however, that women who felt comfortable discussing sex-related
issues were more likely to agree to participate than those who did not.

The sample used in this study included 82 women who reported no abuse
history, 111 women who reported contact child sexual abuse (as defined below),
and 55 women who reported at least one attempted or completed rape incident
(as defined below) at age 18 or older.

In a study of two ethnic groups who cannot be matched on all demographic
characteristics, it is important to determine if women's current demographic
characteristics influenced the prevalence of abuse reported in this study.
Thus, we used chi-square tests to examine women's age, education, marital
status, presence of children, and income by ethnicity. One interesting result
was that women's abuse histories were not significantly associated with any
of these characteristics. This suggests that discrepancies in demographic
characteristics between the two ethnic groups may not influence prevalence
of abuse ($p > 0.05$).

Procedure

Each participant was interviewed face-to-face at a location of her choice
by a trained female interviewer of the same ethnicity. Each interviewee
received $20.00 as reimbursement for her time and up to $2.50 for expenses.
Interviews were generally conducted in two sessions and ranged from three
to eight hours in length. On completion of the interview, referrals for mental
health services were provided for those women who requested it (less than
5% of the sample).

Instrumentation

Few measures exist that assess specifically the circumstances and outcomes of sexually abusive experiences, including sexual, psychological, and
relationship issues. None have been developed for a community sample of
African-American and white American women.

For most data, we used the Wyatt Sex History Questionnaire (WSHQ)
(Wyatt, 1985), a 478-item structured interview appropriate for use with
multiethnic groups. It was used to obtain both retrospective and current data

about women's consensual and abusive sexual experiences and the effects of these experiences on sexual and psychological functioning, as well as on intimate relationships. The instrument was pretested on two ethnic groups (77 female volunteers and 16 pilot respondents) to determine whether it asked for information in a clear and understandable manner (Wyatt, 1982) before it would be used in research.

With one exception, questions were arranged chronologically, beginning with childhood and ending in adulthood, to allow for detection of inconsistencies in the data provided by the respondents. When inconsistencies were noted, it was possible to ask the respondent for clarification immediately. For example, if a woman reported first intercourse at age 19 and a sexual assault at the same age, a series of questions was asked about the circumstances of each event to ensure that they were not identical. Questions about the occurrence of sexual abuse were asked at the end of the interview, and affirmative responses were followed by a series of more detailed questions about each incident.

Reliability was established for various portions of the questionnaire. For example, severity of abuse was rated on a 10-point scale by four interviewers, yielding an interrater reliability of .90. Ten audiotapes were randomly examined for accuracy of interviewers' written transcriptions of participants' responses. In this comparison, only two mistakes were noted out of 4,780 items.

Several additional analyses were conducted to examine the reliability of the data. Pearson correlations between demographic characteristics obtained in the telephone recruitment and those obtained during the interview up to nine months later ranged from .82 to 1.0. Demographic characteristics of participants and their parents, received from 119 women who were reinterviewed for another study one month to two years later (Peters, 1984), yielded test-retest correlations ranging from .65 to .98. Overall, respondents' responses were consistent over time, strengthening the probability that other responses were also reliable.

In addition to the WSHQ, three paper-and-pencil instruments were administered to measure self-esteem, general well-being, and sex guilt, or the need to control one's sexual desires. The Rosenberg Self-Esteem (RSE) Scale, the General Well-Being (GWB) Scale, and the Mosher Forced Choice Sex Guilt Test were each read to the participants in the course of the face-to-face interview.

The RSE is a 10-item scale measuring generally favorable or unfavorable global self-attitudes. Each item is measured on Likert scales, which allows the respondent to weigh her response to each statement. Three scoring methods can be used, although Rosenberg's method of choice (from personal communication in January, 1984) was that of assigning a score of 1 to 4 to each statement. Scores 1 and 2 represent lowest and low self-esteem, respectively, for any one statement. Scores 3 and 4 represent high and highest self-esteem, respectively, for any one item. The total RSE Scale score may range from 10 to 40, with 40 reflecting highest and 10 lowest self-esteem. Rosenberg (1979) reports a coefficient of reproducibility of 92% and a coefficient of scalability of 72%. In a college sample, test-retest reliability after a two-week period revealed r's between .85 and .88. Construct validity of the RSE Scale has been tested in terms of its empirical relationship to depressive affect, anxiety, and peer group reputation (Rosenberg, 1979, pp. 292-295). Tests of the scale's convergent and discriminant validity, as well as factor analyses of the items, also have been conducted (Rosenberg, 1979, pp. 292-295). Rosenberg and Simmons (1971) reported an alpha internal consistency of .85. In our sample, we obtained a Cronbach's alpha of .805 for both ethnic groups.

In a comparison of 12 studies conducted between 1960 and 1968, Rosenberg and Simmons (1971) found that, in 8 of 13 comparisons, blacks rated higher in self-esteem; whites rated higher in 4; and, in 1, no differences were found. Rosenberg conservatively concluded that the weight of evidence did not justify assumptions that blacks have either higher or lower self-esteem than whites, but that there were no appreciable racial differences in self-esteem. Our study demonstrated that African-American and European-American women do not score differently from one another in terms of the range of scores that fall within "high," "medium," and "low" self-esteem. For both African-American and European-American women in this sample, the range of scores falling in the high self-esteem category was 35-40. In the medium self-esteem category, the range of scores for African-American women was 32-34; it was 31-34 for European-American women. The low self-esteem category was represented by a range of scores of 10-31 for the African-American women and 10-30 for European-American women. Nonsignificant differences were found between the African-American and white American women's mean RSE Scale scores: 32.82 ($N = 119$) and 31.9 ($N = 120$), respectively. These data support Rosenberg's conclusions that there are no significant differences in self-esteem between the two ethnic groups of women.

The General Well-Being (GWB) Scale comprises closed-ended questions that tap subjectively perceived psychological functioning during the past month. The 18-item schedule used in this research is a short version developed at the National Center for Health Statistics (NCHS) by Harold Dupuy. Six content areas measure (a) health worry; (b) energy level; (c) satisfying, interesting life; (d) depressed versus cheerful mood; (e) emotional-behavioral control; and (f) relaxed versus tense and anxious mood. An individual's score can range from 0 to 110, with 0 indicating the greatest degree of stress and 110 indicating the most positive adjustment. The internal consistency coefficient of the 18 items with a noninstitutionalized sample of adults (ages 25-79) was found to be .93 (N = 6,913) (Neff & Husaini, 1980). Using the percentage cutoffs provided by Neff and Husaini (1980), the respective range of scores for positive well-being, moderate distress, and severe distress were 63-110, 52-62, and 0-51 for our sample. There was little variation in the range of scores between African-American and European-American women. In this sample, we obtained a Cronbach's alpha of .91 for both ethnic groups. This measure was selected because it included items regarding psychological health, as well as problems. We also were concerned with identifying both healthy and unhealthy sexual practices that were associated with psychological well-being.

The Mosher Sexual Guilt Subscale is one of three scales developed from a sentence-completion measure of guilt. It consists of 27 items. For the purposes of our study, we used a shortened form of the inventory comprising 26 items. For each item, the respondent selects one of two completed phrases most characteristic of her feelings, beliefs, and reactions. Each item is weighted to yield a score to represent the amount of sex guilt the respondent has. The test allows respondents to be divided into high and low sex-guilt groups based on the distribution of scores. Numerous studies have validated the construct, convergent, and discriminant validity of the three subscales (Abramson & Mosher, 1975; Galbraith, 1964; Lamb, 1963), but the most convincing evidence of utility comes from the predictive validity investigations (Abramson, Mosher, Abramson, & Woychowski, 1977). The scale has a possible range of −45 to +37, with positive scores representing greater guilt. In this sample, there was a highly significant ethnic difference, with African-American women scoring in the direction of greater guilt than did European-American women (M = −17.16) [(F(1,242) = 31.80, p .0001)]. The scores for white American women were similar to scores previously generated for this population (for example, see Abramson & Imai-Marquez, 1982). We obtained a Cronbach's alpha of .853 for both ethnic groups in our sample.

The Definition of Child Sexual Abuse

Initially, sexual abuse was defined and read to respondents as "sexual body contact prior to age 18 with someone of any age or relationship to the respondent" (Wyatt, 1985). However, to separate women's childhood sexual victimization experiences from exploratory sexual experimentation before age 12, or any other consensual sexual activity with peers, two additional exclusion criteria were used:

1. An incident was considered sexual abuse if the perpetrator was more than five years older than the respondent at the time.

2. If the age difference was less than five years, only contact that was not desired, or involved coercion, was included.

For these analyses, "sexual abuse" was restricted to incidents involving body contact, including breast or genital fondling and attempted or completed vaginal or oral intercourse. Of the 111 women who reported at least one such sexual contact abuse incident, 40% were African-American and 51% were European-American.

The Definition of Rape

Completed rape was defined as the involuntary penetration of the vagina or anus by the penis or another object. *Attempted rape* was defined as an attempt to penetrate the vagina or anus with the penis or another object against a woman's will. This definition was read to all respondents who were then asked about any sexual experiences in their adult lives that might have occurred without their consent. To separate rape in adulthood from childhood sexual abuse, the former type of experience needed to have occurred since the age of 18. The perpetrator might have been a friend, relative, or stranger.

Women were encouraged to describe particular incidents, regardless of their uncertainty about whether a particular experience constituted rape. Hesitancy was especially common in cases of attempted or completed rapes committed by persons known to the women. Consequently, they sometimes did not consider such incidents to be typical rapes, as other studies have also indicated (Burt, 1980). Nevertheless, these incidents were included as rapes in the study.

Our approach to assessing the prevalence of types of sexual assault since age 18 differs from recent studies that used behavioral descriptions and excluded the term *rape* (Koss & Gidycz, 1985). In this study, we defined incidents of attempted and completed rape and asked about the circumstances of each incident. Rape-related information was requested after rapport was well established, one to two hours into the structured interview. Discrepancies between women's and research definitions of rape and terms such as *anus* (a word with which 9% were unfamiliar) and *vagina* and phrases such as "other objects used for penetration" were clarified. We found it particularly useful to discuss the definition of rape before asking women to describe their experiences. After the completion of the interview, it was not uncommon for women to recontact the interviewers and report additional incidents as they realized that what they had experienced had been rape.

Preparation of the Data

Table 11.2 shows the number and type of items for each variable or factor, the specific content of items, and their coding ranges.

For categorical items, we created scales with at least two and at most six points. Scales with open-ended items were coded in descending order, starting with experiences or information that were self-directed to those involving others. This ordering captured the importance of self-learning over self-related experiences at the hand of someone outside of the family. Relevant questionnaire items from each of the 12 domains were entered into several factor analyses, with orthogonal factor rotation. This procedure yielded several factors for four of the domains: Sexual Socialization, Age of Onset of Sexual Behavior, Voluntary Adult Sexual Behavior, and Sexual Satisfaction. When data were missing because the respondent never had a particular experience, we entered the statistical mean based on all the responses given to the particular item by all respondents. Only those items with loadings above .25 were retained for each factor (see Table 11.2 for a detailed listing of domains, factors, and items). For each factor, reliability analyses were conducted. Table 11.2 lists Cronbach's coefficient alpha for each factor where it was considered relevant.

From the factor analyses, the following three factors emerged for the Sexual Socialization domain: Parental Endorsement of Body Awareness and Nudity (20 items), Endorsement of Sexual Intimacy by Agents of Socialization (18 items), and Parents' Demonstrative Messages about Sexual Expression (13 items). Of the 83 items entered into the analyses originally, a total of 51 items were retained.

For the Age of Onset of Sexual Behavior domain, we obtained two factors: Age of First Sexual Behaviors with Others and Age of First Self-Exploratory Behaviors. The six items entered into these analyses were all retained, with three items loading on each factor.

The factor analyses for the Voluntary Adulthood Sexual Behavior domain generated the following five factors: (a) Frequencies of Adult Sexual Activities (five items), (b) Effective Use of Birth Control (three items), (c) Partner Sex Initiation (two items), (d) Unplanned Pregnancies (two items), and (e) Frequency of Sexual Contact (two items). Of a total of 31 items, 14 items were retained.

Two final factors emerged for the Sexual Satisfaction domain: Current Sexual Satisfaction (11 items) and Partner Sex Dysfunction (5 items). Thus, 16 of the original 31 items were retained.

Other sets of items were retained as separate variables or combined by using composite scores. Some were converted to log scores to account for wide variations in frequencies. These constructs or measured variables were Parent Education, Quality of Family Life, Voluntary Childhood Sexual Behavior, Severity of Intrafamilial Child Sexual Abuse, Severity of Extrafamilial Child Sexual Abuse, Voluntary Adolescent Sexual Behavior, Severity of Attempted Rapes, Severity of Completed Rapes, Need to Control One's Sexual Desires, and General Well-Being.

(Text continued on page 76)

Table 11.2   Variables, Items, and Coding Procedures Used for Data Analyses

---

Sexual Socialization (51 items)
Factor I: Parental endorsement of body awareness and nudity
(Cronbach's alpha = .832) (20 items)

Variables and Items	Coding Range
1. What parents said about nudity in home during subject's childhood[a] (5-point scale)	(1) Negative (3) Nothing (5) It is okay
2. What parents really felt about nudity in home (childhood and adolescence)[a] (3-point scale)	(1) Opposed (3) Not opposed
3. What parents really felt about masturbation (childhood and adolescence)[a] (3-point scale)	(1) Opposed (3) Not opposed
4. Whether parents told subject about sexual intercourse first[c] (2-point scale)	(1) Yes (2) No
5. What was said about necking during subject's adolescence[a] (5-point scale)	(1) Opposed (2) Nothing (5) It is okay
6. What parents really felt about necking during subject's adolescence[a] (3-point scale)	(1) Opposed (3) Not opposed
7. Subject nude or partially nude around house (childhood and adolescence)[a] (3-point scale)	(1) Never (3) A lot
8. Parents nude around house (childhood and adolescence)[a] (3-point scale)	(1) Never (3) A lot
9. Subject completely undressed in front of parents (childhood and adolescence)[a] (3-point scale)	(1) Never (3) A lot
10. Parents completely undressed in front of subject (childhood and adolescence)[a] (3-point scale)	(1) Never (3) A lot
11. Subject and parents bathed or showered nude together (childhood and adolescence)[a] (3-point scale)	(1) Never (3) A lot
12. Subject saw parents nude in bathroom (childhood and adolescence)[a] (3-point scale)	(1) Never (3) A lot

Factor II: Endorsement of sexual intimacy by socialization agents
(Cronbach's alpha = .725) (18 items)

1. Age when first became aware of sex[b]	Age in years
2. How became aware of sex[a] (6-point scale)	(1) Menstruation (3) Peer (6) Experience
3. What was said about masturbation (childhood)[a] (3-point scale)	(1) Prohibitive message (3) Nothing
4. What was said about homosexuality (childhood and adolescence)[a] (3-point scale)	(1) Negative message (2) Nothing (3) Neutral or okay

Table 11.2 Continued

Variables and Items	Coding Range
5. How parents felt about homosexuality (childhood and adolescence)[a] (3-point scale)	(1) Opposed (3) Not opposed
6. What was said about premarital intercourse (childhood and adolescence)[a] (5-point scale)	(1) Negative message (3) Nothing (5) Okay
7. How parents felt about premarital intercourse (childhood and adolescence)[a] (5-point scale)	(1) Negative message (3) Nothing (5) Okay
8. Age when first learned of coitus[b]	Age in years
9. What was said about petting (adolescence)[a] (4-point scale)	(1) Opposed (2) Mixed message (4) Nothing
10. How parents felt about petting (adolescence)[a] (3-point scale)	(1) Opposed (3) Not opposed
11. Religious messages about sex (childhood and adolescence)[a] (3-point scale)	(1) Prohibitive (3) Nothing
12. What recalled being said about possibility of sexual molestation (adolescence)[a] (3-point scale)	(1) Specific prohibitions (3) Nothing
13. Sexual standards told so boys would like and respect you? (adolescence)[a] (4-point scale)	(1) Sex instructions and prohibitions (4) Nothing

Factor III: Parents' demonstrative messages about sexual expression
(Cronbach's alpha = .674) (13 items)

1. What parents communicated about sex by way they acted (childhood and adolescence)[a] (5-point scale)	(1) Negative message (3) Nothing (5) Positive/okay
2. How parents felt about their sex life (childhood and adolescence)[a] (3-point scale)	(1) Did not enjoy it (2) No expression about it (3) Enjoyed it
3. What parents or other adults said about nudity in home (adolescence)[a] (4-point scale)	(1) Negative message (3) Nothing (4) Okay
4. Both bedroom and bathroom doors left open (childhood and adolescence)[c] (2-point scale)	(1) Yes (2) No
5. Both bedroom and bathroom doors left open, except at specific times (childhood and adolescence)[c] (2-point scale)	(1) Yes (2) No
6. Types of behavior by parents demonstrating physical affection toward each other (childhood and adolescence)[a] (3-point scale)	(1) Kissing (2) Hugging (3) Affectionate slap, fondle, etc.
7. How often parents showed physical affection toward each other (childhood and adolescence)[a] (4-point scale)	(1) Occasionally (4) Daily

Variables and Items	Coding Range
Parent Education[t] (2 items)	
1. Mother's education[b]	Number of years
2. Father's education[b]	Number of years
Quality of Family Life (4 items)	
1. Kind of relationship parents had (childhood)[a,t] (6-point scale)	(1) None (2) Very poor (6) Excellent
2. Closeness of immediate family (childhood)[a,t] (4-point scale)	(1) Not very close (4) Very close
Felt Closest to in Family[tt] (2 items)	
1. Who subject felt emotionally closest to in immediate family (childhood)[a] (4-point scale)	(1) Brother (4) Mother/mother substitute
2. Others in extended family subject felt very close to (childhood)[a] (3-point scale)	(1) Other relatives (2) Grandparent (3) Uncle/aunt
Voluntary Childhood Sexual Behaviors (5 items)	
Self-exploration and Masturbation[tt] (2 items)	
1. Number of times explored breast and genitals[b]	Actual number
2. Number of times masturbated per month[b]	Actual number
Childhood Play With Others[tt] (2 items)	
1. Number of times touched genital area of another person's body[b]	Actual number
2. Number of times another person looked at or touched subject's genitals[b]	Actual number
Frequency of Sexual Arousal[ttt] (1 item)	
1. Number of times sexual arousal occurred[a] (3-point scale)	(1) 1-2 times (2) 3 times (3) 4 times or more
Severity of Child Intrafamilial Sexual Abuse[*] (2 items)	
Frequency of Abuse per Incident[ttt]	
1. Number of times abuse occurred with this person[b]	Actual number
Duration of Abuse per Incident[ttt]	
2. Longest duration of an abuse incident in weeks[b]	Actual number
Severity of Child Extrafamilial Sexual Abuse[*] (2 items)	
Frequency of Abuse per Incident[ttt]	
1. Number of times abuse occurred with this person[b]	Actual number
Duration of Abuse per Incident[ttt]	
2. Longest duration of an abuse incident in weeks[b]	Actual number

[*]These scales included two items each. Rather than calculating an alpha for the two items of each scale, we examined correlations for each pair of items. All four correlations were greater than .800, indicating that items were highly interrelated.

Table 11.2 Continued

Variables and Items	Coding Range

Voluntary Adolescent Sexual Behaviors[t]
(Cronbach's alpha = .284) (3 items)

1. Number of times masturbated per month[b] — Actual number
2. Number of sexual partners up to age 17[b,ttt] — Actual number
3. Length of time of sexual relationships[b] — Number of years

Age of Onset of Sexual Behaviors (6 items)
Factor I: Age of first sexual behaviors with others
(Cronbach's alpha = .936) (3 items)

1. Age when boy first touched breasts during — Age in years
petting (adolescence)[b]

2. Age when boy first touched genitals during petting — Age in years
(adolescence)[b]

3. Age at first intercourse (adolescence)[b] — Age in years

Factor II: Age of first self-exploratory behaviors
(Cronbach's alpha = .665) (3 items)

1. Age first looked at or touched breast and genital — Age in years
area (childhood)[b]

2. Age when first masturbated (childhood)[b] — Age in years
3. Age when first experienced orgasm[b] — Age in years

Severity of Attempted Rape in Adulthood[*] (2 items)

Number of rapes per incident[ttt] — Actual number
Amount of physical coercion used[ttt] (2-point scale) — (1) None
                                                        (2) Some

Severity of Completed Rape in Adulthood[*] (2 items)

Number of rapes per incident[ttt] — Actual number
Amount of physical coercion used[ttt] (2-point scale) — (1) None
                                                        (2) Some

[*]These scales included two items each. Rather than calculating an alpha for the two items of each scale, we examined correlations for each pair of items. All four correlations were greater than .800, indicating that items were highly interrelated.

Voluntary Adult Sexual Behavior (14 items)
Factor I: Frequencies of adult sexual activities
(Cronbach's alpha = .702) (5 items)

1. Number of times per month subject performed oral sex[b] — Actual number
2. Number of times per month partner performed oral sex[b] — Actual number
3. Number of times per month intercourse with partner[b] — Actual number
4. Number of times per month anal intercourse with partner[b] — Actual number
5. Number of times per month subject masturbated[b] — Actual number

Variables and Items	Coding Range
Factor II: Effective use of birth control (Cronbach's alpha = .705) (3 items)	
1. Percentage of time using any method of birth control (all methods included) [b]	Actual percentage reported
2. Percentage of time using effective birth control (diaphragm, condom, IUD, pill, tubal ligation)[b]	Actual percentage reported
3. Percentage of time using ineffective birth control ("natural methods" such as rhythm and withdrawal; foam or jelly; etc.)[b]	Actual percentage reported
Factor III: Partner sex initiation (Cronbach's alpha = .955) (2 items)	
1. Percentage of time partner initiates sex[a] (4-point scale)	(1) 25% (4) 100%
2. Percentage of time subject initiates sex[a] (4-point scale)	(1) Never (4) 75%
Factor IV: Unplanned pregnancies (Cronbach's alpha = .825) (2 items)	
1. Number of unplanned pregnancies[b]	Actual number
2. Number of abortions[b]	Actual number
Factor V: Frequency of sexual contact (Cronbach's alpha = .833) (2 items)	
1. Intercourse with number of male partners after age 18[b]	Actual number
2. Length of time of each relationship[a]	(1) One-night stands (3) Combination of long and short relationships (5) One or multiple long-term partner(s)
Sexual Satisfaction (16 items) **Factor I: Current sexual satisfaction** (Cronbach's alpha = .841) (11 items)	
1. Sexual satisfaction with this partner[a] (3-point scale)	(1) Not satisfying (3) Satisfying
2. Percentage of time subject was not adequately lubricated[a] (2-point scale)	(1) 25-100% (2) Almost never
3. Percentage of time subject was not aroused or excited[a] (4-point scale)	(1) 75% (4) Almost never
4. Percentage of time subject did not want to have sex[a] (4-point scale)	(1) 75% (4) Almost never
5. Overall satisfaction of sexual relationships[a] (5-point scale)	(1) Very unsatisfying (3) Some satisfying, some not (5) Very satisfying

Table 11.2 Continued

Variables and Items	Coding Range
6. Sexual experiences/intercourse generally unpleasant and/or painful[a] (3-point scale)	(1) No (2) Somewhat (3) Yes
7. Percentage of time intercourse painful[a] (2-point scale)	(1) 25-100% (2) Almost never
8. Sexual experiences/intercourse pleasant and enjoyable[a] (3-point scale)	(1) No (2) Somewhat (3) Yes
9. Sexual experiences/intercourse brought new and unusual feelings[a] (3-point scale)	(1) No (2) Somewhat (3) Yes
10. Sexual experiences/intercourse one of best things ever to happen to subject[a] (3-point scale)	(1) No (3) Yes
11. Sexual experiences/intercourse rewarding and fulfilling experience[a] (3-point scale)	(1) No (3) Yes
Factor II: Partner sex dysfunction (Cronbach's alpha = .490) (5 items)	
1. Percentage of time partner did not get or maintain an erection[a] (2-point scale)	(1) 25-75% (2) Almost never
2. Percentage of time partner ejaculated before or while entering vagina[a] (2-point scale)	(1) 25-100% (2) Almost never
3. Percentage of time partner did not have control of when he ejaculated[a] (2-point scale)	(1) 25-100% (2) Almost never
4. Percentage of time partner did not become aroused or excited[a] (2-point scale)	(1) 25-75% (2) Almost never
5. Percentage of time partner could not ejaculate[a] (2-point scale)	(1) 25-75% (2) Almost never
Need to Control One's Sexual Desires[t] 26 items from Mosher Forced Choice Sex Guilt Test[tt] (Cronbach's alpha = .853)	
Psychological Well-Being[t] (30 items) 10 items from Rosenberg Self-Esteem Scale[tt] (Cronbach's alpha = .805) 18 items from General Well-Being Scale[tt] (Cronbach's alpha = .906)	

Key to superscripts.
Type of item: a = categorical; b = numerical; c = dichotomous.
Method of variable reduction: t = individual item; tt = composite score; ttt = log score.

The Parent Education latent construct was reflected by two items: the mother's and father's education as measured in years. For the Quality of Family Life construct, we used two single-item variables—the nature of the parental relationship and the degree of closeness within the immediate family—as well as a composite score that indicated who the respondent felt closest to in her immediate or extended family.

The Voluntary Childhood Sexual Behavior construct consisted of two composite scores—self-exploration and masturbation (two items) and childhood play with others (two items)—and one single-item log score—frequency of arousal (one item).

For both the Severity of Intrafamilial and Extrafamilial Child Sexual Abuse variables, which reflect childhood sexual abuse, we used multiplicative variables. Both frequency and duration of these types of childhood sexual abuse were converted to log scores. To capture the magnitude of abuse as accurately as possible, we multiplied frequency and duration of sexual abuse, rather than adding the two items.

The Voluntary Adolescent Sexual Behavior construct was reflected by three single-item variables: frequency of masturbation per month, number of sex partners up to age 17 (which was converted to a log score), and length of sexual relationships (in years).

For the Severity of Attempted and Completed Rapes scales, we used two weighted items each: the number of rapes per incident and the amount of physical coercion applied.

The 26 items of the Mosher Sex Guilt Inventory yielded a composite score for the Need to Control One's Sexual Desires variable. To form a latent control for this measure, we randomly parceled the 26 items into 3 scales that were used to reflect the latent factor (e.g., Newcomb, 1990). As mentioned earlier, the construct of sex guilt was renamed the "need to control one's sexual desires" to create a more neutral and less judgmental perception of sexual standards.

The Psychological Well-Being construct was reflected by the 10-item Rosenberg Self-Esteem Scale (Rosenberg & Simmons, 1971) and the 18-item General Well-Being Scale (Neff & Husaini, 1980). A composite score was generated for each.

■ Ethnic Comparisons

Our sample was chosen to contain about equal numbers of African-American and white American women. Patterns of sexual development and processes related to sexual abuse might be different based on ethnic and cultural variations. Potential differences can emerge in at least two ways: (a) as mean differences on the variable scores for each group and (b) as relational differences on the magnitude of correlations between variables for each group. Thirty variables were included in these two sets of analyses (Need to Control One's Sexual Desires was combined into a total score for these analyses).

Point-biserial correlations were used to test for mean differences between the ethnic groups on all variables. These correlations are presented in the last column of Table 11.3. Ten of these correlations were significant. However, when the Bonferroni adjustment was used to correct for multiple simultaneous comparisons, only three of these differences remained reliable: African-American women reported that they felt their families were closer when they were children. As adults they reported lower frequencies of sexual activities and sexual contact than did European-American women.

To test for relational differences between pairs of variables for the European-American and African-American women, correlation matrices were generated separately for each group. Corresponding correlations in each matrix were statistically compared using the Fisher r-to-z conversion. The Bonferroni method was used to adjust for multiple simultaneous comparisons. Out of the 435 comparisons, only 1 remained statistically reliable at the $p \leq .05$ level when adjusted for the 435 comparisons. This difference revealed no significant correlation between severity of intrafamilial sexual abuse and family closeness for the European-American women but a significant correlation for African-American women. In other words, there was a strong relationship between family closeness and incest for African-American women, whereas for white American women there was no reliable association between these variables. Although several other comparisons between correlations in each group were significant at the unadjusted $p < .001$ level of significance, none of these involved sexual abuse variables. Therefore we concluded that there were very few differences between African-American and European-American women regarding their correlates with sexual abuse and that the two samples could be combined for the remaining analyses. However, this does not preclude future comparisons that may compare more circumscribed sets of variables in light of specific hypotheses. Under these conditions, our harsh restrictions on the alpha level necessary for significance would not be necessary and further differences may emerge as a result in a less exploratory approach.

■ Analyses

Several statistical procedures are used to analyze these data. However, most of our analyses that relate to hypotheses and substantive issues involve (a) structural equation models (SEM) with latent variables for testing direct and mediating effects and (b) comparisons of correlations between distinct groups for testing moderating effects.

Because few substantial differences were found on correlational patterns between ethnic groups, women of both ethnicities will be merged for the SEM

Table 11.3 Summary of Statistics for All Variables

Life Area/Variables	Number of Items	Mean	Range	Variance	r_{pb} Mean Ethnic Difference[a]
Family Context					
Parental endorsement of body awareness and nudity	20	[b]	−1.26-4.16	[c]	.20**
Endorsement of sexual intimacy by socialization agents	18	[b]	−1.77-4.36	[c]	.06
Parent's demonstrative messages about sexual expression	13	[b]	3.48-0.74	[c]	.12
Mother's education	1	2.26	0-20	7.68	.14**
Father's education	1	2.24	1-23	11.44	.19*
Relationship parents had	1	3.75	1-6	1.80	−.03
Family closeness	1	3.96	1-5	1.27	−.25***
Felt closest to in family	2	2.71	0-3	0.29	−.14**
Childhood					
Self-exploration and masturbation	2	1.31	0-4	1.10	−.06
Frequency of arousal	1	0.58	0-4	0.93	.07
Sex play with others	2	1.13	0-4.56	2.70	.03
Severity of intrafamilial abuse	2	1.25	0-31.41	14.10	.05
Severity of extrafamilial abuse	2	1.71	0-31.41	18.55	.02
Adolescence					
Frequency of masturbation	1	0.53	0-3.44	0.70	.19*
Number of sexual partners	1	0.51	0-4.06	0.36	.02
Length of relationships	1	2.33	1-7	1.67	.20**
Age of first sex behaviors with others	3	[b]	−3.25-4.38	[c]	.03
Age of first self-exploratory behaviors	3	[b]	−2.09-2.32	[c]	−.19**
Adulthood					
Severity of rapes	2	4.99	0-63	174.57	.01
Severity of attempted rapes	2	3.37	0-53	124.67	.11
Frequency of adult sexual activities	5	[b]	−1.73-2.37	[c]	.35***
Birth control effectiveness	3	[b]	−1.98-4.03	[c]	.06
Partner sex initiation	2	[b]	−3.06-2.00	[c]	−.05
Frequency of sexual contact	2	[b]	−1.44-3.72	[c]	.24***
Abortions	2	[b]	−1.00-5.66	[c]	−.07
Well-being	18	[b]	−37.09-22.53	[c]	−.11

(*Continued*)

Table 11.3 Continued

Life Area/Variables	Number of Items	Mean	Range	Variance	r_{pb} Mean Ethnic Difference[a]
Self-esteem	10	32.33	17-40	18.97	−.10
Need to control sexual desires (Mosher total score)	26	38.41	32-44		
Current satisfaction	11	[b]	−1.09-3.90	[c]	−.03
Sex dysfunction with partner	5	[b]	−5.09-1.10	[c]	−.02

*$p < .05$; **$p < .01$; ***$p < .001$
[a]A positive correlation indicates that the African-American women had the larger mean.
[b]Variable was standardized; mean = 0.00.
[c]Variable was standardized; variance = 1.00.

analyses. To analyze all variables in one SEM, this aggregated sample is necessary to yield stable and reliable parameter estimates (Newcomb, 1990; Tanaka, 1987).

Our substantive findings are based on a series of SEMs that include both latent and measured variables (Bentler, 1980; Bentler & Newcomb, 1986; Newcomb, 1990). The two scales within each sexual abuse domain are retained as separate variables and not used as latent construct indicators. This was done to capture their unique aspects directly. We expect that many of the measured variables within the other 10 domains will be adequate indicators of latent constructs, and confirmatory factor analyses are used to determine this. Where certain sets of variables do not reliably reflect latent constructs of their domains, these measures are retained and treated as separate variables (single-indicator factors, albeit with measurement error).

Once an appropriate measurement model is established, structural or path modes are constructed. Based on the conclusions of Chou and Bentler (1990) and MacCallum (1986), we will first add paths to create an overfit model and then remove nonsignificant paths and parameters. Both standard paths (i.e., strictly between constructs) and nonstandard parameters (including at least one measured variable) are considered in these analyses (e.g., Newcomb, 1990; Newcomb & Bentler, 1988b, c). Several fit indices are examined to evaluate the adequacy of the models, including the chi-square to degrees-of-freedom ratio, the p value associated with this ratio, the normed fit index (NFI) (Bentler & Bonett, 1980), and the comparative fit index (CFI), which adjusts for small samples (Bentler, 1990). The SEM analyses are conducted with the EQS program (Bentler, 1989) using the maximum likelihood (ML) estimator. Although most of the variables are distributed normally, a few are not. These deviations violate traditional assumptions of ML procedures.

Unfortunately, the more robust methods are only practical with far fewer variables than we want to include and require many more subjects than we have (e.g., Bentler, 1989; Muthén, 1984, 1987; Newcomb, 1990). However, recent theoretical arguments and empirical verifications reveal that ML is much more robust to normality violations than previously assumed (e.g., Bentler, 1989; Mooijaart & Bentler, 1991; Satorra & Bentler, 1990). Based on these convincing breakthroughs, we are confident that the few nonnormal variables will not distort the ML estimates in our SEMs.

A second set of analyses will test for moderator effects between types of sexual abuse and various outcome variables. Ten potential moderator variables were selected, and the sample was partitioned into the upper and lower third of each of these. Correlations among the sexual abuse variables with five selected outcome variables were calculated for those at the extreme ends of each moderator distribution. For each moderator, these correlations were compared to determine whether they differed statistically and thus would reveal a significant interaction or moderator effect.

12

Review of Previous Findings

Several different analyses have been conducted with the data of this study and have subsequently been presented in other publications. They will be summarized here for the interested reader to complement the results of our current structural modeling analyses. Some of the significant findings reported earlier are not included in the structural modeling analyses: Only the most robust of findings were retained at the .0001 level of significance. All of the previous studies can be grouped roughly into five different categories: (a) comparisons with other studies, (b) sexual behavior and attitudes, (c) childhood sexual abuse, (d) adulthood sexual abuse, and (e) methodological considerations. Many of these studies involved ethnic-group comparisons to better understand the role of culturally related socialization in the development of lifelong sexual patterns.

■ Comparisons With Other Studies

Two of the early studies, one focusing on white and the other on black females, contrasted women's sexual socialization and sexual behavior in the 1980s with the landmark study of Alfred Kinsey and his associates (1953). The purpose of these comparisons was to identify changes that had occurred in women's sexual behavior over three decades (Wyatt et al., 1988a,b). Specifically, childhood family characteristics; sexual socialization and education; sexual behavior in childhood, adolescence, and adulthood; contraceptive practices; and child sexual abuse were compared in subsamples of college-educated women in both studies. Generally, the results of those comparisons reflected societal changes in attitudes toward sexuality and changes in patterns of sexual behavior. Except for a few differences in findings for African-American and white American women, the changes in sexual practices were identical or similar for the two ethnic groups, even though the degree of change may have differed.

Compared with women in the 1940s, women in the 1980s recalled learning about sex in general and intercourse in particular from a broader range of sources, such as sex education in school, a variety of media, and through voluntary or abusive sexual experiences. The increased role of media and schools in the process of socializing women about sexuality reflects the greater availability of sexual information in today's society. Furthermore, parental attitudes about nudity in the home were found to be more relaxed than they had been in the 1940s.

Changes in sexual behavior were particularly dramatic. Women in the Wyatt sample, as opposed to the Kinsey women, reported a significant increase in both voluntary and abusive sexual behaviors, with the exception of childhood sexual play. Consistent with society's changing attitudes about masturbation, more women in the 1980s acknowledged having engaged in childhood masturbatory behavior. It is interesting, however, that contemporary women experienced more guilt about masturbation. Differences in methodologies between the Wyatt (1985) and Kinsey and associates (1953) studies and the fact that the latter did not make it possible to differentiate voluntary from abusive first sexual experiences were likely to account for the decrease in reported childhood sexual play in the Wyatt sample and the higher amount of guilt about masturbation. The increase in masturbatory guilt may reflect an increase in the number of women who recalled that, as girls, they masturbated as a result of some underlying problem, such as having been sexually abused.

Women in the Wyatt sample also reported an earlier onset of intercourse, as well as orgasmic responses at younger ages. Furthermore, they were less likely to have a fiance or husband as their first sexual partner and were more sexually active than the Kinsey women: They reported a higher number of sexual partners, participated in a broader range of sexual behaviors, such as oral and anal sex, and were more likely to have experienced childhood sexual abuse. Although there was an increase in extramarital sex for both African-American and European-American women in the 1980s, this increase was only significant for white American women. The findings also suggested that child sexual abuse that occurs before age 13 with adult male perpetrators has been continuing at a consistent rate for the past 33 years. Whether child sexual abuse is on the increase was not clearly established. The higher prevalence of incidents of childhood sexual abuse in the Wyatt sample is likely to be related to differences in the definition of sexual abuse between the two studies. Wyatt and associates' (1988a, b) findings indicate that Kinsey's statistics grossly underrepresented the prevalence of child sexual abuse, given that data on incidents of sexual abuse between women older than 12 with perpetrators who were not adults was not collected.

Several other aspects of abuse incidents differed significantly between the Wyatt and Kinsey samples of white American women. The majority of women in the 1980s had been abused by someone they knew as opposed to the reported stranger abuse in the earlier study. Abuse involving physical contact between perpetrator and victim was more prevalent for the Wyatt sample, and women were more likely to have had multiple occurrences of abuse. For the comparisons of African-American women, only one statistically significant difference emerged: The proportion of women who had two or more incidents with different perpetrators was much higher in the Wyatt sample. Overall, the likelihood of revictimization was higher in the 1980s than in the 1940s.

Changes in contraceptive use were also found for both African-American and European-American women, revealing a shift toward newer, more effective methods, such as the birth control pill and IUD, and greater availability of contraception to nonmarried women. The interested reader is referred to the Wyatt, Peters, and Guthrie articles (1988a,b) for a more detailed description of these two comparative studies.

■ Sexual Behavior and Attitudes

Several studies focused on ethnic differences in a variety of sexual attitudes and behaviors in adolescence and adulthood. In one study, the changing patterns of and influences on adolescent sexuality over the past 40 years were examined by comparing the data of the Wyatt study to other relevant research (Wyatt, 1990d). In Wyatt's (1990d) study, the overall sample mean age at first coitus was 16.9 years, and 91% of the women had experienced first sex by age 19. Findings indicated that the age of first coitus was decreasing and ethnic differences were diminishing. These trends suggested that factors other than ethnicity, such as family income, might be more helpful in predicting the early onset of sexual behaviors. Wyatt's results (1990d) also confirmed previous reports that the rate of adolescent sexual activity among African-American women may be more moderate than among their white American peers. Specifically, African-American women reported engaging in sex less frequently with partners in longer-term sexual relationships. Furthermore, women of either ethnic group who experienced consistent parenting or who grew up in homes with two parenting adults tended to delay intercourse as compared to women from homes in which the number or composition of parenting figures changed during adolescence. On the other hand, early necking and petting appeared to contribute to early intercourse for both ethnic groups. Women who experienced first coitus before age 18, but who had decided against it at some point before actually becoming sexually active, tended to be more strongly motivated to defer sex, because of fear of pregnancy or parental disapproval, as compared to women who had coitus since age 18. When the latter group of women considered first coitus, they were more likely to experience it. Both age groups anticipated that intercourse would be painful, especially younger and African-American women. For women who were initiated into sex at younger ages, however, first intercourse appeared to be less of what they expected. Women who were older apparently had a more realistic expectation of the experience. Perhaps as women mature and are exposed to more factual information about first coitus, they become more aware of what the first experience entails. While African-American women were slightly more realistic about intercourse and the discomfort that is sometimes experienced the first time, they were also more likely to engage in first intercourse out of "curiosity" than were their European-American peers who were influenced more by peer and partner pressure.

Regardless of ethnicity, however, women who were at least 18 years old or older at first coitus appeared to be influenced more by their own feelings or readiness to have sex than younger women. Women who had experienced at least one incident of contact sexual abuse had consensual intercourse 15 months earlier on the average than women in the nonabuse group. The abused women were also found to begin necking and petting earlier than their nonabused peers, to have more sexual partners, and to have shorter-term sexual relationships between the ages of 13 and 17. For women who had experienced sexual abuse before the age of 18, sexual abuse appeared to be a better predictor than ethnicity when age at first intercourse and subsequent sexual activity were considered.

In another study, Wyatt (1989) examined demographic, socialization, and decision-making factors, as well as potential differences between African-American and European-American women with regard to these variables as predictors of age at first coitus. The results indicated that, similarly for both groups, the following were the predictors of an older age at first intercourse: women's perceptions of their parents as more influential on their adolescent sexual behavior than peers, being in love and ready for sex, having more education, attending religious services more frequently during adolescence, and having an older mother. When demographic variables were controlled, ethnicity was not significantly associated with the strongest predictors or with first coitus. The interested reader is referred to Wyatt (1989) for more detailed information.

Another study investigated ethnic and cultural differences in women's sexual behavior in a more comprehensive fashion (Wyatt, 1991a). Overall, significant ethnic differences were found between African-American and European-American women in their sexual preferences for cunnilingus, fellatio, anal intercourse, and sex with more than one partner (group sex). White American women reported that they engaged in these practices more often than did their African-American cohort.

African-American women were slightly, but not significantly, younger at the time of first intercourse. A significantly smaller percentage of African-American than white women had ever masturbated or had 13 or more partners and between 4 and 7 one-night encounters since age 18. Both groups of women reported that their easiest method of achieving orgasm involved vaginal intercourse, followed by a second preference for cunnilingus and masturbation for white American women. No significant differences between ethnic groups were found for extramarital affairs and partner swapping.

Almost twice as many African-American women as European-American women (65% to 35%) reported that they were not currently using any form of contraception. Furthermore, a fairly large proportion of African-American women used nonprescription methods of birth control, such as the rhythm method or coitus interruptus. As a consequence, they also reported more unintended pregnancies than did the white cohort. It appeared that African-American women tended to use contraceptives ineffectively or used birth control pills rather than barrier methods of disease transmission. When asked about their nonuse of contraceptives, approximately twice as many African-American women stated that "they were not available at the time." Similarly, twice as many African-American than European-American women expressed a dislike of contraceptives. It was concluded that, contrary to some beliefs (MIRA, 1987), the sexual patterns of African-American women appear to contribute less to the risk of AIDS than do their patterns of contraceptive use and nonuse. Risk factors for AIDS and other STDs among African-American women evidently are the ineffective use of contraceptives, a preference for contraceptive methods that do not prevent transmission of body fluids, and the onset of sexual activity at ages at which women were often too young or too poorly educated to appreciate the importance of consistently using barrier methods of contraception. European-American women, on the other hand, appeared to be most at risk as a result of a repertoire of sexual behaviors likely to facilitate the transmission of body fluids. They were, however, more likely to have their partners use condoms to prevent infection.

Sexual attitudes, such as sex guilt, have been shown to influence the nature and type of sexual practices (see for example, Sack et al., 1984). Wyatt and Dunn (1991) examined the relationship of SES, ethnicity, and religiosity to sex guilt and sexual permissiveness as it pertains to attitudes toward premarital sexual relations. The findings revealed that the association between church attendance and sex guilt was stronger for European-American than for African-American women. Furthermore, no significant differences in sex guilt by frequency of church attendance emerged for African-American women. In contrast to previous research (Reiss, 1967; Slane & Morrow, 1981), African-American women reported higher levels of sex guilt than did their white peers. Even at lower church attendance levels (less than once a week), this relationship was retained. Furthermore, African-American women reported less sexually permissive attitudes toward premarital sex than did the white comparison group. African-American women from lower SES backgrounds scored significantly lower on permissiveness items than did African-American women of higher SES. They also had significantly higher sex guilt scores than did white American women of all SES levels. In conclusion, women's religiosity was suggested to be the best predictor of sex guilt over ethnicity and SES (for more details, see Wyatt & Dunn, 1991).

African-American women's sexual satisfaction in heterosexual relationships was examined as a dimension of their sex roles in another study (Wyatt & Lyons-Rowe, 1990). Data were collected within the context of each woman's longest relationship with a primary partner. Three factors—sexual responsiveness, sexual expression, and sexual interest and enthusiasm—emerged from a principal components factor analysis of 18 variables that included frequencies of and attitudes toward sexual behaviors, percentage of time orgasmic, the nature of the couple's sexual communication, as well as women's and their parents' demographic characteristics. Overall, women who were sexually satisfied in their primary relationships had positive feelings about sex, engaged in and initiated sex frequently, were highly orgasmic, and verbally expressed their sexual needs in their relationships. Specifically, sexual responsiveness reflected both affective and behavioral responses to intercourse with the primary partner. From these data, a profile emerged of women who were less sexually satisfied when they were unsure if engaging in intercourse was right or wrong, when they felt guilty about sex, when they were fearful of the consequences of intercourse, and when they did not feel that sex with their partner was a rewarding experience, and who were orgasmic less than 25% of the time. Sexual expression, on the other hand, reflected a more behavioral description of sexual satisfaction and suggested a profile of women who were more sexually satisfied with high frequencies of intercourse, mutual oral stimulation, and both verbal and nonverbal expression of sexual needs. Finally, sexual interest and enthusiasm indicated that when women initiated sex a high percentage of the time and their partners seldom initiated sex, women felt sex with this partner brought new and exciting feelings and was one of the best things that ever happened to them. Subsidiary analyses also found that women whose mothers had more education showed an increase in their sexual interest and enthusiasm. Furthermore, while early religious socialization was associated with sexual satisfaction, church attendance in childhood was linked to less sexual responsiveness in

88   SEXUAL ABUSE AND CONSENSUAL SEX

adulthood. Please see Wyatt and Lyons-Rowe (1990) for a more detailed description of the study.

■ Child Sexual Abuse

These data examined the prevalence and circumstances of child sexual abuse among African-American and white American women ages 18 to 36 (Wyatt, 1985). Sexual abuse incidents included both a range of physical contact experiences—such as fondling and attempted and completed incidents of intercourse and oral sex—and non-body-contact experiences involving solicitations to engage in sexual behavior, perpetrators who masturbated publicly, and exhibitionists. Given the broadest definition, 62% of women reported at least one incident of sexual abuse before age 18, with 57% of African-American women and 67% of European-American women having been abused. This prevalence rate was higher than in any previously cited studies of comparable methodology (Finkelhor, 1979; Russell, 1983). One in 2.5 African-American women had experienced some form of abuse involving body contact, as did 1 in 2 white American women. The latter women experienced significantly more abuse in the early childhood period (6 to 8 years), whereas their African-American cohorts reportedly experienced more abuse as preadolescents (9 to 12 years). No significant differences for the two ethnic groups were found with regard to the number of occurrences with the same perpetrator (most of whom were male and matched the victim's ethnicity), the percentage of physical coercion involved, or the most common locations—the home of the child or perpetrator and on the street in the neighborhood—in which the abuse occurred (for more detail, see Wyatt, 1985).

Another study focused on several aspects of the victim's personal experience in the aftermath of child sexual abuse (Wyatt, 1990b). For both African-American and European-American victims, the following were examined: the survivor's immediate response, first disclosure of the abuse, reasons for nondisclosure, short-term effects (up to three months), lasting effects (including feelings about both sex and men), and the victim's attributions regarding the causes of the abuse. Few ethnic differences were noted in terms of the survivor's immediate response and short-term effects. African-American women expressed more negative reactions to fondling incidents than in response to those involving intercourse, but the trend was reversed for white American women. A factor that was likely to account for this finding is that fondling incidents for African-American women involved more physical coercion, whereas abuse incidents involving intercourse for white women were accompanied by more physical coercion. In more than one third of incidents reported by both ethnic groups, victims did not tell anyone about the abuse, and 70% of the undisclosed incidents involved contact abuse. For the other incidents, approximately 80% of women of both ethnic groups most often told a parent or primary caretaker. African-American women, however, tended to disclose more to extended family members than did their European-American peers. External reasons for nondisclosure, such as threats by the perpetrator and fear of blame, were reported by more than half of the sample. No significant differences between the two ethnic groups emerged with respect to initial and lasting effects. Although not statistically significant, it was interesting to note that the vast majority of incidents that resulted in lasting effects on African-American women's sexual functioning involved more severe abuse, whereas for white American women the negative lasting effects were associated with less severe types of abuse. Lasting effects of sexual abuse on women overall included sexual problems and feeling less trustful, more cautious, and more fearful of men. Avoidance of men resembling the perpetrator was identified among African-American women. Growing up as a African-American woman in a white society may have been a factor contributing to adjustment problems later in life, in addition to child sexual victimization (Wyatt, 1990b).

The relationship between child sexual abuse and adolescent sexual functioning for African-American and white American women was examined in other analyses (Wyatt, 1988a). Significant relationships between several aspects of women's child abuse experiences and their voluntary sexual behavior before age 18 revealed that women who reported contact sexual abuse had voluntary sexual intercourse 15.4 months earlier than did women who had either noncontact abuse or no abuse. Likewise, women with contact abuse engaged in necking and petting behaviors at earlier ages and had more sexual partners during adolescence and briefer sexual relationships than did women who had noncontact abuse or no abuse histories. Similar relationships between interviewers' ratings of the severity of child sexual abuse and women's adolescent sexual behaviors were also noted. Women whose child sexual abuse was rated to be most severe had significantly earlier ages of necking, petting, and coitus and more sexual partners and shorter-term relationships than did women with moderately severe, least severe, or no abuse experiences. Ethnic differences were not statistically significant. These findings indicate that child sexual abuse, rather than women's ethnicity alone, may contribute to the early onset and higher frequency of adolescent sexual behaviors.

A different design using observed variable simultaneous path analysis models analyzed retrospective assessments of the circumstances and coping strategies that mediated the immediate and lasting effects of women's sexual abuse in childhood (Wyatt & Newcomb, 1990). Circumstances related to sexual abuse were assumed to affect several intervening or mediating variables that in turn were predicted to influence later outcomes in adulthood. Age at last abuse, duration of abuse, proximity of abuse (which included the relation-ship of victim to perpetrator, location of abuse, and effect of abuse on the family), severity of abuse (which included the number and type of abuse incidents and use of physical coercion), psychological coercion, and abuse by a teenage perpetrator represented the six circumstances of abuse that were examined. The four variables constituting internal and external mediators were (a) immediate negative reactions to the abuse, (b) internal attributions (self-blame), (c) extent of disclosure, and (d) involvement of authorities. One variable —negative effects of abuse, including emotional, sexual, and relationship-specific problems—reflected adult outcomes. Findings supported both media-tional and direct effects models of child sexual abuse on adult functioning. Of the six circumstances of abuse variables, two had direct effects on adult negative outcomes. Severity of abuse had a direct (nonmediated) influence on these later outcomes, and proximity of abuse had both direct and mediated influences on adverse adult functioning. The internal mediators, immediate negative responses and internal attributions, were most important because one or both fully explained the impact of age at last abuse, duration of abuse, and psychological coercion on negative outcomes.

Specifically, four circumstances of abuse were found to predict immediate negative reactions to the abuse: (a) an older age when the abuse ended, (b) shorter duration of victimization, (c) abuse close to home (perpetrated by a family member [incest] or leading to family breakup), and (d) no use of psychological coercion. Internal attributions were predicted by the presence of psychological coercion and the occurrence of abuse away from the home (perpetrated by a stranger or not leading to family disruption). Involvement of authorities (police and other agencies) was more likely when the abuse was more severe, whereas less disclosure was affected by a closer proximity of abuse. Finally, negative effects of abuse were predicted by a closer proximity to the abuse, in particular a closer relationship to the perpetrator, greater severity of abuse, more immediate negative responses, internal at-tributions, and lower likelihood of abuse disclosure (see Wyatt & Newcomb, 1990, for more information).

Wyatt (1988b) also examined the relationship between the cumulative impact of a range of child sexual abuse experiences and African-American and European-American women's psychological well-being in adulthood. The four indicators used to define the extent and severity of each sexual abuse experience reported were (a) the total number of abuse incidents, (b) the duration of abuse by a given perpetrator, (c) the frequency of sexual contact with a given perpetrator, and (d) ratings of the overall severity of each respondent's abuse experiences. These four indicators were also compared to identify the best predictors of women's later psychological problems. Psychological well-being in adulthood was measured in terms of self-esteem and general well-being. Abuse experiences that did not involve body contact, such as incidents with exhibitionists and masturbators, apparently had little or no effects on women's later sense of well-being. Although frightening, these experiences seemed to have temporary rather than lasting and traumatic effects.

However, sexual abuse that involved fondling, attempted and completed intercourse, and oral or vaginal sex tended to have stronger relationships to diminished self-esteem and decreased well-being, with the lasting effects increasing with the amount of body intrusion involved in the type of sexual behavior that had occurred. The best predictor of problems related to the self-esteem and well-being of women who experienced contact abuse involving either fondling or sexual intercourse was the severity of the sexual abuse experience. Specifically, women who reported one or more fondling incidents not only manifested diminished self-esteem, but also fewer positive expressions of well-being, less energy, more tension, and less emotional stability in the past month. Women who had experienced one or more incidents involving vaginal intercourse exhibited a similar pattern of lower self-esteem, more worries about health, less cheerful moods, diminished energy, and more tension. It was concluded that subjective assessments of the severity of child abuse obtained following face-to-face interviews with respondents may provide a more comprehensive evaluation of several aspects of the extent of sexual abuse than a single index rating.

Although the overall severity of abuse proved to be the best indicator of diminished self-esteem for women who reported experiences including vaginal intercourse and oral sex, the duration of one or more abuse experiences was strongly associated with women's general well-being and specifically their positive expressions, emotional stability, and cheerful moods. The latter results suggested that when the length of time of each abuse experience was extended, women's later overall positive outlook on their lives was influenced. For more details, see Wyatt (1988b).

In another study, Wyatt, Guthrie, and Notgrass (1992) examined the effects of women's child sexual abuse and subsequent sexual revictimization. To assess the effects on later sexual and psychological functioning, two methods of defining sexual revictimization over the life course were used. The first classification included incidents of sexual abuse involving contact and non-contact sexual abuse in women before and after age 18. The second classification included the total number of incidents women reported. The cumulative effects of victimization on women's relationship problems, sexual dysfunction, the severity and frequency of sexual practices (some of which increase the STD risk), contraceptive use, and psychological well-being were assessed. Women who were sexually abused during childhood were found to be 2.4 times more likely to be revictimized as adults, and women who were abused in childhood and revictimized in adulthood had significantly higher rates of unintended and aborted pregnancies. Furthermore, women with two or more incidents in both childhood and adulthood were most likely to have unintended and aborted pregnancies; to engage in masturbation, cunnilingus, fellatio, vaginal and anal sex, group sex, and partner swapping on a frequent basis; and have brief sexual relationships. These findings suggested that certain aspects of women's sexual decision making were influenced by the severity of abuse, at what point the abuse had occurred over the life span, and the number of incidents per person. For a more detailed description of the study, see Wyatt, Guthrie, and Notgrass (1992).

In a 1990 article, Wyatt attempted to identify various dimensions of victimization—specifically, racial discrimination and frequent exposure to other forms of violence—that may affect sexually abused ethnic minority children in addition to their sexual victimization experiences. The dynamics and effects of these forms of victimization were likened to the traumatizing dynamics of child sexual abuse and of posttraumatic stress disorder. Finkel-hor and Browne's (1985) traumagenic dynamics model of child sexual abuse, which describes four dynamics of the effects of child sexual abuse, was applied to other experiences of victimization. Wyatt (1990c) emphasized the importance of assessing the effects of multiple forms of victimization that children of ethnic-group affiliation may face apart from those related to child sexual abuse. It was suggested that effective treatment needs to address all forms of victimization an ethnic child of color has encountered, as well as account for the cumulative effect of multiple victimization experiences, rather than focusing only on one form of abuse.

Using a form of log-linear analyses, Wyatt and Mickey (1988) examined the effects of the support of nonabusing parents and others on survivors' adjustment to childhood sexual abuse and on survivors' attitudes toward men. Findings revealed that negative attitudes toward men tended not to be related to the severity of the sexual abuse experience if nonabusing parents and others supported survivors when they disclosed the incidents. For more information, including the limitations of the study, see Wyatt and Mickey (1988).

■ Adult Sexual Abuse

Wyatt (1992) investigated initial effects of rape or attempted rape, including attributions of victimization, as well as lasting effects of attempted or completed rape on African-American and European-American women's intimate relationships and sexual functioning. Ethnic and cultural factors affecting women's reactions and adjustment to sexual assault were emphasized. No statistically significant difference in prevalence of rape incidents was found between the two ethnic groups. Of all the women in the sample, 20%

to 25% had experienced at least one rape or attempted rape incident since age 18. Significantly more African-American women did not disclose their assault experiences until years later. Among the reasons for this nondisclosure may be that the credibility of African-American women as rape victims has been even less firmly established than that of white American women. Furthermore, African-American rape victims may not perceive police to be supportive because of past racial incidents in which racism mediated police responses to other crimes or to rape incidents in the black community. African-American women might also minimize their rape or attempted rape experiences and cautiously discuss only the most severe incidents that might have approximated culturally sanctioned rape—incidents in which strangers were the perpetrators or where physical violence or weapons were involved.

Similar percentages of women in both ethnic groups reported immediate physical effects, negative psychological effects, and problems in their sex lives. Physical effects—including injuries of varying degrees of severity, sleep or appetite disturbances, STD infection, and pregnancy—were identified in more than 39% of the incidents involving African-American women and 46% of those involving European-American women. Negative psychological effects—such as fear, anger, anxiety, depression, and preoccupation with the abuse incident—were identified in 85% of African-American women's incidents and 86% of white women's reports. Problems in women's sex lives were found in 48% of incidents reported by African-American women and 55% of those reported by European-American women. Among these effects were avoidance of sex, decreased frequency of sexual activity, diminished enjoyment of sex, the development of specific sexual problems, and avoidance of men resembling the perpetrator.

Twenty-eight percent of African-American women and 17% of white American women reported long-lasting negative effects on their sex lives, effects that were similar in nature to the types of sexual difficulties reported as immediate effects. Long-term psychological effects—including mistrust of men, negative attitudes toward men, chronic depression, and specific fears of being left alone and being out at night—were reported by more than half of all women with rape or attempted-rape experiences. African-American women were significantly more likely than their European-American comparison group to attribute their assaults to the fact that they lived in unsafe neighborhoods. Women of both ethnic groups who had rape histories—and European-American women, in particular—also reported high frequencies of sexual behaviors, including fellatio, cunnilingus, vaginal intercourse, anal sex, extramarital affairs, higher numbers of partners, and shorter-term sexual relationships since age 18. Finally, all rape survivors were more likely to have unintended and aborted pregnancies and histories of prostitution. It was suggested that research needs to include ethnicity, particularly the experiences women encounter as members of ethnic minority groups, as a factor contributing to their self-perceptions as rape survivors.

Another study examined internal and external mediators that link aspects of women's rape or attempted rape experiences to the initial and lasting effects on their postrape adjustment, attitude toward sex and intimacy, and life-style changes designed to prevent future assaults (Wyatt, Newcomb, & Notgrass, 1990). Measured variable simultaneous path analyses were performed to test the relationships among traumatic rape or attempted rape circumstances, mediating factors, and outcome variables. Four variables represented the circumstances of abuse: (a) age at most recent abuse, (b) severity of abuse, (c) maximum rapes per incident, and (d) proximity of the perpetrator to the victim. Internal attributions (self-blame), a supportive response from a confidant, and the involvement of authorities (police officers, mental health counselors, or rape-treatment clinics) constituted the three mediator variables. The two outcome variables consisted of negative effects and adaptive life-style changes (for example, changing locks on doors or taking a self-defense class). "Negative effects" was a composite score of initial and lasting psychological effects, lasting effects on women's sexual functioning, and attitudes toward men. Two circumstances of the rape experience predicted two mediating factors. From older age at the time of the most recent rape and greater severity of abuse more consistent internal attributions (self-blame) were predicted, and less severe abuse predicted a supportive response from someone whom the victim told about the assault. Women's negative initial and lasting attitudes toward sex and intimacy were predicted by the mediators, internal attributions, and greater involvement of authorities, as well as by the rape circumstances, greater severity of abuse, and more rapes per incident. Older age at most recent assault and abuse perpetrated away from home and by a stranger predicted adaptive life-style changes. Please see the original publication (Wyatt, Newcomb, & Notgrass, 1990) for more details.

■ Methodological Considerations

Issues in the definition of child sexual abuse in prevalence research were the focus of another study (Wyatt & Peters, 1986a). Four representative studies of the prevalence of child sexual abuse were reviewed and contrasted. Two of them involved samples in the Northeast (Finkelhor, 1979, 1984) and two were conducted with samples in the West (Russell, 1986; Wyatt, 1985). Similarities and dissimilarities were identified in terms of the upper age limit for child sexual abuse, the criteria used to define a given sexual experience as abusive, the inclusion or exclusion of experiences involving age peers, and the use of different criteria for incidents occurring during adolescence. Prevalence rates from one study that used a slightly less restrictive definition of abuse were recalculated based on the definitions of the other research studies. This resulted in a 14% decrease in the number of individuals identified as abused. Three definitions of sexual abuse were compared in terms of their consideration of the age difference between the victim and the perpetrator and the types of behaviors examined between nonfamily and family members. Finkelhor (1979, 1984) used age differences as part of the criteria for child sexual abuse in both of his studies. Russell (1986) deleted most types of extrafamilial abuse from her definition of abuse occurring at ages 14 through 17, although she did collect a full range of contact and noncontact abuse experiences for ages 13 and younger. Thus, in three of the four studies the criteria for sexual abuse in childhood have been defined by the age of the subject, the age of the perpetrator, or by the type of abuse. The differences in prevalence and the 14% decrease on the basis of recalculations of prevalence in the less restrictive study indicated that altering the definition of child sexual abuse did affect the prevalence rates and also suggested that other factors such as methodological differences need to be examined to determine their impact on prevalence rates. The interested reader is referred to Wyatt and Peters (1986a) for a more extensive description of this research.

In an attempt to describe how differences in methodology and sample characteristics may contribute to the variation in child sexual abuse prevalence rates, Wyatt and Peters (1986b) compared the same four studies (Finkelhor, 1979, 1984; Russell, 1986; Wyatt, 1985). Sampling procedures included nonprobability and probability samples of men and women. Data collection ranged from self-administered questionnaires to face-to-face interviews. The tentative conclusions drawn on the basis of the limited evidence from this small number of studies indicated that two aspects of data collection were the most significant factors accounting for discrepant prevalence findings. The use of face-to-face interviews and inverted funnel questioning (asking multiple questions about specific types of abusive behaviors) were associated with much higher prevalence rates than was the use of self-administered questionnaires with broad funnel questioning. The variation in the age range of respondents was also considered to be a potential factor in discrepant prevalence reporting.

Several aspects of methodology and sample characteristics did not seem to influence prevalence rates. Those were the use of random-sampling techniques, the area of the country in which the study was conducted, the educational level of subjects, and the sample's ethnic composition.

In summary, methodological and sampling considerations of sex research can influence our understanding of sociocultural factors and how they impact consensual and nonconsensual sexual experiences.

13

Results of Structural Equation Model (SEM) Analyses

The statistical results from this chapter are organized into three distinct sections. Each section repeats the findings of the previous section but with greater detail and statistical justification. All results in this chapter are based on linear structural equations models (SEMs), which are used to analyze all data simultaneously. The emergent findings capture correlations between variables, as well as direct and mediated relationships from one variable to another, and they establish where no association exists between variables.

The first section below describes several of the substantive findings we found most interesting in these analyses. These are presented in the next section. Based on our judgment, these results represent a select and incomplete group of the total set of findings. All findings are completely summarized in the section titled "Complete Summary of SEM Results." This section describes all of the significant results from the SEM analyses but without their technical or statistical details. Finally, the section "Technical Details of Analyses" is provided for those readers who want complete details of all aspects of model development, including both confirmatory factor analyses (CFA) and structural models.

■ Highlights of SEM Results

The following points are brief descriptions of several major conclusions captured in our SEM analyses.

Healthy Consensual Sexual Practices

- Consensual childhood sexual behaviors established a trajectory for voluntary sexual involvement in adolescence and a broader range of activities in adulthood.

- In general, earlier consensual sexual involvement and activities had few serious sexual or psychological consequences in adulthood. In fact, adolescent sexual involvement was associated with higher adult sexual satisfaction.

- Women who recalled that both their parents and religious affiliations communicated negative messages about sexual intimacy reported less childhood sexual behavior, less voluntary adolescent sexual behavior, effective use of birth control, and greater sexual satisfaction. Although they were more restrained in their sexual patterns, they were amongst the groups of women who effectively used barrier methods of birth control and reported sexual satisfaction in their primary adult sexual relationship. The latter two patterns highlight different aspects of sexual health.

- Adult psychological well-being (including self-esteem and general well-being) was not directly related to either type of childhood sexual abuse. However, women's psychological well-being in adulthood was related to less parent education and higher quality of family life in childhood. In essence, women from at least working-class families that were very close were happiest overall.

Patterns Compromising Sexual Health

- Being raised in a family with conflict and little closeness increased the likelihood and severity of both intra- and extrafamilial childhood sexual abuse. However, these associations and all others we present were not perfect, emphasizing that sexual abuse can occur in many types of families.

- Having parents with little formal education increased the likelihood and severity of both intra- and extrafamilial childhood sexual abuse. Again this association was not perfect, reminding us that sexual abuse does occur even in families with highly educated parents.

- The occurrence and severity of both intra- and extrafamilial childhood sexual abuse were strongly associated (if one type occurred it was quite possible that the other type occurred). This indicates that vulnerability to childhood sexual abuse and victimization is often not limited to one perpetrator or to one context.

- Both types of childhood sexual abuse were associated with an earlier age of sexual behavior onset and more voluntary childhood sexual activities.

- Furthermore, child or adolescent sexual involvement was unrelated to the need to control sexual desires or psychological well-being in adulthood. However, adolescent sexual behavior reduced the effective use of birth control in adulthood, and child sexual play with others increased the likelihood of severe rapes in adulthood. Childhood sexual abuse experiences affected various aspects of adult sexual activities, decisions, and responses beyond the influence exerted by patterns of consensual sexual behavior established earlier in life.

- Victims of both intra- and extrafamilial childhood sexual abuse were at high risk of sexual revictimization as adults in the form of increased likelihood and severity of completed rapes (but not attempted rapes).

- Adult sexual attitudes and behaviors that increased the risk of disease transmission and unintended pregnancies were related to intrafamilial childhood sexual abuse as opposed to extrafamilial childhood sexual abuse.
- The severity of intrafamilial childhood sexual abuse contributed to several adult outcomes, including reduced sexual satisfaction, a greater need to control sexual desires, more unplanned pregnancies, a higher frequency of sexual contact, and less frequent partner initiation of sexual activities, according to women's reports.
- The severity of intrafamilial sexual abuse was only specifically associated with less effective use of birth control as an adult. The latter two findings strongly suggest that sexual abuse is associated with negative aspects of sexual health.
- Severe incidents of completed rapes in adulthood were predicted by both types of childhood sexual abuse (mentioned above), as well as by not feeling close to anyone in one's family of origin and infrequent or no masturbation activity as a teenager. These women experienced severe childhood sexual abuse that occurred in multiple contexts with multiple perpetrators, had no one to turn to in their family to whom they felt close, and avoided autoerotic sexual stimulation as a teenager (perhaps denying and being unwilling to learn about channeling sexual impulses and desires).
- Severe incidents of attempted rapes in adulthood were related to a background of conflicting sexual messages and activities, including no endorsement of sexual intimacy by childhood socialization figures, having mothers with little formal education, and frequent sexual play with others as a child but little masturbatory experience as an adolescent.
- The severity of attempted rapes in adulthood had no serious repercussions on or associations with any aspect of these women's psychosexual functioning that we assessed, with the one exception of completed rapes that were less severe. Although this negative relationship was small, it may indicate that either (a) women who had experienced the trauma of a completed rape were less likely to place themselves in circumstances that might lead to attempted rape or may feel that they cannot resist an attempted incident of sexual assault that results in a completed rape; or (b) women who had survived an attempted rape realized that they could successfully resist a sexual assault and thereby reduce the likelihood of a future completed rape.
- Severe incidents of completed rapes were related to more unintended pregnancies and more frequent sexual contact as adults.
- Neither type of adult sexual abuse (attempted or completed rape) was associated with any aspect of psychological well-being, sexual satisfaction, or a need to control sexual desires in this community sample of women after childhood and adolescent influences on these characteristics were considered. However, these well-being measures were not specifically designed to assess aspects of sexual trauma.

■ Complete Summary of SEM Results

The information and findings captured in the complete final structural or path model are numerous and complex, and they may be appreciated from several different perspectives. Variables from many domains were included that reflected various aspects and stages of female sexual development. These results provide empirical multivariate tests of several theories and processes related to women's psychosexual maturation and trauma experiences. Some of these areas include family influences on sexual development and sexual abuse, developmental patterns of sexual behavior, the impact of early family qualities on adult sexual behavior and well-being, and the antecedents, concomitants, and consequences of childhood sexual abuse and adult sexual trauma. In this book, we focus primarily on two of these general areas of concern and inquiry: sexual abuse and sexual development of women.

Sexual Abuse

Table 13.1 summarizes the findings related to the sexual abuse variables from the final structural model. Significant predictors, correlates, and consequences for each of the four types of sexual abuse are listed.
We found that the severity of intrafamilial sexual abuse was:

1. predicted by less endorsement of sexual intimacy by socialization agents, lower parent education, and poorer quality of family life;
2. correlated with more voluntary child sexual behavior, an earlier age of sexual onset, higher severity of extrafamilial sexual abuse, and more sexual play with others; and
3. correlated with more completed rapes, less partner sex initiation, a higher frequency of sexual contact, more unplanned pregnancies, a greater need to control desires, and more partner sex dysfunction.

The severity of extrafamilial sexual abuse was:

1. predicted by more parent endorsement of body awareness and nudity, lower parent education, and poorer quality of family life;
2. correlated with more voluntary child sexual behavior and earlier age of sexual onset; and
3. correlated with more completed rapes and more effective use of birth control.

The severity of completed rapes was:

Table 13.1 Summary of Significant Predictors, Correlates, and Consequences of Four Types of Severity of Sexual Abuse From the Final Structural Model

Intrafamilial	Extrafamilial	Completed Rapes	Attempted Rapes
		Predictors	
(-) Endorsement of sexual intimacy by socialization agents	(+) Parent endorsement of body awareness and nudity	(+) Intrafamilial	(-) Endorsement of sexual intimacy by socialization agents
(-) Parent education	(-) Parent education	(+) Extrafamilial	(-) Mother's education
(-) Quality of family life	(-) Quality of family life	(-) Felt closest to in family	(+) Sexual play with others
		(-) Frequency of arousal	(-) Frequency of masturbation
		(-) Frequency of masturbation	
		Correlates	
(+) Voluntary child sexual behavior	(+) Voluntary child sexual behavior	(-) Frequency of sexual contact	(-) Completed rapes
(-) Age of sexual onset	(-) Age of sexual onset	(+) Unplanned pregnancies	(+) Frequency of sexual contact
(+) Extrafamilial			
(+) Mutual contact			
		Consequences	
(+) Completed rapes	(+) Effective use of birth control		
(-) Partner sex initiation	(+) Completed rapes		
(+) Frequency of sexual contact			
(+) Unplanned pregnancies			
(+) Need to control sexual desires			
(+) Partner sex dysfunction			

Note: (-) indicates a negative relationship with the above variable, while (+) indicates a positive relationship with the above variable. Capitalized variables are latent constructs, and lower case variables are measured.

1. predicted by greater severity of both intra- and extrafamilial sexual abuse, women feeling less close to someone in their families as children, and lower frequencies of both arousal and masturbation in childhood; and
2. correlated with a lower frequency of sexual contact and more unintended pregnancies.

Finally, the severity of attempted rapes was:

1. predicted by less endorsement of sexual intimacy by socialization agents, lower maternal education, more sexual play with others, and lower frequency of masturbation; and
2. correlated with reduced severity of completed rapes and lower frequency of sexual contact.

It is noteworthy that in this final path model, none of the four indices of sexual abuse severity were significantly associated (as predictors or correlates) with any aspects of adult psychological well-being (including self-esteem and general well-being). Although both of the childhood scales of sexual abuse in the final CFA model were correlated significantly with (less) adult psychological well-being, these associations were apparently mediated or spurious and therefore fully accounted for by family context influences (parent education and family quality) in the final structural model (because these paths were not significant in the structural model and were therefore removed—that is, constrained to zero). These findings emphasize the importance of accounting for many potential influences when studying a complex ecology of psychosocial forces and processes to minimize the likelihood of obtaining erroneous, misleading, or spurious results and conclusions.

However, in this particular case, it appears that the lack of effects between childhood sexual abuse variables and adulthood psychological well-being may also be explained by mediating and moderating effects of the women's internal versus external attributions of responsibility for the sexual abuse (Wyatt, Newcomb, & Skidmore, 1992). Therefore, effects of childhood sexual abuse on adult psychological findings do occur but are explained by family context variables and women's attributions of responsibility for the sexual abuse.

Sexual Development

The second focus of this study is on general patterns (antecedents, correlates, and outcomes) of women's sexual development. These results are also captured in the final path SEM when viewed from a slightly different perspective. These findings are summarized according to three types of patterns or associations related to sexual behavior at each age period covered by our retrospective assessments: (a) predictors of sexual behavior at each life stage, (b) adult consequences of earlier sexual practices and patterns, and (c) associations (correlations) among different aspects of sexual functioning within each developmental period. Several of these patterns involve experiences with sexual abuse (as captured in our four scales of these events) and thus are repetitions of certain findings already reviewed above (regarding the predictors, correlates, and consequences of sexual abuse).

Table 13.2 summarizes these significant patterns of women's sexual development. Columns are organized into significant predictors, correlates, and consequences of the various sexual variables (both measured and latent). These are discussed according to each column in the table.

Beginning with predictors (column 1 of Table 13.2), childhood voluntary sexual behavior was increased by parental endorsement of body awareness and nudity and decreased by endorsement of sexual intimacy by socialization agents (parents and religious sources). Adolescent voluntary sexual behavior was positively predicted by the amount of childhood voluntary sexual behavior. The length of relationships (one indicator of adolescent voluntary sexual behavior) was affected specifically by greater parental endorsement of body awareness and nudity, higher parent education, and poorer family quality of life. An earlier age of sexual behavior onset was influenced by greater parental endorsement of body awareness and nudity, while an older age of first sex with others was influenced by higher parent education.

Turning to adult sexual behaviors, the frequency of adult sexual activities was influenced by an earlier age of sexual behavior onset and greater parental endorsement of body awareness and nudity. The effective use of birth control in adulthood was increased by lower voluntary adolescent sexual behavior, a greater severity of extrafamilial sexual abuse, and an older age of first intercourse with others. Adult partner sex initiation was increased by an earlier age of sexual behavior onset and little or no exposure to intrafamilial sexual abuse. Adult frequency of sexual contact was increased by an early age of sexual behavior onset and greater severity of intrafamilial sexual abuse. More unintended pregnancies in adulthood resulted from a greater severity of intrafamilial sexual abuse. Increased adult sexual satisfaction was predicted by more voluntary adolescent sexual behavior, little or no experience with intrafamilial sexual abuse, and more endorsement of sexual intimacy by socialization agents received as a child. Adult sexual dysfunction with one's primary partner (one indicator of sexual satisfaction) was specifically affected by a greater severity of intrafamilial sexual abuse and more childhood voluntary sexual behavior.

Four within-age-period correlates of sexual behavior did not involve the sexual abuse measures. These are listed in column 2 of Table 13.2, and three are repeated to maintain consistency of this table's organization. A later age of sexual behavior onset was related to both lower childhood and adolescent voluntary sexual behavior. In adulthood, greater sexual satisfaction was related to more psychological well-being and a higher frequency of adult sexual activities.

Finally, we turn to later consequences or outcomes of prior sexual behavior that involve a sexual behavior predictor. Those findings are summarized in column 3 of Table 13.2. We present only those not associated with sexual abuse, because these were presented earlier, although some findings are related to the consequences of nonsexual behavior variables, which are presented. Adolescent voluntary sexual behavior was significantly predicted by childhood voluntary sexual behavior. The latent construct of psychological well-being was not affected by any aspect or type of earlier sexual behavior or trauma, although greater psychological well-being was associated with lower parent education and better family quality (not given in Table 13.2). General well-being (one indicator of psychological well-being) was specifically enhanced by greater parental endorsement of body awareness and nudity. An increased need for control of sexual desires was influenced by a later age of sexual behavior onset and less parental endorsement of body awareness and nudity. One indicator of the need to control sexual desires construct was also increased by fewer parental demonstrative messages about sexual expression. Adult partner sex dysfunction, according to women's reports, was predicted by a greater amount of childhood voluntary sexual behavior and an earlier age of sexual behavior onset. Adult frequency of sexual activities and sexual contact were predicted by an earlier age of sexual behavior onset. Finally, greater adult sexual satisfaction and less effective use of birth control were predicted by more adolescent voluntary sexual behavior.

■ Technical Details of Analyses

Confirmatory Factor Analysis (CFA) Models

A series of CFA models was run to determine an adequate measurement or factor structure for the 30 measured variables that represented the 12 domains. In the initial CFA model, 10 latent factors were hypothesized to reflect 26 measured variables, excluding the four sexual abuse variables that accounted for two domains. These 10 factors perfectly reflected the 10 domains of variables that were assessed. The indicators of each latent factor were the measured variables within each domain. The factor structure was pure (each variable loaded only on one factor), and no multiple or complex factor loadings were allowed (loadings on all other factors were fixed at zero). The

Table 13.2 Summary of Significant Predictor Correlates and Consequences of Childhood, Adolescent, and Adult Sexual Behaviors From the Final Structural Model

Type of Sexual Behavior	Predictors	Correlates	Consequences
Childhood			
Voluntary sexual behavior	Parental endorsement of body awareness and nudity (+) Endorsement of sexual intimacy by socialization agents (-)	Severity of intrafamilial sexual abuse (+) Severity of extrafamilial sexual abuse (+) Age of sexual behavior onset (-)	Adolescent voluntary sexual behavior (+) Partner sex dysfunction (+)
Self-exploration and masturbation	—	—	
Frequency of arousal	—	—	—
Sexual play with others	—	Severity of intrafamilial sexual abuse (+)	Severity of attempted rapes (+)
Adolescence			
Voluntary sexual behavior	Childhood voluntary sexual behavior (+)	Age of sexual behavior onset (-)	Effective use of birth control (-) Sexual satisfaction (+) Severity of completed rapes (-)
Frequency of masturbation	—	—	—
Number of sexual partners	—	—	
Length of relationship	Parent endorsement of body awareness and nudity (+) Parent education (+) Family quality (-)	—	
Age of sexual behavior onset	Parental endorsement of body awareness and nudity (-)	Severity of intrafamilial sexual abuse (-) Severity of extrafamilial sexual abuse (-) Childhood voluntary sexual behavior (-)	Frequency of adult sexual activities (-) Partner sex initiation (-) Frequency of sexual contact (-)

Variable	Correlates
Age of first sex behavior with others	Parent education (+); Need to control sexual desires (−); Effective use of birth control (+) —
Age of first self-exploratory behaviors	—
Adulthood	
Frequency of adult sexual activities	Parental endorsement of body awareness and nudity (+); Age of sexual behavior onset (−); Sexual satisfaction (+) —
Effective use of birth control	Age of first sex with others (+); Adolescent voluntary sexual behavior (−); Severity of extrafamilial sexual abuse (+); Severity of intrafamilial sexual abuse (−) — —
Partner sex initiation	Age of sexual behavior onset (−) —
Frequency of sexual contact	Severity of intrafamilial sexual abuse (+); Age of sexual behavior onset (−); Severity of attempted rapes (+) — —
Unplanned pregnancies	Severity of intrafamilial sexual abuse (+); Severity of completed rapes (+) —
Sexual satisfaction	Adolescent voluntary sexual behavior (+); Endorsement of sexual intimacy by socialization agents (+); Severity of intrafamilial sexual abuse (−); Psychological well-being (+) —
Current sexual satisfaction	Frequency of adult sexual activities (+) —
Sex dysfunction with partner	Severity of intrafamilial sexual abuse (+); Childhood voluntary sexual behavior (+) — —

four sexual abuse scales were included as separate variables and correlated with all 10 factors, although they were not used as indicators of any constructs.

In each CFA model, the variance of latent factors was fixed at unity, all factor loadings were freely estimated, and correlations were allowed among all latent constructs (including all measured variables that were not indicators of latent factors, but which were treated as latent constructs—that is, single-indicator factors).

Results from this initial model indicated that it was not an adequate representation of the data. The fit indices were poor, and loadings on several factors were nonsignificant or extremely small. This information suggested how the initial CFA model should be modified to reflect more accurately the data.

A second CFA model was tested that included these revisions. In particular, two of the latent factors in the initial CFA model were weak and poorly captured by their measured-variable indicators. In other words, these two latent constructs, representing two domains of variables, did not exist as hypothesized. These two domains included sexual socialization (from family context) and voluntary sexual behavior (from adulthood). In the second, revised CFA model, all variables within these two domains were kept as separate variables but treated like latent constructs (i.e., as single-indicator factors). For instance, frequency of sexual contact was allowed to correlate with all eight remaining latent constructs (reflecting the eight domains) and all measured variables from the other four domains.

This second model was a vast improvement over the first model. All eight latent constructs had significant factor loadings that ranged in magnitude from modest (in a few cases) to large. The fit indices also improved in this modified CFA model, $\chi^2(286, N = 248) = 426.91, p < .001, NFI = .80, CFI = .92$. Criteria for not rejecting a model vary, and some would consider the fit of this model adequate (i.e., the chi-square value is less than two times the degrees of freedom). Others prefer a closer approximation to the data. We followed the latter course and modified the model again. However, we will also estimate our final structural model without the modifications that follow to ascertain whether these changes affected the path coefficients.

Our third CFA model included the identical factor structure of the second model. This time the changes involved adding correlations among measured variables (if they were not indicators of a construct) or residuals of measured variables (if they were indicators of a latent construct). The multivariate Lagrangian multiplier test was used to select empirically these additional correlations. These correlations reflect small, unanticipated associations between aspects of measured variables. These may reflect meaningful but unexpected relations between variables, method or response biases, or sample-specific variations.

In the third CFA model, 22 of these correlations were added. These are neither presented nor interpreted, because their meaning can be unclear or misleading (i.e., suppressor effects). With these additions, the CFA model fit quite well, χ^2 (264, $N = 248$) = 244.77, $p = .80$, NFI = .89, CFI = 1.00. A comparison of the factor loadings and intercorrelations among the 8 latent constructs and 12 measured variables (treated like factors) in the second and third models shows that they were essentially identical or only slightly different. In other words, adding the additional correlations did not disturb the critical features of the model. Thus, the third model can be trusted as a reasonable approximation of the data, regardless of whether the correlations were included.

The standardized factor loadings and unique variance estimates for this third CFA model are presented in Table 13.3. Table 13.4 presents the intercorrelations of the four sexual abuse scales from this final CFA model. The severity of intra- and extrafamilial sexual abuse incidents and rapes were all positively and significantly correlated. The severity of attempted rapes was only significantly correlated with less severity of rapes. Table 13.4 also presents the correlations between these four sexual abuse scales and the eight latent constructs (indicated by initial capitalization) and eight measured variables from the final CFA model. Intrafamilial sexual abuse was significantly correlated with 14 of these other variables, as was extrafamilial sexual abuse. The severity of rapes was significantly correlated with 8 of these variables, while severity of attempted rapes was significantly correlated with only 3 of these 12 variables.

Structural or Path Models

The structural or path model was developed in several stages. These stages involved creating an initial model, adding parameters to generate an overfit model, and finally deleting parameters to arrive at the final structural model.

Initial Structural Model

Using the factor structure from the final CFA model, many of the factor and variable intercorrelations were replaced with unidirectional paths. Figure 11.1 in Chapter 11 displays the general flow of these directional effects. Overall, the direction of influence progressed developmentally across the four global areas of life: from family context to childhood to adolescence to adulthood. This sequential order was considered a plausible, defensible, and conservative causal pattern. Variables within each of the four life areas were allowed to correlate freely without imposing any causal priority. Several hypotheses could have been used to specify reasonable directional paths

Table 13.3 Standardized Factor Loadings and Unique Variances From the Final Confirmatory Factor Analysis Model

Factor/Variable	Loading	Unique Variance	Factor/Variable	Loading	Unique Variance
Family Content			*Adulthood*		
Parental endorsement of body awareness and nudity	a		Severity of completed rapes	a	
Endorsement of sexual intimacy by socialization agents	a		Severity of attempted rapes	a	
Parent's demonstrative messages about sexual expressions	a		Frequency of adult sexual activities	a	
Parent education			Effective use of birth control	a	
Mother's education	.62***	.62			
Father's education	.71***	.49	Partner sex initiation	a	
Family quality			Frequency of sexual contact	a	
Relationship parents had	.50***	.75			
Family closeness	-.51***	.74	Unplanned pregnancies	a	
Felt closest to in family	.61***	.62			
Childhood			Psychological well-being		
Voluntary sexual behavior			General well-being	.86***	.26
Self-exploration and masturbation	.74***	.45	Self-esteem	.62***	.62
Frequency of arousal	.42***	.82	Need to control sexual desires		
Sexual play with others	.62***	.62	Mosher 1	.84***	.29
Severity of intrafamilial sexual abuse	a		Mosher 2	.86***	.25
Severity of extrafamilial sexual abuse	a		Mosher 3	.84***	.29
			Sexual satisfaction		
			Current sexual satisfaction	.95***	.11
			Partner sex dysfunction	-.32***	.90

Adolescence	
Voluntary sexual behavior	
Frequency of masturbation	.72***	.48
Number of sexual partners	.45***	.80
Length of relationship	.33***	.89
Age of sexual behavior onset	
Age of first sex behavior with others	.71***	.71
Age of first self-exploratory behaviors	.93***	.12

**p < .01; ***p < .001.
aNot an indicator of a latent construct.

Table 13.4 Correlations Between the Four Sexual Abuse Variables and All Latent
Factors and Single-Item Factors in the Final CFA Model

	Severity of Sexual Abuse			
	Intrafamilial	Extrafamilial	Rapes	Attempted Rapes
Severity of sexual abuse				
Intrafamilial	—			
Extrafamilial	.57***	—		
Rapes	.28***	.30***	—	
Attempted rapes	.02	−.05	−.11*	—
Family context				
Parent endorsement				
of body awareness				
and nudity	.01	.12*	.11*	.07
Endorsement of sexual				
intimacy by sociali-				
zation agents	−.09	.03	.08	.16**
Parent's demonstrative				
messages about sexual				
behavior	−.10*	−.12*	.00	−.10*
Parent education	−.20**	−.09	−.06	−.01
Family quality	−.28***	−.41***	−.28***	.06
Childhood				
Voluntary sexual behavior	.28***	.23**	.18**	.13*
Adolescence				
Voluntary sexual behavior	.61***	.33***	.03	.07
Age of sexual behavior onset	−.23***	−.23***	−.16**	−.04
Adulthood				
Frequency of adult sexual				
activities	.08	.12*	.14*	−.05
Birth control effectiveness	.19**	.22**	.17**	−.06
Partner sex initiation	−.10	−.01	−.02	.06
Rate of sexual contact	.18**	.15**	.36***	.08
Abortions	.28***	.19**	.38***	.02
Psychological well-being	−.12*	−.10*	−.08	.06
Need to control sexual desires	.01	.03	−.01	.00
Sexual satisfaction	−.16*	−.04	.01	.04

*p < .05; **p < .01; ***p < .001.

between variables within each life area. However, this approach was not
used, because the temporal order of variables within each life area could
not be accurately established, leaving any causal interpretations uncertain and

equivocal. In addition, other results or conclusions of the model are dependent on the total structural configuration. If causal paths within life areas are not accurate, all other findings may be distorted or biased and should not be trusted (Newcomb, in press).

Variables in the family context were considered solely independent influences and were allowed to correlate freely with each other. Initially, each predicted all variables within the other three areas. Variables from adulthood were solely dependent consequences and were initially predicted by each variable in all three other areas; their residuals were allowed to correlate freely. All childhood variables were initially allowed to predict all adolescence variables. Two domains of variables (Childhood Sexual Abuse and Age of Sexual Behavior Onset) spanned the childhood and adolescence life areas. As a result, variables within these two domains were not directionally related to variables in either childhood or adolescence; all of these associations were captured as correlations.

The final CFA model included 22 correlations between measured variables or their residuals. In this initial structural model, all of these were retained except for those that correlated variables between domains at different places in the sequential order and that are now joined with directional paths. These correlations were removed to allow for the possibility that they might reflect directional influences that could be included as structural paths.

The fit of this model was slightly worse than the final CFA model. The decrement in fit is solely the result of deleting the several correlations between measured variables (or their residuals). If these had not been removed, the fit would have been identical to the final CFA model, because this is a saturated structural model (all factor and variable intercorrelations in the final CFA model were accounted for by a path or correlation in this initial structural model).

Overfit Structural Model

The initial structural model was modified by adding 14 more paths. Each was a significant path, and all represent nonstandard effects (Newcomb, 1990; Newcomb & Bentler, 1988b,c). These were empirically determined by using the Lagrangian multiplier modification indices (Bentler, 1989) to examine specific types of effects within carefully selected aspects of the model. Two types of nonstandard effects were added: (a) latent factor predicting measured variable and (b) measured variable (or its residual) predicting measured variable.

These additions yielded a model that fit the data exceptionally well. However, it also contained numerous unnecessary (nonsignificant) paths and correlations.

Final Structural Model

The last stage of model modification involved removing all nonsignificant parameters. This was accomplished using the Wald test (Bentler, 1989) and resulted in the final structural model. This model fit the data quite well; χ^2 (408, N = 248) = 389.93, p = .66, NFI = .83, CFI = 1.00.

This final model includes only significant parameters. Even so, it is quite large and complex. There are far more variables and parameters to present from this final structural model than can be depicted in a single table or figure. To facilitate presentation of the results, the final model is separated into three components, and each is summarized in a figure and two tables. Factor loadings for the latent constructs are not presented, because they are essentially the same as those in the final CFA model presented above. Although the final structural model is presented as three components, they are in fact all interdependent aspects of the one final, simultaneous, structural equation model. All results must be interpreted in the overall context of the complete model. Components are separated only for ease of presentation.

Figure 13.1 depicts the structural paths among the 8 latent constructs and 12 measured variables not used as indicators of latent factors. Correlations among the family context variables and the two child sexual abuse scales are also provided.

Table 13.5 contains the 14 nonstandard paths that were not depicted in Figure 13.1. Table 13.6 summarizes all of the remaining correlations within each sequential domain representing a developmental life period.

An additional structural model was run that did not include any of the correlations added in the final CFA model. This tests whether the addition of these empirically determined parameters somehow distorted or changed the outcome of the final SEM. Results of this SEM revealed that all significant paths remained significant. The primary and only substantive difference was that this model had a poorer fit to the data, as would be expected. Nevertheless, the χ^2/df ratio was far less than 2.00, indicating an acceptable fit by many experts (e.g., Bentler & Bonett, 1980; Newcomb, 1990).

It could be argued further that the added 14 nonstandard paths also distorted the model and simply capitalized on chance in this specific sample (e.g., MacCallum, Roznowski, & Necowitz, 1992). A final structural model was tested that excluded these 14 parameters. As in the additional model presented above, all estimated paths and correlations remained significant, despite a substantial expected decrement in the fit of model. Therefore, we conclude that the final SEM presented in Figure 13.1 and Tables 13.5 and 13.6 is an acceptable representation of the data and is not distorted by model modifications. In fact, the nonstandard path additions to the model contributed substantially to the practical and theoretical importance of the findings

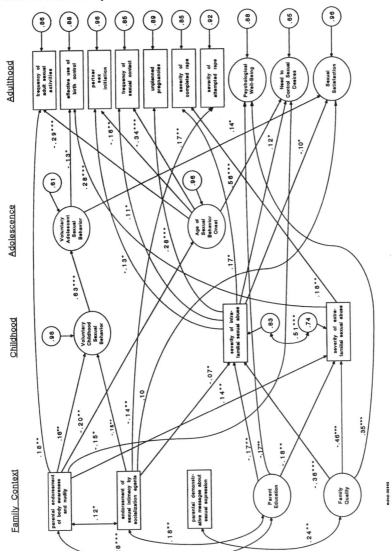

Figure 13.1.

(Newcomb, in press). These nonstandard paths can be readily implemented in EQS (Bentler, 1989), which is not the case in other SEM procedures and programs where it is practically impossible (i.e., LISREL; see Jöreskog & Sörbom, 1988).

Table 13.5 Additional Nonstandard Paths From the Final Structural Model Not Depicted in Figure 13.1

Predictor Variable		Consequent Variable		Standardized Parameter Estimate
Observed	Latent	Observed	Latent	
Parent endorsement of body awareness and nudity		Length of relationships		.17**
Parent's demonstrative messages about sexual expression		General well-being		.12*
Parent's demonstrative messages about sexual expression		Mosher 3		-.14***
	Parent education	Length of relationships		.12*
	Parent education	Age of first sex with others		.15**
Mother's education (R)[a]		Severity of attempted rapes		-.11*
	Family quality	Length of relationships		-.21**
Severity of intrafamilial sexual abuse		Severity of completed rapes		-.14**
	Child voluntary sexual behavior	Partner sex dysfunction		.19**
Sexual play with others (childhood) (R)		Partner sex dysfunction		.11*
Frequency of masturbation (adolescence) (R)		Severity of attempted rapes		.16**
Frequency of masturbation (adolescence) (R)		Severity of completed rapes		-.10*
Age of first sex with others (R)		Severity of attempted rapes		-.12*
		Effective use of birth control		.24***

[a](R) denotes residual of the variable.
*p < .05; **p < .01; ***p < .001.

Table 13.6 Additional Correlations From the Final Structural Model

Variable		Variable		Standardized Parameter Estimate
Observed	Latent	Observed	Latent	
Severity of intrafamilial sexual abuse (R)[a]			Child voluntary sexual behavior (R)	.33***
Severity of intrafamilial sexual abuse (R)		Sexual play with others (R)		.12*
Severity of intrafamilial sexual abuse (R)			Age of sexual behavior onset (R)	−.28***
Severity of extrafamilial sexual abuse (R)			Child voluntary sexual behavior (R)	.31***
Severity of extrafamilial sexual abuse (R)			Age of sexual behavior onset (R)	−.24***
Severity of extrafamilial sexual abuse (R)		Age of first sex with others (R)		−.52***
Severity of completed rapes (R)		Frequency of sexual contact (R)		.31***
Severity of completed rapes (R)		Unplanned pregnancies (R)		.33***
Severity of completed rapes (R)		Severity of attempted rapes (R)		−.11*
	Child voluntary sexual behavior (R)		Age of sexual behavior onset (R)	−.89***
	Adolescent voluntary sexual behavior (R)		Age of sexual behavior onset (R)	−.18*
	Sexual satisfaction (R)		Psychological well-being (R)	.26***
	Sexual satisfaction (R)	Frequency of adult sexual activities (R)		.40***

[a] (R) denotes the residual of the observed or latent variable.
*$p < .05$; **$p < .01$; ***$p < .001$.

115

14

Discussion of SEM Results

To review, this study examined a community sample of African-American and European-American women's voluntary and coercive sexual experiences across developmental periods of their lives and their effects on adult sexual and psychological functioning. Women recalled their past and current sexual histories during structured face-to-face interviews administered by highly trained female interviewers who matched the women's ethnicity. This data-collection format differs radically from earlier methods that assumed that women would be willing and comfortable to discuss sexual matters with mature white men (Kinsey et al., 1953). It also acknowledges that many Americans know little about sexual terminology, anatomy, and physiology and that an ongoing clarification of definitions and locations of sexual body organs and behavior is necessary to obtain this information. Although certainly influenced by memory performance error (see Wyatt, 1990d, for further discussion), women were asked to discuss as many of their sex-related experiences over their lives as they could recall. This was a time-consuming and often tedious process, but it was necessary to understand the context of sexual experiences and women's perceptions of the effects of these experiences on their lives.

This study investigated the effects of family of origin characteristics, sexual socialization, and consensual and nonconsensual sexual experiences on women's sexual and psychological functioning during the life course. Our findings reveal several mechanisms that make women more vulnerable to engaging in risky sexual practices, as well as other conditions that render them less vulnerable to such behaviors. The mechanisms associated with women's risky sexual decision making appear to be different for childhood, adolescence, and adulthood. In the following, we attempt to clarify these mechanisms in our descriptions of the patterns of sexual functioning we encountered. In our discussion, we emphasize those life-experience factors that appear to be instrumental in determining subsequent sexual behaviors and decision making.

■ Sexually Active Women Without Sexual Abuse Histories

A composite picture of women who did not experience sexual abuse and who enjoyed a lifetime of sexual activity emerged. Apparently, these women were raised by parents who had, verbally or nonverbally, endorsed body awareness and nudity in childhood and adolescence. In accordance with social learning theory (Bandura, 1977; Goffman, 1967; Murphy, 1947), we found that this kind of parental endorsement had a significant effect on women's voluntary sexual behavior during their life course. In childhood, these women engaged in more sexual behavior, including self-exploration, masturbation, and sexual play with others, and they experienced a higher frequency of sexual arousal. They had begun to be sexually active at younger ages in adolescence but maintained long-term sexual relationships with their partners. As adults, they reported having intercourse and both oral and anal sex more frequently and experienced greater sexual satisfaction.

Previous research has confirmed a relationship between parental attitudes and women's sexual practices later in life (see, for example, Newcomb, 1984). Our own findings lend further support to some of the existing evidence about the association between parental endorsement of body awareness, nudity, and sexuality and a woman's lifetime sexual practices (Friedrich et al., 1991; Newcomb, 1984; Shelley, 1981). In light of these findings, it appears that young women may adopt sexual attitudes and associated behaviors similar to those of their parents.

In accordance with the idea that children and adolescents use their parents as sexual role models, women who were less likely to have engaged in childhood sexual behaviors described their parents as people who implicitly and explicitly conveyed that they prohibited nudity and did not endorse sexual intimacy. As indicated by prior research, other sources of socialization (such as the church, temple, hall, or religious institution) appear to have further reinforced nonendorsing parental attitudes, extending their influence into adulthood (Barrett, 1980; Libby et al., 1978; Murstein & Holden, 1979; Newcomb, 1985; Wyatt & Lyons-Rowe, 1990). Apparently, women who grew up with more restrictive parental sexual attitudes and religious influences were likely to adopt more prohibitive attitudes about sex in childhood and subsequently were less sexually active. We did not find, however, that prohibitive parental and religious attitudes toward sex and sexuality resulted in similar attitudes in adolescence and adulthood. It is likely that other influences, such as peers, and the process of physiological maturation into adolescence and adulthood, as well as the emotional separation from parents, counteracted prohibitive messages from parents and religious institutions.

More endorsement of body awareness and nudity by parents predicted less need to control sexual desires in adulthood, an earlier age of sexual behavior onset, and a high frequency of adult sexual activities, more childhood sexual behaviors, and less severe extrafamilial abuse. Conversely, women raised in homes in which parents had not endorsed body awareness and nudity may delay engaging in sexual behavior and report strict standards of sexual conduct, but they also are more vulnerable to childhood sexual abuse away from the home, perhaps because of their overly restrictive and unrealistic socialization about sex at home. However, prolonged and frequent sexual abuse by a family member may also facilitate strict standards about sex (Browne & Finkelhor, 1986), as well as a sense of having been stigmatized (Finkelhor & Browne, 1985), although we did not examine such an association. It is also very common for adult perpetrators of incest to espouse a strict moral code while engaging in sex with their own daughters (Herman, 1981). Parents in these homes may limit the amount and type of sex education offered to children apart from the victimization experiences themselves.

Obviously, parents did not exert their influence only by conveying their attitudes about sex and sexuality. Other factors such as socioeconomic status can influence the financial resources and types of activities in which families engage. Financial resources however, do not always influence the emotional climate of the home. Thus, lengthier sexual relationships in adolescence were predicted by recollections of endorsing parental attitudes about the body and nudity, as well as by higher parent education and poorer family relationships. Even though educated parents may have conveyed more information about sex-related topics, women who grew up in homes that lacked marital harmony and emotional closeness became involved in longer-term sexual relationships in adolescence. According to Strasberger (1985), adolescents have a special need for closeness. Perhaps the pattern of adequate family income and emotional distance among family members for women who identified themselves as sexually active female adolescents resulted in an attempt to meet needs for closeness that went unfulfilled within the family through adolescent love interests. Unfortunately, not all of the partners with whom adolescents seek to have close relationships are their age peers. Similarly, other influences such as substance use, school problems, and family estrangement can facilitate early sexual activity (McGee & Newcomb, 1992; Newcomb & McGee, 1991).

■ Early Involvement in Sexual Activity

Apart from the lasting impact of parental variables, we noted a pattern of sexual behavior reinforcement that is consistent with social learning theory. Thus, early sexual activity tended to facilitate or reinforce subsequent sexual behavior. When women recalled having engaged in more voluntary sexual behavior as children, they were also highly likely to have masturbated more, maintained longer sexual relationships, and had more sexual partners during adolescence. Previous research suggests that early childhood or early adolescent sexual experiences involving genital contact with another child increase both the likelihood of intercourse by young adulthood and the number of intercourse partners (Leitenberg et al., 1989). Similarly, Newcomb (1984) found that an older age at first sexual contact and intercourse was related to fewer sexual partners. Corroborating these prior findings, we found that a high frequency and number of voluntary childhood and adolescent sexual behaviors were associated with a younger age of onset of sexual behavior.

■ Factors Associated With Early Intercourse

The age at which women first engage in sex appears to be important in other respects as well. An earlier onset of self-exploration and sex with partners in adolescence, in conjunction with certain childhood and adolescence family characteristics, had lasting effects on women's sexual behavior in adulthood. First, adult women whose parents had endorsed body awareness and nudity and who had begun to engage in sex earlier reported a higher frequency of sexual practices such as masturbation, intercourse, and oral and anal sex. Apparently, these women experimented with sexual patterns at younger ages in adolescence and continued to do so in adulthood. This finding is consistent with research reporting that women who recall their parents' influence in childhood and adolescence are likely to be affected by parental attitudes (Libby et al., 1978; McNab, 1976; Thornton & Camburn, 1987; Yarber & Greer, 1986). Furthermore, the findings support earlier studies on sexual behavior. For instance, Newcomb (1984) found that later ages of first sexual contact, first intercourse, and first masturbation were associated with decreased later sexual behavior, defined as the number of sexual partners and monthly masturbation and intercourse frequencies in adulthood. Based on prospective data, Newcomb and Bentler (1988) found that the frequency of intercourse among young adult women was higher when these women, as teenagers, had an early age of sexual involvement, had a higher frequency of adolescent sexual events, had more sexually active peers, and reported satisfaction with opposite-sex relationships. The frequency of intercourse for young adult men was significantly predicted by a younger age of sexual involvement and lower law abidance.

An earlier onset of sexual behavior and more severe sexual abuse by a family member in childhood led to a higher rate of sexaul contact in adulthood and more frequent initiation of sex by the partner. This pattern of heightened sexual activity is likely to be the result of inappropriate childhood sexualization (Finkelhor, 1988; Finkelhor & Browne, 1985) which, once established, appears to continue into adulthood. Interestingly, women who had a high rate of childhood voluntary sexual behaviors also initiated sex with their partners less as adults. Without further knowledge of the nature of these women's sexual socialization experiences, however, it is difficult to draw conclusions about the antecedents of their attitudes with regard to sexual initiation. More research is needed to identify factors associated with establishing patterns of sexual noninitiation among women. Nevertheless, it is quite clear that early sexual experiences, both voluntary or coerced, are linked to greater partner initiation of sexual behavior in adulthood. This pattern may reflect an early sexual socialization process in which others instigate or coerce women into early sexual activity that continues into adulthood.

Finally, we found that women who were younger at first sex with others tended to have parents with less education. This was true for both ethnic groups of women included in this study (Wyatt, 1989). Daughters of better-educated parents tended to delay intercourse.

Implicit in these findings is the assumption that educated parents may have been more likely to convey important information about sex to their daughters, including possible consequences of sexual activities, than parents with less education. Although the data do not necessarily indicate that parents' education results in more sex education information in the home, these findings are supported by other results indicating that adolescents of higher SES parents, defined by higher education or family income, are more knowledgeable about midcycle fertility than adolescents from lower SES families (Morrison, 1985). On the basis of information obtained from women about their parents' education and occupations, it appears that women from more educationally privileged backgrounds were likely to delay sex with others until late adolescence. Given that adolescents prefer obtaining information about sex from their parents (Dickinson, 1978), women whose parents were less educated may have had insufficient or inaccurate parental information available to them, thus leaving them less aware of potential sexual risks and more susceptible to engaging in early sexual activity as a means of satisfying sexual curiosity (Wyatt, 1990d).

■ Influences on Effective Use of Birth Control and Unplanned Pregnancies

Other adult outcomes, such as effective use of birth control and unintended pregnancies, were also influenced by various sexual experiences in women's childhood and adolescence. Early sexual abuse experiences had differential effects on increasing women's vulnerability to inadequate contraceptive use.

We found that effective use of birth control in adult women was predicted by less voluntary adolescent sexual behavior, greater severity of extrafamilial sexual abuse, and older age of first sex with others. Therefore, effective adult women contraceptors delayed their age of voluntary sexual intercourse, engaged in adolescent sexual activities to a limited extent, and were likely to have been sexually abused by a nonfamily member as children. The latter finding perhaps represents a healthy defensive or coping reaction against unwanted and harmful sexual intercourse and the potentially traumatic consequences (i.e., pregnancy and STDs).

In their prospective study, Newcomb and Bentler (1988a) found only two predictions of effective young adult birth control for women and only two for men. For young adult women, effectiveness of future birth control methods was related to greater religious commitment and having more sexually active friends as teenagers. For young adult men, general birth control effectiveness was predicted by an older age of sexual behavior onset (corroborating our present findings for women) and fewer sexually active friends as teenagers.

We found that adult unintended pregnancies were significantly predicted only by greater severity of intrafamilial sexual abuse as children. This finding was also significantly correlated with severity of completed rapes in adulthood. Again from their prospective results, Newcomb and Bentler (1988a) found that the higher occurrence of abortions among young adult women was predicted by lower social conformity, an earlier age of sexual involvement, and greater frequency of sexual events as teenagers. Therefore, unintended pregnancies and abortions among adult women are related to both coercive sexual abuse in the home as a child, early and greater sexual involvement as adolescents, and completed rapes as adults.

In general, female sexual abuse survivors, regardless of whether the abuse occurred intra- or extrafamilially, have previously been found to be three times more likely to become pregnant before age 18 than women not abused in childhood (Zierler, Feingold, Laufer, Velentgas, Kantrowitz-Gordon, & Mayer, 1991). It is likely, however, that incestuous abuse resulted in a greater sense of powerlessness and inability to protect oneself, even with respect to contraception, than did incidents involving extrafamilial abuse. Survivors of incest often also suffer from body image distortion and an aversion to touching their own bodies and may, consequently, have difficulty with contraceptive devices that require body exploration (Wyatt, 1991a; Wyatt, Guthrie, & Notgrass, 1992). Our findings are consistent with the fact that father-daughter incest has been linked to more severe effects on women's psychological functioning than have other forms of sexual abuse (Browne & Finkelhor, 1986). Tharinger's (1990) statement is most appropriate here: The decision-making and problem-solving abilities of children sexually abused within the family become impaired with regard to sexual issues as a result of inappropriate and ineffectual sexual socialization both before and during the abuse.

■ Predictors of Partner Dysfunction

One interesting fact is that women who had been sexually abused by a family member and had subsequently engaged in more childhood sexual behavior were more likely to report as adults that their sexual partners had sexual dysfunctions. There are three possible interpretations of this finding that are not mutually exclusive. First, given that survivors sometimes avoid or are reluctant to discover their own sexual needs and to communicate them, these women may not have developed the skills with which to choose sexually functional partners. Second, in selecting a passive or nonthreatening partner, they may have unconsciously made such a choice to alleviate any guilt they might have in experiencing pleasure during sex. At least some portion of their early sexual experiences and socialization provided distorted expectations and inappropriate models. In fact, the perpetrator of sexual abuse may have been sexually dysfunctional, as are many men who force sex on women and children (Masters et al., 1992). Sexual pleasure also may be avoided because survivors experienced pleasant sexual feelings with their perpetrators. To experience sexual pleasure would be similar to experiencing the guilt and shame of having been victimized, even though some or all aspects of the sexual encounter were enjoyable. Third, survivors may have had difficulty initiating and expressing their sexual needs with their partners. Their partners may subsequently experience problems of sexual arousal (Maltz, 1988) and consequently may be dysfunctional (Wyatt, 1991a).

■ Factors Affecting Psychological Well-Being

In contrast to studies that have identified specific adverse psychological effects of childhood sexual abuse (for example, Browne & Finkelhor, 1986; Orr & Downes, 1985), we found that psychological well-being in adulthood, including self-esteem and general well-being, were not directly related to any type of childhood, adolescence, or adulthood sexual experience when the entire sample was used in the analyses. There are some reasons for the overall lack of association between sexual abuse and psychological variables. First, psychological distress in a community as opposed to a clinical sample may be less severe. These women rarely received mental health services for their victimization experiences, and many appear to have developed adequate coping strategies to facilitate their psychological well-being. Furthermore, the average span of time that had elapsed since the last childhood sexual abuse incident was 15.5 years and 5.5 years for incidents of attempted or completed rape. It is also possible that the measures of general well-being for the sample as a whole did not adequately assess the extent of very severe mental health problems in this population. They were designed to assess healthy coping strategies as well as psychological distress among community samples.

On the other hand, more detailed analyses presented elsewhere (Wyatt, Newcomb, & Skidmore, 1992) revealed the critical role of attribution in sexual abuse. Personal attributions (i.e., self-blame) for childhood sexual abuse both mediated and moderated the associations between circumstances of the abuse and adult psychological well-being. Those women with internal attributions (self-blame) for their abuse suffered from diminished psychological well-being in adulthood. External attributions for their abuse protected women's psychological well-being from the adversity of their childhood sexual trauma, whereas internal attributions had the opposite effect, leading to deteriorated adult psychological adjustment.

■ Other Factors Affecting Psychological Well-Being

The impact of certain family characteristics, childhood socialization, and later sexual experiences on adult women's well-being and self-esteem were particularly apparent from these findings. A higher quality of family life and low parent education were associated with greater psychological well-being in adulthood. Apparently, children of less educated parents and those who had observed marital harmony and experienced emotional family closeness gained an adequate foundation for general well-being and self-esteem in adulthood. This relationship has been confirmed in other studies of self-esteem (Cole, 1978; Cole & Putnam, 1992). Greater parental endorsement of body awareness and nudity was also associated with general well-being in adulthood. Once again, this finding lends support to the notion that women from homes where nudity and body touching were allowed tended to incorporate positive messages about sex and sexuality modeled by their parents in childhood and adolescence. This may have resulted in greater well-being in adulthood. Greater sexual satisfaction in adulthood was correlated with psychological well-being, as well as with a higher frequency of sexual activities. These characteristics suggest that women enjoyed a range of sexual behaviors in the context of satisfying relationships. It is likely that women who report high levels of self-esteem and high sexual satisfaction in their relationships are more responsive to educational information about the use of barrier methods of contraception and to changes in sexual behavior. Being in satisfying relationships may allow women to feel free to communicate about sex with their partners and to be motivated to prevent health risks.

■ The Cycle of Revictimization

Various groups of women appear to be at risk of being revictimized. First, women severely sexually abused in childhood by a family or nonfamily member were highly likely to have been revictimized throughout their life course, a finding that is consistent with other studies (e.g., Browne & Finkelhor, 1986; Russell, 1986; Wyatt, Guthrie, & Notgrass, 1992). More research on the cycle of revictimization needs to be conducted to identify the lasting effects of repeated sexual victimization on women. Second, women who reported less family closeness and who had engaged infrequently in sexual behaviors in childhood were also at risk for victimization later in life. This finding suggests that family life has a salient impact on increasing women's vulnerability to encountering abusive sexual experiences in the future. In contrast, attempted rape victims in adulthood were less likely to experience revictimization in the form of completed rapes and had a lower frequency of sexual contact in their primary relationships with partners. Having survived incidents of attempted rape, these women may have attempted to avoid sexual contact and became more wary and cautious about intimacy and potential rape situations. Relationship factors placing them at risk for attempted rape, however, are less clear and may be different from those involved in completed rapes. On the other hand, women who have been raped may feel powerless to resist subsequent attempted rapes and therefore fail to prevent a coercive attempt at sex (reducing attempted rapes, increasing the likelihood of completed rapes, and revictimization). More research is needed to determine additional factors that result in the cycle of revictimization among rape victims.

Sadly, patterns of revictimization begin quite early. We found a strong positive association between severity of intra- and extrafamilial childhood sexual abuse. Therefore, there is a good likelihood that a girl experiencing incest in the home will also be sexually abused away from home. At this young age, sexually abused girls may learn that they are powerless and helpless with regard to unwanted and inappropriate sexual invasion and that there is no safety either in or outside of the home. This learning may help explain continued victimization throughout some survivors' lives and other adverse outcomes of childhood sexual abuse.

Women's reports of severe rape experiences were correlated with a higher frequency of sexual contact and a greater likelihood of obtaining an abortion for an unintended pregnancy. Because these findings do not suggest cause and effect, it is not clear whether these women faced a higher risk of rape because of their increased exposure to sexual contact or whether they felt less able to protect themselves adequately by using effective birth control as a result of having been victimized.

This study identified other predictions of incidents of attempted rape. Women who had experienced severe rape attempts reported growing up in homes in which their mothers had less education and where sexual intimacy was not endorsed. These women also reported less teenage masturbation but more sexual play with others in childhood. Apparently, less information given at home was associated with peer-initiated sex play. The pattern that emerges is one of the sexually unsophisticated child who agrees to exploratory sex play initiated by others and an interest in self-stimulation. This pattern may reinforce partner-initiated sexual contact later in life, some of which may be rape attempts.

■ General Conclusions

Overall, it appears that the most salient sex-related experiences were those described as sexually abusive. Our results revealed that childhood sexual victimization had a significant impact on women's sexual behaviors throughout the life course, regardless of the relationship between perpetrator and victim. Women who as children had experienced more severe sexual abuse by family or nonfamily members, including longer duration and repeated incidents, reported that their parents were likely to have less education and poorer marital relationships and that their families were likely to be estranged. Poor family quality has been confirmed in other studies as a risk factor for sexual abuse (Bagley & Ramsay, 1985; Briere, 1988a; Brunold, 1980; Finkelhor, 1984; Finkelhor, Hotaling, Lewis, & Smith, 1990; Fromuth, 1983; Kaufman, Peck, & Tagiuri, 1954; Lustig, Dresser, Spellman, & Murray, 1966), even though parent education has not been consistently linked to childhood victimization (see for example, Finkelhor et al., 1990). Less closeness between fathers and daughters, however, has been associated with both intra- and extrafamilial sexual abuse (Fromuth, 1983).

Thus, child sexual abuse does not occur independent of other factors involved in the emotional climate of the marriage and family. These factors tend to interact with one another and contribute to poor mental health and diminished self-esteem (Bagley & Ramsay, 1985; Browne & Finkelhor, 1986). In contrast to some earlier studies (Finkelhor, 1984; Fromuth, 1983; Landis, 1956; Russell, Schurman, & Trocki, 1988; Sedney & Brooks, 1984; Tormes, 1968), we found that less parental education increased these women's vulnerability to being sexually victimized. Children of less educated parents may be at a higher risk for sexual abuse because of the variety of financial and other stressors that lesser-educated families encounter.

Incest victims reported a poor quality of family life, had parents with less education, and had received less adequate and appropriate information about sexuality and the consequences of becoming sexually active. Although some incest perpetrators are frequently described as outwardly espousing moral values about sex, they often justify having sex with their daughters as being a part of their parental role (Herman, 1981). The lack of sex-related information and the failure of abusive or nonoffending parents to have an open dialogue within the family about human sexuality and its appropriate role in life often reinforce the shroud of secrecy about ongoing sexual abuse. Victims of more severe extrafamilial sexual abuse also reported poor quality of family life and low parental education. In contrast to incest survivors, they were more likely to have received parental endorsement with respect to body awareness and nudity. Apparently, however, for this sample of women, information about body awareness and nudity did not provide these women with sufficient information or caution to prepare them for exploitative and coercive sexual experiences outside of the family.

Furthermore, women who reported sexual abuse, regardless of the relationship between perpetrator and victim, were also likely to have reported an earlier onset and a greater frequency of childhood and adolescent sexual activities. These findings may reflect female children's attempts to process the traumatic experience of sexual abuse by a compulsive reenactment of sexual activity (Friedrich, 1988; Wyatt, 1988a). Other interpretations of these correlates suggest that children who engage in more voluntary sexual activities may be perceived as highly sexualized by family and nonfamily members, which may increase their risk of being singled out for coercive sexual activities.

Our most disturbing findings concern the effects of abusive childhood sexual experiences on later sexual activities that appear to place child sexual abuse victims at increased risk of contracting STDS, including HIV. High-risk behaviors such as vaginal, oral, and anal intercourse; ineffective use of birth control; and multiple partners often resulted in unintended and aborted pregnancies. However, the risk of disease transmission was also increased by ineffective use of barrier methods or the nonuse of contraceptives. These findings are consistent with another study that reported women survivors of childhood rape as more likely than women with no reported abuse histories in childhood to work as prostitutes, have unintended pregnancies, change sex partners frequently, and engage in sexual activities with casual acquaintances (Zierler et al., 1991). Among the abused women, adult survivors of incest were most likely to be poor contraceptors. Few studies, however, have yet identified incest victims as a group at particularly high risk for contracting STDs, including HIV. These findings identify women who report incidents of child sexual abuse as surviving the abuse but still as potential victims of STDs, including HIV.

Although this retrospective study has been helpful in understanding the relationship between child sexual abuse and later consensual sexual experiences throughout the life course, more research on specific experiences such as sexual abuse is needed to determine the range of its effects on women's risk of contracting AIDS. Recent national statistics report African-American women to be at highest risk of becoming infected with HIV (CDC, 1992). Future research that identifies sociocultural factors in women's sexual development and decision making will enhance the available information about women's sexual experiences over the life course and the impact of sexual abuse on their consensual sexual practices.

15

Results of Moderator Analyses

As in Chapter 13, the statistical results from this chapter are organized into three distinct sections. All findings in this chapter are based on moderated effects between the four types of sexual abuse and various outcomes.

The extensive set of SEM analyses presented in Chapter 13 examined how four sets of variables representing influences, occurrences, and outcomes of female sexual behavior and trauma were significantly related to each other. Within-set associations were tested with correlations, and between-set linkages were evaluated as regression paths in the large SEM. These results revealed whether and how variables were linearly related to each other and could take the form of direct effects, indirect (mediated) effects, correlations, or no relation at all.

We did not always expect that sexual abuse would have a direct effect on other aspects of women's psychosexual functioning, but that "various intervening cognitive interpretations, decisions, and reactions may mediate and help explain the effects of child sexual abuse on later attitudes and behavior" (Wyatt & Newcomb, 1990, p. 759). We also examined women's voluntary sexual behavior in childhood, adolescence, and adulthood as possible mediators between childhood sexual abuse and adult psychosexual satisfaction and behavior (including rapes and attempted rapes). A mediator variable captures "the generative mechanism through which the focal independent variable is able to influence the dependent variable" (Baron & Kenny, 1986, p. 1173). In other words, sexual abuse is assumed to affect the mediator variable, which in turn affects later psychosexual functioning. In this manner and via this mechanism, "mediators explain how external physical events take on internal psychological significance" (Baron & Kenny, 1986, p. 1176).

Nevertheless, these SEM analyses examined only the linear relations between variables, assuming that such associations would be similar for all women. This set of analyses, however, did not consider another type of association between variables—that of a moderated or interactive relationship (e.g., Baron & Kenny, 1986). In some areas of psychology and sociology it is referred to as a *buffering effect* (e.g., Cohen & Wills, 1985) or as *vulnerability versus resistance* (e.g., Newcomb, 1992; Newcomb & Felix-Ortiz, in press). In this chapter, we examine several possible moderated associations between sexual abuse and selected outcome variables.

An interactive or moderated relationship suggests that the extent or degree of association between two or more variables is different for some individuals as compared to other individuals. The variable that differentiates groups of individuals who have different associations between independent and dependent variables is considered the *moderator variable*. A moderator variable may have a direct or main effect on the criterion or dependent variable (that would have been revealed in the SEM analyses of the previous chapter), as well as interact with or moderate the effects of independent variables on the dependent variable(s). Baron and Kenny (1986) define moderating effects as those situations where various conditions of the moderator variable create or are associated with different causal or correlational relations between two or more variables. Thereby, "moderator variables specify when certain effects will hold" (Baron & Kenny, 1986, p. 1176).

In the present analyses, we have selected several potential moderator variables and test whether they are associated with different degrees of relationship between measures of sexual abuse and selected outcome measures from adulthood. These analyses will determine if, how, and in what manner our selected moderator variables may exacerbate, nullify, or attenuate the associations between various types of sexual abuse and selected outcome measures.

■ Selection of Variables

Given the large number of variables available in our rich data set, it was necessary to select variables for our moderator analyses. These variables were chosen on the bases of prior research, theory, and potential importance for practitioners. We selected 4 independent variables, 5 outcome or dependent variables, and 10 potential moderator variables.

Independent Variables

The four independent variables were the severity of sexual abuse scales. These included:

1. the severity of intrafamilial childhood sexual abuse,
2. the severity of extrafamilial childhood sexual abuse,
3. the severity of completed rapes in adulthood, and
4. the severity of attempted rapes in adulthood.

Outcome or Dependent Variables

Five scales were selected as potential outcome or correlates of sexual abuse. These five scales were all from adulthood and included:

1. frequency of adult sexual activities,
2. frequency of sexual contact,
3. self-esteem,
4. psychological well-being, and
5. a need to control sexual desires.

Need to control sexual desires was also included as a potential moderator variable.

Moderator Variables

Ten variables were chosen to be tested as potential moderator or interaction variables. Eight of these reflect parent and family background scales and include:

1. parent endorsement of body awareness and nudity,
2. parent endorsement of sexual intimacy,
3. parent demonstrative messages about sexual expression,
4. mother's education,
5. father's education,
6. good parent relationship,
7. family closeness, and
8. feeling close to a family member during childhood.

The other two variables are:

9. voluntary adolescent sexual behavior, and
10. a need to control sexual desires.

This chapter is organized in a manner similar to Chapter 13. The first section below describes several of the substantive findings we found most interesting. These are presented in "Highlights of the Moderator Results" and represent a select and biased group of these findings (based on our judgments). However, all findings are completely summarized in the section titled "Complete Summary of Moderator Results." Finally, a section called "Technical Details of the Moderator Analyses" is provided for those readers who want complete details of all aspects of the moderator analyses.

■ Highlights of the Moderator Results

Family Patterns Promoting Sexual Health

• Family closeness had a moderator effect, including serving as a buffer from consequences of extrafamilial sexual abuse in a close family.

Family Patterns Compromising Sexual Health

• The moderator variable regarding feeling closest to a family member was associated with the greatest number of significant interaction effects. In general, not feeling close to someone in one's family increased the association between sexual and negative psychological effects and a greater need to control sexual desires. On the other hand, feeling close to someone in the family increased the association between both types of child sexual abuse.

• Parent endorsement of body awareness and nudity also had a high number of significant interaction effects. Intrafamilial sexual abuse negatively affected adult self-esteem and general well-being only for those who were raised in homes that did not endorse body awareness and nudity. Low parent endorsement of body awareness and nudity was also associated with a greater vulnerability to being raped if extrafamilial sexual abuse had occurred and much stronger needs to control adult sexual desires, if the women had been sexually abused as children.

• The fewest significant interaction effects were found for mother's education as a moderator variable and were related only to variations in associations among the sexual abuse variables. For instance, highly educated mothers increased the vulnerability of experiencing one type of childhood sexual abuse if the other type had occurred.

• Moderator effects had the greatest impact on altering associations with the childhood sexual abuse traumas, compared to the adult sexual traumas. Indeed, by far the greatest number of associations altered by the moderators were for intrafamilial sexual abuse.

• Those women who experienced greater endorsement of sexual intimacy by socialization agents had greater negative outcomes associated with intrafamilial sexual abuse, including a greater likelihood of extrafamilial sexual abuse, lower adult self-esteem and general well-being, and a greater need to control sexual desires in adulthood.

• On the other hand, those women exposed to demonstrative messages about sexual expression by parents were protected from certain consequences of intrafamilial sexual abuse, including also experiencing extrafamilial sexual abuse, vulnerability to adult sexual revictimization in the form of completed rapes, and the need to control their adult sexual desires.

• Although those women who had highly educated fathers and experienced intrafamilial sexual abuse were not at risk for sexual revictimization as adults in terms of completed rapes, their adult self-esteem and general well-being was negatively affected, and they had a greater need to control their sexual desires if childhood incest occurred (as compared with those women with poorly educated fathers).

• Growing up in a family with a poor relationship between parents and experiencing intrafamilial sexual abuse increased the likelihood of extrafamilial sexual abuse, as well as both low self-esteem and general well-being in adulthood. Conversely, being raised by parents with a good relationship severed the high connection between intra- and extrafamilial sexual abuse, and preserved adult self-esteem and general well-being if incest occurred.

• Those women who felt a strong need to control sexual desires experienced greater damage to their general well-being when exposed to either type of childhood sexual abuse or adulthood completed rapes.

■ Complete Summary of the Moderator Results

Because the information in the technical section below (associated with 10 tables of moderator results) is quite involved and complex, we have attempted to summarize and organize the most important findings. Table 15.1 organizes the numerous findings that can be categorized in several ways.

The first column of Table 15.1 presents instances where two significant correlations were found between a specific type of sexual abuse and a specific outcome variable, but the difference between these two correlations was not significant (this is neither an interaction nor a moderator effect). The remaining three columns of Table 15.1 reflect several types of significant moderator effects (identified by significant differences between correlations in each moderator group). The rows of Table 15.1 are broken down by all 4 sexual abuse variables within each of the 10 moderator variables. Entries in the table are abbreviations for each of the several outcome variables where significant effects were found. Each abbreviation is accompanied by two signs: The upper sign indicates the direction of the correlation for those high on the moderator variable, and the lower sign indicates the direction of the correlation for those low on the moderate variable.

One general result from the 10 tables presented in the technical section occurs when a sexual abuse variable is significantly correlated with an outcome variable in the same direction for both of the moderator groups, but the between-set correlation is not significant. This does *not* represent a moderator effect. It does represent a significant main effect or association between the sexual abuse variable and the outcome variable. In many of these instances, the two significant correlations will have been captured in the SEM as either a significant path or correlation. For example, in many of the moderator analyses, significant correlations were found between intra- and extrafamilial sexual abuse, although these two correlations were themselves not significantly different (as tested by the z-score). In the CFA this is reflected in the significant correlation between these two variables and in the SEM by the significant correlation between the residual variable of these two variables. There are two situations where two such significant correlations will not be in the SEM. First, the significant correlations were captured in the SEM as indirect effects and not direct paths or correlations. And second, because the SEM was based on the total sample of 248 women and the moderator analyses study only approximately two thirds of this total sample (because of trichotomizing the moderator variable), the missing subjects in the moderator analyses (representing approximately the middle third of the moderator distribution) may have washed out any significant associations found in the two extreme groups. On the other hand, there are at least two explanations for when there is a significant path or correlation in the SEM model and not two significant correlations in the moderator analyses. One is where the excluded subjects in the moderator analyses (and not combining the groups together) reduced the power to detect significant associations in the moderator analyses; with the combined sample in the SEM analyses, there was sufficient power to detect the association. In the second case, in the moderator analyses, one correlation may have been significant and the other not (but themselves not significantly different), so that in the SEM significant associations were found, although in the moderator analyses both correlations were not significant.

Perusing Table 15.1 and the SEM results, it appears that in many cases the latter two circumstances were more prevalent than the former situations. In other words, there were often more significant paths or correlations in the SEM than there were the two correlations between the same variables in the moderator analyses. This is not a matter of concern but must be understood according to the explanations reviewed above. Where discrepancies of this nature occur, it makes most sense to rely on the SEM findings because they are based on the total sample and are more reliable and valid.

Of most interest to this chapter on moderator effects are the types of significant interaction or moderator effects. These were identified by obtaining significant differences when comparing two correlations—between sexual abuse and outcome variables—for each of the moderator groups. Although there are many ways to categorize the various patterns of association where these significant effects arise, we have selected three that have important implications for theory, research, and practice.

Table 15.1 Summary of Interaction Effects by Type of Moderator

Moderator/ Type of Sexual Offense	No Significant z-Difference/ Both Correlations Significant	Significant z-Difference		Same Sign Both Correlations Significant
		Sign Reversal	One Correlation Significant	
Parent Endorsement of Body Awareness and Nudity				
Intrafamilial	Extra$_+^+$/Rape$_+^+$	NCSD$_+^-$[b]	FASA$_+^+$/SE$_-^0$/WB$_-^0$	
Extrafamilial	FASA$_+^+$	SE$_-^+$[a]/NCSD$_+^-$		Rape$_+^+$
Rape				
Attempted Rape				
Endorsement of Sexual Intimacy by Socialization Agents				
Intrafamilial	Rape$_+^+$/FASA$_+^+$	NCSD$_-^+$[b]	SE$_-^0$/WB$_-^0$	Extra$_+^+$
Extrafamilial	Rape$_+^+$			
Rape	FASA$_+^+$	NCSD$_+^-$		
Attempted Rape				
Parent Demonstrative Messages about Sexual Expression				
Intrafamilial	Rape$_+^+$		Rape$_+^0$/NCSD$_-^0$	Extra$_+^+$
Extrafamilial	FASA$_+^+$			
Rape		SE$_-^+$[a]	WB$_-^0$	
Attempted Rape				
Mother's Education				
Intrafamilial				
Extrafamilial	FASA$_+^+$	Att Rape$_-^+$	Att Rape$_+^0$	Extra$_+^+$
Rape				
Attempted Rape				
Father's Education				
Intrafamilial	Extra$_+^+$	NCSD$_-^+$[b]/SE$_+^-$/WB$_+^-$	Rape$_+^0$	
Extrafamilial			Rape$_0^+$	

	Column 1	Column 2	Column 3
Rape			FASA$^+_+$
Attempted Rape		SE$^+_-$[a]	
Good Parent Relationship			
Intrafamilial	Rape$^+_+$/FASA$^+_+$	SE$^+_-$[b]/WB$^+_-$	Extra$^0_+$
Extrafamilial	Rape$^+_+$	WB$^+_-$[b]	
Rape	FASA$^+_+$		
Attempted Rape			
Family Closeness			
Intrafamilial	Rape$^+_+$	SE$^+_-$[a]	FASA$^0_+$/WB$^0_-$
Extrafamilial	Rape$^+_+$	WB$^+_-$	FSC$^0_+$
Rape			Extra$^+_+$
Attempted Rape			FASA$^+_+$
Felt Closest to in Family			
Intrafamilial	Rape$^+_+$/FASA$^+_+$	NCSD$^+_-$	SE$^0_-$/WB$^0_-$
Extrafamilial	Rape$^+_+$	NCSD$^+_-$[a]	WB$^0_-$
Rape	FASA$^+_+$	NCSD$^+_-$[b]	FSC$^0_+$
Attempted Rape			SE$^0_+$
Voluntary Adolescent Sexual Behavior			
Intrafamilial			FASA$^0_+$/NCSD$^0_+$
Extrafamilial	FASA$^+_+$		
Rape			Extra$^+_0$
Attempted Rape			Rape$^+_+$
Need to Control Sexual Desires			
Intrafamilial	Extra$^+_+$	WB$^+_0$	WB$^0_-$
Extrafamilial	Rape$^+_+$	WB$^-_+$	FSC$^0_+$
Rape	FASA$^+_+$/FSC$^+_+$	FSC$^+_-$[a]	SE$^0_-$
Attempted Rape			Rape$^+_+$

Extra = extrafamilial sexual abuse; Rape = severity of completed rapes; Att Rape = severity of attempted rapes; FASA = frequency of adult sexual activity; FSC = frequency of sexual contact; SE = self-esteem; WB = well-being; NCSD = need to control sexual desires

[a] Both correlations are not significant despite a significant z-difference between the correlations. This represents a slightly different/opposing process occurring in the two groups. [b] Both correlations are significant and have opposite signs.

Note: +, o, - indicate direction of correlation in each moderator group. The upper symbol reflects the group high on the moderator variable and the lower symbol reflects the group low on the moderator variable. "o" captures nonsignificant correlations between $-.10 \leq r \geq .10$.

The first type is where there is a sign reversal on the two correlations. The correlations may or may not be significant in the opposite directions. These are presented in column 2 of Table 15.1. For the current summary, we chose to include in this category all significant z-score differences where the two correlations had opposite signs and both were greater than .10 (absolute value). This type of interaction represents a particularly important moderating effect where opposite processes occur within the two groups. In other words, levels of the moderator variable represent groups wherein opposite associations were found between sexual abuse and outcome variables.

Certainly, the most important and theoretically interesting differences of this type occur where both of the correlations are each significant in their opposite directions and they were themselves significantly different. These are denoted with a superscript "b" in column 2 of Table 15.1. There were six of this type of moderating effect among all of the interactions tested. For instance, need to control sexual desires was inversely correlated (significantly so) with severity of intrafamilial sexual abuse for those women who reported high levels of parent endorsement of body awareness and nudity (moderator variable), while a significantly positive correlation was found between severity of intrafamilial sexual abuse and need to control sexual desires for those who reported low parent endorsement of body awareness and nudity. This type of interaction was found one time for parent endorsement of body awareness and nudity, parent endorsement of sexual intimacy, father education, and felt closest to in family, and it was found two times for good parent relationship.

A variant of this type of interaction is where the correlation is significant in one group (defined by the moderator variable) but is nonsignificant in the other moderator groups (although greater than .10), and both correlations were significantly different as evidenced by the z-score. For example, those women with highly educated fathers had a significant correlation between intrafamilial sexual abuse and self-esteem, while for those with fathers who had little education, this correlation was positive ($r = .17$) but not significant. These two correlations were significantly different. Therefore, the self-esteem of women with high father education was quite vulnerable to damage by intrafamilial sexual abuse, whereas if women had fathers with low education, their self-esteem was less affected if they were exposed to intrafamilial sexual abuse. This variation was certainly the most prevalent of this type of interaction; there was at least one of this variant on every moderator variable, and these are indicated in column 2 of Table 15.1 with no superscript. There was one such type of interaction for parent demonstrative messages about sexual expression, mother education, good parent relationship, and voluntary adolescent sexual behavior; two such interactions for parent endorsement of body awareness and nudity, parent endorsement of sexual intimacy, and family closeness; three for father education and feeling closest to a family member; and four for need to control sexual desires.

Finally, a third variant of this type of interaction represented by reversed correlation signs occurred where there was a significant difference between the correlations: The correlations had reversed signs and were greater than .10, but neither was significant on its own. Such results are denoted by a superscript "a" in column 2 of Table 15.1. There were six such types of moderator effects. These are the weakest of the reversed-sign moderator, but they still reveal that opposing processes are evident in the two moderator groups and that these opposing processes are significantly different. The weakness results from the fact that neither of the two correlations is significant in its own right and is only different in contrast to the other group. These are still quite important because they actually reveal opposite processes occurring in the two contrasting moderator groups. For instance, those women with fathers who were well educated had a positive (but nonsignificant) correlation between attempted rapes and self-esteem, while those with poorly educated fathers had a negative (nonsignificant) correlation between these. However, the z-score difference between these correlations was significant, revealing a reliably distinct process occurring in each of the two groups defined by extremes of the moderator variables (father education).

Some of these results present a very complex interpretation when combined with the SEM results. For instance, in the SEM analyses, those women who had parents (both fathers and mothers) with high education were less likely to be sexually abused in the home. Conversely, lower parent education was related to greater likelihood of sexual abuse in the home. However, those women who had been sexually abused in the home and had mothers with little education were somehow protected from attempted rapes in adult life. As another example, let us look at completed rapes and self-esteem for the moderator variable of parent demonstrative messages about sexual expression. Those high on this moderator variable had a positive (but nonsignificant) correlation between completed rapes and self-esteem (revealing an enhancing or at least protective process), while those low on this moderator variable had a negative (but again nonsignificant) correlation between completed rapes and self-esteem (highlighting a vulnerability process).

A second type of significant interaction or moderator result occurs when one of the correlations is significant and the other is nonsignificant (and .10 or less), and there is a significant z-score difference between the two correlations. This indicates that one of the groups designated by the moderator variable is uniquely vulnerable or protected from sexual abuse as related to other outcomes. In other words, one group has a strong association between a sexual and an outcome variable that is not found in the other group. This may also indicate that a high (or low) level of a moderator variable activates a buffering or susceptibility process that is not present in the group low (or high) on the same moderator variable. For instance, those women who reported low family closeness had a significant positive correlation between extrafamilial sexual abuse and frequency of sexual contact, and there was essentially no relation between these two variables for those with high family closeness. These moderator effects are listed in column 3 of Table 15.1.

A final type of moderator finding summarized in Table 15.1 occurred when both correlations were significant and in the same direction (identical signs), and there was a significant z-score difference between the two correlations. These results reveal a similar process (sign or direction of effect) between sexual abuse and outcome variables but indicate differential sensitivity to the process. These moderator effects are listed in column 4 of Table 15.1. There were 9 such significant types of interactions captured by the 10 moderator variable analyses. In all but one instance, these reflected different magnitudes of positive correlations among the four severity of sexual abuse variables. As one example, those high on parent endorsement of body awareness and nudity had a significantly positive but lower correlation between extrafamilial sexual abuse and completed rapes in adulthood compared to a much higher correlation between these two sexual abuse variables for those low on parent endorsement of body awareness and nudity. In this case, those women who perceived their parents as endorsing body awareness and nudity became less susceptible to the continuation of sexual abuse from childhood to adulthood than did those women who felt that their parents were restrictive about body awareness and nudity and whose vulnerability or victim-proneness was exacerbated from childhood to adulthood.

Table 15.2 gives a summary of the number of significant interactions revealed in the technical results (Tables 15.3 through 15.12).

Only interactions are summarized here that exclude column 1 of Table 15.1 where no significant differences between correlations were found. The row totals of Table 15.2 reveal the number of significant interactions associated with each of the 10 moderator variables, whereas column totals of Table 15.2 indicate the number of significant interactions related to each of the four types of sexual abuse.

■ Integration of Findings

Both the SEM and moderator analyses revealed important but complex relationships among sexual abuse experiences and how these relate to other psychosocial family predictors and later adult outcomes. There are far more significant relationships than can be completely integrated in one book.

Table 15.2   Number of Significant Moderator Effects

		Severity of Sexual Abuse			
Moderator Variable	*Intra-familial*	*Extra-familial*	*Completed Rapes*	*Attempted Rapes*	*Total*
Parent endorsement of body awareness and nudity	4	3	1	0	8
Endorsement of sexual intimacy by socialization agents	4	0	0	1	5
Parent demonstrative messages about sexual expression	3	0	2	0	5
Mother's education	2	1	0	0	3
Father's education	4	1	0	1	6
Good parent relationship	3	1	0	0	4
Family closeness	4	2	1	0	7
Felt closest to in family	4	2	2	1	9
Voluntary adolescent sexual behavior	1	1	0	2	4
Need to control sexual desires	2	2	2	1	7
Total	31	13	8	6	58

On the one hand, this reveals that there are definitely many important and reliable predictors, associations, and outcomes related to both child and adult sexual abuse experiences. In terms of significant associations, most are related to severity of intrafamilial sexual abuse, followed by severity of extrafamilial sexual abuse, adult completed rapes, and adult attempted rapes. This would indicate that sexual abuse that occurs earlier in life and is more closely associated with one's family is more directly related to earlier family conditions and later adult outcomes. Childhood sexual abuse incidents are the second most powerful events that are related to family characteristics. Thus childhood sexual abuse seems to have the strongest and most profound association between family characteristics and later psychosexual functioning as an adult. Although sexual abuse in adulthood clearly has many precursors, correlates, and moderators, there were far fewer of these than for child sexual abuse experiences. It was quite evident that the severity of completed rapes in adulthood was substantially more related to early vulnerability conditions and contemporaneous psychosocial qualities than was severity of attempted rapes.

On the other hand, many of the results reveal quite important and groundbreaking evidence regarding associations and outcomes of both childhood and adult sexual abuse experiences of women that need to be integrated and understood more fully. These results are profound and meaningful. They will take a long time to appreciate fully. Nevertheless, in our final chapters, we will struggle to integrate and comment on the more obvious and interesting patterns that have emerged from these analyses. We cannot address them all, although we have presented the reader, scientist, and clinician with our completed set of results. Those findings that we do not address can be tackled by others in this field. We can only discuss a selected set of the more consistent and provocative findings.

We must reiterate that the analyses in the present chapter and those given in the previous chapter address substantially different issues. Chapter 13 examined direct and mediated relationships between sexual abuse experiences and family-of-origin characteristics; child, adolescent, and adult voluntary sexual behavior; and adult psychosexual characteristics. This chapter attempts to test how these relationships may not occur, or under what circumstances they do or do not occur, or how the process may differ depending on a selected set of 10 moderator variables.

In subsequent chapters we will try to interpret findings from each of these analytic and theoretical perspectives and integrate these explanations. These results should have unique importance to the theory, research, and clinical practice related to women's sexual abuse experiences in both childhood and adulthood.

■ Technical Details of the Moderator Analyses

Analytic Approach

There are various methods to operationalize or test for interactions or moderating effects (e.g., Baron & Kenny, 1986; Newcomb, 1990). These include multiplicative terms in multiple-regression analyses (e.g., Cronbach, 1987; Dunlap & Kemmery, 1987), multiple-group SEM analyses (e.g., Newcomb, 1990), or direct tests of the magnitudes of the associations (correlations) between two variables compared across two or more groups (e.g., Games, 1978; Newcomb, 1986). We have selected the last method for this investigation because it provides the degree of association between the variables in the two groups, as well as the statistical comparison between the magnitudes of these two associations.

In the current analyses, we used correlations to examine the degrees of association between each of the four independent and the dependent or outcomes variables. These correlations are generated for each of two groups created from the moderator variables. Each of the 10 moderator variables was trichotomized, and subjects falling in the upper and lower thirds of each distribution were used to create subsamples for comparison of correlations.

Thus we avoid the ambiguity and difficulties involved with interpreting associations (correlations) among those who fall in the middle of the distribution of the moderator variables and so enhance the chances of detecting an interaction or moderating effect.

The size of the two groups created based on each of the 10 moderator variables may differ substantially as a result of uneven distributions. For each moderator, we made our best attempt to create groups representing the upper and lower thirds of the sample. In many cases this worked well, although in a few cases larger or smaller groups had to be made based on the distribution of the moderator. In a few cases, the moderator variable is dichotomous so that the division actually represents a median split and all subjects will be in one group or the other. In a couple of other instances, there were so few levels of the moderator variable that it was necessary to generate groups with numbers quite different from one third of the sample. In each instance, however, we made the best attempt to create groups from the upper and lower thirds of the sample. The sample size for each subgroup is given in the footnote of each moderator table.

Finally, each pair of analogous correlations (one from each group created by the moderator variable) is compared statistically to determine if it is reliably different in magnitude. This was accomplished using the Fisher r-to-z conversion (e.g., Games, 1978; Newcomb, 1986). This test results in a z-score that reflects the likelihood that the correlations are similar. Because it is quite difficult to detect interaction effects in psychosocial research (e.g., Stacy, Newcomb, & Bentler, in press), we used a one-tailed test of significance for this z-score. This increases our sensitivity to detect the elusive interaction or moderator effects.

Results

This section presents the statistical results. These are organized into 10 tables, each reflecting analyses based on one moderator variable. Each table includes two correlations between each of the four sexual abuse scales and each of the five psychosexual outcome variables: one correlation for the group representing the upper third of the moderator variable and the other correlation calculated on the group representing the lower third of the moderator variable. The z-scores that test the similarity of each of these pairs of correlations are also given in the tables. One-tailed tests of significance were used ($p < .05$) to increase our power to assess interactions, which are notoriously difficult to detect (e.g., Stacy et al., in press).

The following 10 subsections describe the information given in each table. Each section is devoted to one moderator variable, and the results are summarized for that moderator variable in a table. There are many significant

Table 15.3 Correlations Between Sexual Abuse and Outcomes With Parent Endorsement of Body Awareness and Nudity (PBN) as Moderator Variable

		Intra-familial	Extra-familial	Completed Rapes	Attempted Rapes
			Severity of Sexual Abuse		
Severity of Sexual Abuse					
Extrafamilial	PBN[a]	.65***	—	—	—
	PBN[b]	.61***	—	—	—
z-diff		0.40			
Rapes	PBN[a]	.34**	.24*	—	—
	PBN[b]	.33**	.48***	—	—
z-diff		0.07	1.66*		
Attempted rapes	PBN[a]	−.09	−.10	−.13	—
	PBN[b]	.01	−.11	−.16	—
z-diff		0.60	0.06	0.18	—
Outcomes					
Frequency of adult sexual activities	PBN[a]	.50***	.17	.44***	.05
	PBN[b]	.15	.16	.30*	.20*
z-diff		2.38**	0.06	0.97	−0.91
Frequency sexual contact	PBN[a]	.06	.14	.05	.09
	PBN[b]	.14	.11	.21*	−.14
z-diff		−0.48	0.18	−0.98	1.38
Self-esteem	PBN[a]	−.01	.14	−.09	.03
	PBN[b]	−.26*	−.14	.08	.14
z-diff		−1.65*	1.69*	−1.02	−0.66
General well-being	PBN[a]	.00	−.15	−.04	.19*
	PBN[b]	−.38***	−.13	−.11	.10
z-diff		2.39**	−0.12	0.42	0.55
Need to control sexual desires	PBN[a]	−.30**	−.19*	−.08	−.03
	PBN[b]	.30**	.15	.03	−.04
z-diff		−3.70***	−2.05*	−0.60	0.06

*p < .05; **p < .01; ***p < .001.
[a] PBN = high parent endorsement of body awareness and nudity (N = 74).
[b] PBN = low parent endorsement of body awareness and nudity (N = 75).

relationships, and these are summarized across all 10 moderator variables in the final section of this chapter. For those readers not interested in all of the specific analyses, it is possible to review the 10 tables and skip to the summary at the end of this chapter.

Parent Endorsement of Body Awareness and Nudity

Results based on the parent endorsement of body awareness and nudity moderator variable are presented in Table 15.3.

For women who reported high parent endorsement of body awareness and nudity, the following pattern of results was found:

1. Intra- and extrafamilial sexual abuse and completed rapes were all correlated significantly with one another, and all three were not significantly correlated with attempted rapes.
2. Intrafamilial sexual abuse was significantly correlated with two of the five outcome variables (higher frequency of adult sexual activities and lower need to control sexual desires).
3. Extrafamilial sexual abuse was significantly correlated with one of the five outcome variables (lower need to control sexual desires).
4. Completed rapes were significantly correlated with one of the outcome variables (higher frequency of adult sexual activities).
5. Attempted rapes were significantly associated with one of the outcome variables (higher general well-being).

Turning next to the correlations among variables for the group low on parent endorsement of body awareness and nudity, the following pattern of results was found:

1. Intra- and extrafamilial sexual abuse and completed rapes were all correlated significantly with one another, and all three were not significantly correlated with attempted rapes.
2. Intrafamilial sexual abuse was significantly correlated with two of the five outcome variables (lower self-esteem and a greater need to control sexual desires).
3. Extrafamilial sexual abuse was not significantly correlated with any of the five outcome variables.
4. Completed rapes were significantly correlated with two of the outcome variables (a higher frequency of adult sexual activities and more frequent sexual contact).
5. Attempted rapes were significantly associated with one of the five outcome variables (higher frequency of adult sexual activities).

Finally, in regard to z-score differences between correlations, there was one significant z-score among the sexual abuse correlations and six for correlations between sexual abuse and outcome scales. Extrafamilial sexual abuse was correlated significantly lower with completed rapes (although still significant) for the group high on parent endorsement of body awareness and nudity than for those who scored lower on this moderator variable (and who had a much larger correlation). Significant z-differences were found on correlations between intrafamilial sexual abuse and the frequency of adult sexual activities, self-esteem, general well-being, and need to control sexual desires. Extrafamilial sexual abuse was correlated significantly differently between the two groups with self-esteem and a need to control sexual desires. No significant z-differences were found in terms of outcome correlates of completed rapes or attempted rapes.

Endorsement of Sexual Intimacy by Socialization Agents

Results based on the endorsement of sexual intimacy by the socialization agents moderator variable are presented in Table 15.4.

For those high on endorsement of sexual intimacy by socialization agents, the following pattern of results was found:

1. Intra- and extrafamilial sexual abuse and completed rapes were all correlated significantly with one another, and all three were not significantly correlated with attempted rapes.
2. Intrafamilial sexual abuse was significantly correlated with four of the five outcome variables (higher frequency of adult sexual activities, lower self-esteem, less general well-being, and a greater need to control sexual desires).
3. Extrafamilial sexual abuse was significantly correlated with two of the five outcome variables (more frequent sexual contact and lower general well-being).
4. Completed rapes were significantly correlated with two of the outcome variables (a higher frequency of adult sexual activities and more frequent sexual contact).
5. Attempted rapes were not significantly associated with any of the outcome variables.

Turning next to the correlations among variables for the group low on endorsement of sexual intimacy by socialization agents, the following pattern of results was found:

1. Intra- and extrafamilial sexual abuse and completed rapes were all correlated significantly with one another, and all three were not significantly correlated with attempted rapes.
2. Intrafamilial sexual abuse was significantly correlated with two of the five outcome variables (a higher frequency of adult sexual activities and less need to control sexual desires).
3. Extrafamilial sexual abuse was significantly correlated with one of the five outcome variables (a higher frequency of adult sexual activities).
4. Completed rapes were significantly correlated with one of the outcome variables (a greater frequency of adult sexual activities).
5. Attempted rapes were significantly associated with one of the five outcome variables (a greater need to control sexual desires).

Table 15.4 Correlations Between Sexual Abuse and Outcomes With Endorsement of Sexual Intimacy by Socialization Agents (ESI) as Moderator Variable

		Severity of Sexual Abuse			
		Intra-familial	Extra-familial	Completed Rapes	Attempted Rapes
Severity of Sexual Abuse					
Extrafamilial	ESI[a]	.68***	—	—	—
	ESI[b]	.47***	—	—	—
z-diff		2.01*			
Rapes	ESI[a]	.44***	.37***	—	—
	ESI[b]	.33***	.31***	—	—
z-diff		0.81	0.43	—	—
Attempted rapes	ESI[a]	.01	−.06	−.14	—
	ESI[b]	−.04	−.08	−.12	—
z-diff		−0.31	0.13	−0.13	—
Outcomes					
Frequency of adult sexual activities	ESI[a]	.22*	.13	.36***	.02
	ESI[b]	.37***	.26**	.38***	−.00
z-diff		−0.36	−0.85	−0.15	0.13
Frequency of sexual contact	ESI[a]	.11	.27**	.27**	−.01
	ESI[b]	.14	.04	.14	−.07
z-diff		−0.19	1.49	0.85	0.38
Self-esteem	ESI[a]	−.23*	.05	−.06	.05
	ESI[b]	.06	.02	−.14	−.01
z-diff		−1.85*	0.19	0.51	0.38
General well-being	ESI[a]	−.37***	−.18*	−.16	−.05
	ESI[b]	.03	.01	−.17	.17
z-diff		−2.63**	−1.21	0.06	−1.39
Need to control sexual desires	ESI[a]	.26**	.07	.02	−.16
	ESI[b]	−.33***	−.16	−.16	.20*
z-diff		3.83***	1.45	1.14	−2.29*

$*p < .05; **p < .01; ***p < .001.$
[a] ESI = high parent endorsement of sexual intimacy ($N = 82$).
[b] ESI = low parent endorsement of sexual intimacy ($N = 82$).

Finally, in regard to z-score differences between correlations, there was one significant z-score among the sexual abuse correlations and four for correlations between sexual abuse and outcome scales. Intrafamilial sexual abuse was correlated significantly higher with extrafamilial sexual abuse for the group high on endorsement of sexual intimacy by socialization agents than for those who scored low on this moderator variable (and who had a smaller but still significant correlation). Significant z-differences were found on correlations between intrafamilial sexual abuse and self-esteem, general well-being, and a need to control sexual desires. No significant z-scores appeared for correlates of extrafamilial sexual abuse or completed rapes. Attempted rapes were correlated negatively with a need to control sexual desires for those high on endorsement of sexual intimacy by socialization agents and positively for those low on this same moderator variable.

Parents' Demonstrative Messages About Sexual Expression

Results based on the parent demonstrative messages about the sexual expression moderator variable are presented in Table 15.5.

For those scoring high on parent demonstrative messages about sexual expression, the following pattern of results was found:

1. Extrafamilial sexual abuse was correlated significantly with intrafamilial sexual abuse and completed rapes; no other sexual abuse variables were significantly correlated.

2. Intrafamilial sexual abuse was not significantly correlated with any of the five outcome variables.

3. Extrafamilial sexual abuse was also not significantly correlated with any of the five outcome variables.

4. Completed rapes were significantly correlated with one of the outcome variables (higher frequency of adult sexual activities).

5. Attempted rapes were significantly associated with one of the outcome variables (a higher frequency of adult sexual activities).

Turning next to the correlations among variables for the group scoring low on parent demonstrative messages about sexual expression, the following pattern of results was found:

1. Intrafamilial sexual abuse, extrafamilial sexual abuse, and completed rapes were all significantly correlated, and all of these were not significantly related to attempted rapes.

2. Intrafamilial sexual abuse was significantly correlated with two of the five outcome variables (a higher frequency of adult sexual activities and less need to control sexual desires).

3. Extrafamilial sexual abuse was significantly correlated with two of the five outcome variables (a higher frequency of adult sexual activities and less need to control sexual desires).

4. Completed rapes were significantly correlated with two of the outcome variables (a higher frequency of adult sexual activities and lower general well-being).

Table 15.5 Correlations Between Sexual Abuse and Outcomes With Parent Demonstrative Messages About Sexual Expressions (PMS) as Moderator Variable

		Intra-familial	Extra-familial	Completed Rapes	Attempted Rapes
			Severity of Sexual Abuse		
Severity of Sexual Abuse					
Extrafamilial	PMS[a]	.39***	—	—	—
	PMS[b]	.87***	—	—	—
z-diff		−5.53***	—	—	—
Rapes	PMS[a]	−.03	.24*	—	—
	PMS[b]	.37***	.35***	—	—
z-diff		−2.51**	−0.72	—	—
Attempted rapes	PMS[a]	.10	.02	−.10	—
	PMS[b]	−.07	−.13	−.15	—
z-diff		1.02	0.90	0.30	—
Outcomes					
Frequency of adult sexual activities	PMS[a]	.12	.10	.39***	.25*
	PMS[b]	.27*	.25*	.35***	.07
z-diff		−0.94	−0.93	0.28	1.11
Frequency of sexual contact	PMS[a]	.04	.17	.18	.09
	PMS[b]	.05	.01	−.07	−.11
z-diff		−0.06	0.97	1.51	1.20
Self-esteem	PMS[a]	−.02	.14	.15	−.00
	PMS[b]	−.01	.02	−.15	.03
z-diff		−0.06	0.73	1.81*	−0.18
General well-being	PMS[a]	−.09	.16	.09	−.10
	PMS[b]	−.04	.07	−.19*	.12
z-diff		−0.30	0.55	1.70*	−1.33
Need to control sexual desires	PMS[a]	.07	−.14	.02	−.17
	PMS[b]	−.26*	−.22*	−.12	.07
z-diff		2.02*	0.50	0.84	−1.45

*$p < .05$; **$p < .01$; ***$p < .001$.
[a] PMS = high parent demonstrative messages about sexual expressions ($N = 76$).
[b] PMS = low parent demonstrative messages about sexual expressions ($N = 74$).

5. Attempted rapes were not significantly associated with any of the five outcome variables.

Finally, in regard to z-score differences between correlations, there were two significant z-scores among the sexual abuse correlations and three for correlations between sexual abuse and outcome scales. Intrafamilial sexual abuse was correlated significantly lower with extrafamilial sexual abuse and completed rapes for the group high on parental demonstrative messages about sexual expression compared to those women who scored low on this moderator variable (and who had smaller correlations that were still significant for extrafamilial abuse but not significant for completed rapes). Significant z-differences were found on correlations between intrafamilial sexual abuse and need to control sexual desires. No significant z-scores appeared for correlates of extrafamilial sexual abuse or attempted rapes. There were two significant z-score differences on correlations between completed rapes and self-esteem and general well-being: Completed rapes were correlated positively with self-esteem and general well-being for those high on parent demonstrative messages about sexual expression and negatively for those low on this same moderator variable.

Mother's Education

Results based on the mother's education moderator variable are presented in Table 15.6.

For those scoring high on mother education, the following patterns of results were found:

1. Extrafamilial sexual abuse was significantly positively correlated with intrafamilial sexual abuse and with attempted rapes; no other correlations among the sexual abuse variables were significant.
2. Intrafamilial sexual abuse was significantly correlated with two of the five outcome variables (a higher frequency of adult sexual activities and less general well-being).
3. Extrafamilial sexual abuse was not significantly correlated with any of the five outcome variables.
4. Completed rapes were significantly correlated with two of the outcome variables (higher frequencies of adult sexual activities and sexual contact).
5. Attempted rapes were significantly associated with one of the outcome variables (higher frequency of adult sexual activities).

Turning next to the correlations among variables for the group low on mother education, the following patterns of results were found:

1. Intrafamilial sexual abuse was significantly positively correlated with extrafamilial sexual abuse and negatively with attempted rapes; no other correlations among the sexual abuse variables were significant.
2. Intrafamilial sexual abuse was not significantly correlated with any of the five outcome variables.

Table 15.6 Correlations Between Sexual Abuse and Outcomes With Mother Education (ME) as Moderator Variable

| | | | Severity of Sexual Abuse | | |
		Intra- familial	*Extra- familial*	*Completed Rapes*	*Attempted Rapes*
Severity of Sexual Abuse					
Extrafamilial	ME[a]	.89***	—	—	—
	ME[b]	.41***	—	—	—
z-diff		5.55***	—	—	—
Rapes	ME[a]	−.04	.17	—·	—
	ME[b]	.06	.04	—	—
z-diff		−0.56	0.74	—	—
Attempted rapes	ME[a]	−.07	.27**	−.09	—
	ME[b]	.41***	−.17	−.16	—
z-diff		−2.85**	2.52**	0.40	—
Outcomes					
Frequency of adult	ME[a]	.23*	.12	.31***	.20*
sexual activities					
	ME[b]	.19	.17	.42***	.04
z-diff		0.24	−0.29	−0.72	0.92
Frequency of	ME[a]	−.05	.18	.23*	−.06
sexual contact					
	ME[b]	−.03	.00	−.03	−.03
z-diff		−0.11	1.02	1.49	−0.06
Self-esteem	ME[a]	−.12	−.03	−.04	.03
	ME[b]	−.07	−.06	.08	−.17
z-diff		−0.28	0.17	−0.68	1.14
General well-being	ME[a]	−.23*	−.07	−.04	−.04
	ME[b]	−.07	−.09	−.19	−.04
z-diff		−0.92	0.11	0.86	0.00
Need to control					
sexual desires	ME[a]	.01	−.12	−.18	−.00
	ME[b]	−.15	−.16	0.13	.06
z-diff		0.91	0.23	−0.29	−0.34

*p < .05; **p < .01; ***p < .001.
[a] ME = high mother education (N = 76: some college or more).
[b] ME = low mother education (N = 59: 11th grade or less).

3. Extrafamilial sexual abuse was not significantly correlated with any of the five outcome variables.

4. Completed rapes were significantly correlated with one of the five outcome variables (a higher frequency of adult sexual activities).

5. Attempted rapes were not significantly associated with any of the five outcome variables.

Finally, in regard to z-score differences between correlations, there were three significant z-scores among the sexual abuse correlations and none for correlations between sexual abuse and outcome scales. Intrafamilial sexual abuse was correlated significantly higher with extrafamilial sexual abuse for those women who reported that their mothers were well educated than for those who scored low on this moderator variable (and who had a smaller but still significant correlation). Intrafamilial sexual abuse was positively associated with attempted rapes (significantly so) for those low on mother education and negatively related (but not significantly so) for those high on mother's education. Finally, extrafamilial sexual abuse was significantly associated with more attempted rapes for those with highly educated mothers and with nonsignificantly fewer attempted rapes than for those with less educated mothers.

Father's Education

Results based on the father's education moderator variable are presented in Table 15.7.

For those who reported that their fathers were well educated, the following patterns of results were found:

1. Extrafamilial sexual abuse was significantly correlated with intrafamilial sexual abuse and completed rapes; there were no other significant correlations among the sexual abuse variables.
2. Intrafamilial sexual abuse was significantly correlated with three of the five outcome variables (lower self-esteem, lower general well-being, and a greater need to control sexual desires).
3. Extrafamilial sexual abuse was significantly correlated with one of the five outcome variables (a higher frequency of sexual contact).
4. Completed rapes were significantly correlated with one of the outcome variables (higher frequency of adult sexual activities).
5. Attempted rapes were significantly associated with one of the outcome variables (a higher frequency of adult sexual activities).

Turning next to the correlations among variables for the group low on father education, the following pattern of results was found:

1. Intrafamilial sexual abuse was significantly correlated with extrafamilial sexual abuse and completed rapes; no other correlations among the sexual abuse variables were significant.
2. Intrafamilial sexual abuse was significantly correlated with one of the five outcome variables (lower need to control sexual desires).

Table 15.7 Correlations Between Sexual Abuse and Outcomes With Father Education (FE) as Moderator Variable

| | | *Severity of Sexual Abuse* | | | |
		Intra-familial	*Extra-familial*	*Completed Rapes*	*Attempted Rapes*
Severity of Sexual Abuse					
Extrafamilial	FE[a]	.49***	—	—	—
	FE[b]	.60***	—	—	—
z-diff		−0.93	—	—	—
Rapes	FE[a]	.08	.51***	—	—
	FE[b]	.40***	−.09	—	—
z-diff		−2.04*	3.89***	—	—
Attempted rapes	FE[a]	−.12	.02	−.12	—
	FE[b]	.11	−.11	−.08	—
z-diff		−1.38	0.78	−0.24	—
Outcomes					
Frequency of adult sexual activities	FE[a]	.25**	.15	.35***	.19*
	FE[b]	.20	.15	.26*	.06
z-diff		0.31	0.00	0.59	0.79
Frequency of sexual contact	FE[a]	.09	.16*	.20	−.03
	FE[b]	.08	.13	.12	−.06
z-diff		0.06	0.18	0.49	0.18
Self-esteem	FE[a]	−.21*	−.10	−.06	.13
	FE[b]	.17	.13	.08	−.15
z-diff		−2.29*	−1.38	−0.83	−1.68*
General well-being	FE[a]	−.36***	−.11	−.08	.12
	FE[b]	.11	−.21	.06	−.07
z-diff		−2.90**	0.61	−0.83	1.14
Need to control sexual desires	FE[a]	.23**	.09	.01	.09
	FE[b]	−.26*	−.08	−.13	−.15
z-diff		2.98**	1.01	0.84	1.44

*p < .05; **p < .01; ***p < .001
[a] FE = high father education (N = 106: some college or more).
[b] FE = low father education (N = 57: 11th grade or less).

3. Extrafamilial sexual abuse was not significantly correlated with any of the five outcome variables.

4. Completed rapes were significantly correlated with one of the outcome variables (a higher frequency of adult sexual activities).

5. Attempted rapes were not significantly associated with any of the five outcome variables.

Finally, in regard to z-score differences between correlations, there were two significant z-scores among the sexual abuse correlations and four for correlations between sexual abuse and outcome scales. Intrafamilial sexual abuse was correlated significantly lower with extrafamilial sexual abuse for the women who reported that their fathers were well educated than for those who scored low on this moderator variable (both correlations were positive, but only the one for low father education was significant). Extrafamilial sexual abuse was correlated positively and significantly with completed rapes for those with high father education and slightly negatively (but nonsignificant) for those with low father education. There were three significant z-score differences on correlations between intrafamilial sexual abuse and self-esteem, general well-being, and a need to control sexual desires: Intrafamilial abuse was negatively and significantly correlated with self-esteem and general well-being for those scoring highly on father education and positively (but not significantly so) for those scoring low on this same moderator variable. Intrafamilial sexual abuse was significantly and positively correlated with a need to control sexual desires for those with high father education and significantly negatively for those with low father education. Finally, attempted rapes were positively associated with self-esteem for those with high father education and negatively correlated for those with low father education (neither correlation was significant).

Good Parent Relationship

Results based on the good parent relationship variable are presented in Table 15.8.

For those with very good parent relationships (the upper third), the following patterns of results were found:

1. Completed rapes were significantly correlated with intrafamilial sexual abuse and extrafamilial sexual abuse, and both in positive directions; there were no other significant correlations between these variables or with attempted rapes.
2. Intrafamilial sexual abuse was significantly correlated with two of the five outcome variables (a higher frequency of adult sexual activities and higher self-esteem).
3. Extrafamilial sexual abuse was significantly correlated with one of the five outcome variables (higher general well-being).
4. Completed rapes were significantly correlated with two of the outcome variables (higher adult sexual activities and more frequent sexual contact).
5. Attempted rapes were not significantly associated with any of the outcome variables.

Table 15.8 Correlations Between Sexual Abuse and Outcomes With Good Parent Relationship (GPR) as Moderator Variable

| | | Severity of Sexual Abuse | | | |
		Intra-familial	Extra-familial	Completed Rapes	Attempted Rapes
Severity of Sexual Abuse					
Extrafamilial	GPR[a]	.04	—	—	—
	GPR[b]	.74***	—	—	—
z-diff		−5.94***	—	—	—
Rapes	GPR[a]	.43***	.46***	—	—
	GPR[b]	.30**	.30**	—	—
z-diff		0.98	1.22	—	—
Attempted rapes	GPR[a]	.04	−.09	−.12	—
	GPR[b]	.06	.02	−.12	—
z-diff		−0.13	−0.72	0.00	—
Outcomes					
Frequency of adult sexual activities	GPR[a]	.19*	.07	.23*	−.03
	GPR[b]	.27**	.20*	.35***	.18*
z-diff		−0.55	−0.87	−0.86	−1.38
Frequency of sexual contact	GPR[a]	.14	.10	.21*	−.14
	GPR[b]	.09	.17*	.09	.01
z-diff		0.33	−0.47	0.80	−0.98
Self-esteem	GPR[a]	.26*	.09	.05	.04
	GPR[b]	−.17*	−.01	.07	.11
z-diff		2.86**	0.65	−0.13	−0.46
General well-being	GPR[a]	.14	.23*	.16	−.07
	GPR[b]	−.19*	−.21*	−.06	.10
z-diff		2.17*	2.92**	1.44	−1.11
Need to control sexual desires	GPR[a]	−.06	−.10	.03	−.03
	GPR[b]	.04	.02	−.03	.00
z-diff		−0.65	−0.78	0.39	−0.20

*p < .05; **p < .01; ***p < .001.
[a] GPR = high quality of parent relationship (N = 75).
[b] GPR = low quality of parent relationship (N = 107).

Turning next to the correlations among variables for the group with a poor parent relationship, the following pattern of results was found:

1. Extra- and intrafamilial sexual abuse and completed rapes were all significantly correlated; no other correlations among the sexual abuse variables were significant.

2. Intrafamilial sexual abuse was significantly correlated with three of the five outcome variables (a higher frequency of adult sexual activities, lower self-esteem, and lower general well-being).

3. Extrafamilial sexual abuse was significantly correlated with three of the five outcome variables (more frequent adult sexual activities, more frequent sexual contact, and lower general well-being).

4. Completed rapes were significantly correlated with one of the outcome variables (a higher frequency of adult sexual activities).

5. Attempted rapes were significantly associated with one of the five outcome variables (a higher frequency of adult sexual activities).

Finally, in regard to z-score differences between correlations, there was one significant z-score among the sexual abuse correlations and three for correlations between sexual abuse and outcome scales. Intrafamilial sexual abuse was correlated significantly higher with extrafamilial sexual abuse for the group with poor parent relationships than those who reported good parent relationship (where the correlation was nonsignificant). Significant z-score differences were found on correlations between intrafamilial sexual abuse, self-esteem, and general well-being: Intrafamilial abuse was positively correlated with self-esteem (significantly) and well-being (nonsignificantly) for those with good parent relationships and negatively and significantly for those reporting a poor parent relationship. A similar pattern was found between extrafamilial sexual abuse and general well-being: a significant positive correlation for those with a good parent relationship and a significant negative association for those with a poor parent relationship. No significant z-differences were found between groups for correlations with completed rapes and attempted rapes and the five outcome measures.

Family Closeness

Results based on the family closeness moderator variable are presented in Table 15.9.

For those scoring high on family closeness, the following pattern of results was found:

1. Intra- and extrafamilial sexual abuse and completed rapes were all correlated significantly with one another; all three were not significantly correlated with attempted rapes.

2. Intrafamilial sexual abuse was not significantly correlated with any of the five outcome variables.

3. Extrafamilial sexual abuse was also not significantly correlated with any of the five outcome variables.

Table 15.9 Correlations Between Sexual Abuse and Outcomes With Family Closeness
(FC) as Moderator Variable

		Intra-familial	Extra-familial	Completed Rapes	Attempted Rapes
			Severity of Sexual Abuse		
Severity of Sexual Abuse					
Extrafamilial	FC^a	.41***	—	—	—
	FC^b	.70***	—	—	—
z-diff		−2.87**	—	—	—
Rapes	FC^a	.20*	.28**	—	—
	FC^b	.38***	.33***	—	—
z-diff		−1.31	−0.37	—	—
Attempted rapes	FC^a	−.03	−.10	−.12	—
	FC^b	.00	−.09	−.14	—
z-diff		−0.20	−0.07	0.14	—
Outcomes					
Frequency of adult sexual activities	FC^a	.03	.09	.48***	.11
	FC^b	.32***	.21*	.26**	.05
z-diff		−2.00*	−0.82	1.71*	0.40
Frequency of sexual contact	FC^a	.07	.00	.11	.00
	FC^b	.11	.26**	−.02	−.20*
z-diff		−0.27	−1.77*	0.87	1.35
Self-esteem	FC^a	.15	.09	−.01	−.02
	FC^b	−.15	.03	−.04	.14
z-diff		2.01*	0.40	0.20	−1.07
General well-being	FC^a	.06	.12	−.05	.12
	FC^b	−.23*	−.24**	−.12	.16*
z-diff		1.95*	2.43*	0.47	−0.27
Need to control sexual desires	FC^a	−.05	−.07	−.05	−.04
	FC^b	.11	.06	.06	−.01
z-diff		−1.07	−0.86	−0.73	−0.20

*p < .05; **p < .01; ***p < .001.
^a FC = high family closeness (N = 79).
^b FC = low family closeness (N = 108).

4. Completed rapes were significantly correlated with one of the outcome variables (higher frequency of adult sexual activities).
5. Attempted rapes were not significantly associated with any of the outcome variables.

Turning next to the correlations among variables for the group low on family closeness, the following pattern of results was found:

1. Intra- and extrafamilial sexual abuse and completed rapes were all correlated significantly with one another, and all three of these were not significantly correlated with attempted rapes.
2. Intrafamilial sexual abuse was significantly correlated with one of the five outcome variables (a higher frequency of adult sexual activities).
3. Extrafamilial sexual abuse was significantly correlated with three of the five outcome variables (a higher frequency of adult sexual activities, more frequent sexual contact, and less general well-being).
4. Completed rapes were significantly correlated with one of the outcome variables (a higher frequency of adult sexual activities).
5. Attempted rapes were significantly associated with two of the five outcome variables (less frequent sexual contact and higher general well-being).

Finally, in regard to z-score differences between correlations, there was one significant z-score among the sexual abuse correlations and six between correlations relating sexual abuse to outcome scales. Intrafamilial sexual abuse was correlated significantly lower with extrafamilial sexual abuse for the group high on family closeness (but still significant) than for those who scored low on this moderator variable (and who had a higher correlation). Significant z-differences were found on correlations between intrafamilial sexual abuse and frequency of adult sexual activities, self-esteem, and general well-being. Intrafamilial sexual abuse was positively related with higher frequency of adult sexual activities, lower self-esteem (nonsignificant correlation), and less general well-being for those scoring low in family closeness. Extrafamilial sexual abuse was correlated significantly differently between the two groups in regard to frequency of sexual contact and general well-being. Extrafamilial sexual abuse was related more positively with sexual contact and more negatively with general well-being (all significant correlations) for those with little family closeness compared to those with a high degree of family closeness (where these correlations were nonsignificant). No significant z-scores appeared for correlates of attempted rapes with the five outcome variables for the two groups.

Felt Closest to in Family

Results based on the moderator variable of women who felt close to a family member are presented in Table 15.10.

For those who felt closest to a family member, the following pattern of results was found:

1. Intra- and extrafamilial sexual abuse and completed rapes were all correlated significantly with one another; all three were not significantly correlated with attempted rapes.

Table 15.10 Correlations Between Sexual Abuse and Outcomes With Felt Closest to in Family (CF) as Moderator Variable

		Intra-familial	Severity of Sexual Abuse Extra-familial	Completed Rapes	Attempted Rapes
Severity of Sexual Abuse					
Extrafamilial	CF[a]	.71***	—	—	—
	CF[b]	.53***	—	—	—
z-diff		2.20*	—	—	—
Rapes	CF[a]	.35**	.32***	—	—
	CF[b]	.22***	.26**	—	—
z-diff		1.05	0.49	—	—
Attempted rapes	CF[a]	.01	−.03	−.11	—
	CF[b]	.03	−.10	−.16	—
z-diff		−0.15	0.52	0.38	—
Outcomes					
Frequency of adult sexual activities	CF[a]	.19**	.14*	.41***	.06
	CF[b]	.21*	.15	.24*	.18
z-diff		−0.15	−0.08	1.42	−0.90
Frequency of sexual contact	CF[a]	.06	.06	.19**	−.08
	CF[b]	.14	.22*	−.06	.07
z-diff		−0.60	−1.21	1.87*	−1.12
Self-esteem	CF[a]	.04	.07	.04	−.05
	CF[b]	−.23*	−.03	−.04	.23*
z-diff		2.04*	0.74	0.59	−2.11*
General well-being	CF[a]	.01	.06	.01	.03
	CF[b]	−.34**	−.30**	−.15	.19*
z-diff		2.70**	2.74**	1.05	−1.20
Need to control sexual desires	CF[a]	−.11	−.13	−.23**	.03
	CF[b]	.20*	.14	.35***	−.07
z-diff		−2.32*	−2.02*	−4.45***	0.74

*p < .05; **p < .01; ***p < .001.
[a] CF = high felt closest to in family (N = 185).
[b] CF = low felt closest to in family (N = 63).

2. Intrafamilial sexual abuse was significantly correlated with one of the five outcome variables (higher frequency of adult sexual activities).

3. Extrafamilial sexual abuse was significantly correlated with one of the five outcome variables (a higher frequency of adult sexual activities).

4. Completed rapes were significantly correlated with three of the outcome variables (higher frequency of adult sexual activities, more frequent sexual contact, and lower need to control sexual desires).

5. Attempted rapes were not significantly associated with any of the outcome variables.

Turning next to the correlations among variables for the women who reported that they felt less close to another in the family, the following pattern of results was found:

1. Intra- and extrafamilial sexual abuse and completed rapes were all correlated significantly with one another; all three of these were not significantly correlated with attempted rapes.
2. Intrafamilial sexual abuse was significantly correlated with four of the five outcome variables (higher frequency of adult sexual activities, lower self-esteem, less general well-being, and higher need to control sexual desires).
3. Extrafamilial sexual abuse was significantly correlated with two of the five outcome variables (a higher frequency of sexual contact and less general well-being).
4. Completed rapes were significantly correlated with two of the outcome variables (a higher frequency of adult sexual activities and higher need to control sexual desires).
5. Attempted rapes were significantly associated with two of the five outcome variables (higher self-esteem and more general well-being).

Finally, in regard to z-score differences between correlations, there was one significant z-score among the sexual abuse correlations and eight between correlations relating sexual abuse to outcome scales. Intrafamilial sexual abuse was correlated significantly higher with extrafamilial sexual abuse for the group who felt closest to a family member than for those who scored low on this moderator variable. Significant z-differences were found on correlations between intrafamilial sexual abuse and self-esteem, general well-being, and a need to control sexual desires. Extrafamilial sexual abuse was correlated significantly different between the two groups in regard to general well-being and need to control sexual desires. Completed rapes were correlated significantly differently with frequency of sexual contact and need to control sexual desires for the two groups based on the moderator variable regarding feeling close to a family member. Finally, attempted rapes were correlated significantly differently with self-esteem for the two groups differing on the moderator variable of felt closest to in family.

Voluntary Adolescent Sexual Behavior

Results based on the voluntary adolescent sexual behavior moderator variable are presented in Table 15.11.

Table 15.11 Correlations Between Sexual Abuse and Outcomes With Voluntary Adolescent Sexual Behavior (ASB) as Moderator Variable

		Intra-familial	Extra-familial	Completed Rapes	Attempted Rapes
			Severity of Sexual Abuse		
Severity of Sexual Abuse					
Extrafamilial	ASB[a]	.70***	—	—	—
	ASB[b]	.04	—	—	—
z-diff		6.17***	—	—	—
Rapes	ASB[a]	.18*	.16*	—	—
	ASB[b]	.07	.53***	—	—
z-diff		0.83	−3.20**	—	—
Attempted rapes	ASB[a]	.07	.02	−.13	—
	ASB[b]	−.04	−.09	−.09	—
z-diff		0.82	0.82	−0.30	—
Outcomes					
Frequency of adult sexual activities	ASB[a]	.26**	.24**	.37***	−.05
	ASB[b]	.06	.03	.31***	.20**
z-diff		1.54	1.60	0.51	−1.88*
Frequency of sexual contact	ASB[a]	.07	.07	.12	−.15
	ASB[b]	−.10	.05	.12	.05
z-diff		1.27	0.15	0.00	−1.50
Self-esteem	ASB[a]	.04	.06	−.02	.01
	ASB[b]	−.01	.03	.05	.08
z-diff		0.37	0.22	−0.52	−0.52
General well-being	ASB[a]	.02	.02	−.03	.09
	ASB[b]	−.11	.09	−.03	.07
z-diff		0.67	−0.52	0.00	0.15
Need to control sexual desires	ASB[a]	−.17*	−.25**	−.09	.17*
	ASB[b]	−.04	−.04	−.08	.05
z-diff		−0.61	−1.61	−0.08	1.65*

*$p < .05$; **$p < .01$; ***$p < .001$.
[a] ASB = high voluntary adolescent sexual behavior ($N = 98$).
[b] ASB = low voluntary adolescent sexual behavior ($N = 137$).

For those scoring high on voluntary adolescent sexual behavior, the following pattern of results was found:

1. Intra- and extrafamilial sexual abuse and completed rapes were all positively and significantly correlated, whereas none were significantly correlated with attempted rapes.

2. Intrafamilial sexual abuse was significantly correlated with two of the five outcome variables (a higher frequency of adult sexual activities and less need to control sexual desires).

3. Extrafamilial sexual abuse was significantly correlated with two of the five outcome variables (a higher frequency of adult sexual activities and less need to control sexual desires).

4. Completed rapes were significantly correlated with one of the outcome variables (a higher frequency of adult sexual activities).

5. Attempted rapes were significantly associated with one of the outcome variables (a higher need to control sexual desires).

Turning next to the correlations among variables for the group scoring low on voluntary adolescent sexual behavior, the following pattern of results was found:

1. Extrafamilial sexual abuse was significantly correlated with completed rapes; no other correlations among the sexual abuse variables were significant.

2. Intrafamilial sexual abuse was not significantly correlated with any of the five outcome variables.

3. Extrafamilial sexual abuse was also not significantly correlated with any of the five outcome variables.

4. Completed rapes were significantly correlated with one of the outcome variables (a higher frequency of adult sexual activities).

5. Attempted rapes were significantly associated with one of the five outcome variables (a higher frequency of adult sexual activities).

Finally, in regard to z-score differences between correlations, there were two significant z-scores among the sexual abuse correlations and two for correlations between sexual abuse variables and outcome scales. Intra- and extrafamilial sexual abuse were highly positively correlated for those high on voluntary adolescent sexual behavior, and they were unrelated for those scoring low on this moderator variable. Those scoring low on voluntary adolescent sexual behavior had a much higher correlation between extrafamilial sexual abuse and completed rapes than those scoring low on this moderator variable, although both correlations were significantly positive. Those scoring high on voluntary adolescent sexual behavior had a significant negative association between extrafamilial sexual abuse and need to control sexual desires in contrast to no reliable association between these variables for women scoring low on voluntary adolescent sexual experiences. Two significant z-score differences were found on correlations between attempted rape and frequency of adult sexual activities and need to control sexual desires: Those with little adolescent sexual experience had a more positive association between attempted rape and frequency of adult sexual activities than did those with higher levels of adolescent voluntary sexual behavior. Similarly, those with more adolescent sexual experience had a more positive association between attempted rape and need to control sexual desires than did those with little voluntary adolescent sexual experience.

A Need to Control Sexual Desires

Results based on the adult moderator variable of need to control sexual desires are presented in Table 15.12. This moderator variable was used as an outcome scale in the previous analyses. Therefore, only four outcome or dependent adult psychosocial measures are used in these analyses.

For those reporting a high need to control sexual desires, the following patterns of results were found:

1. Intra- and extrafamilial sexual abuse and completed rapes were all correlated significantly with one another, and all three were not significantly correlated with attempted rapes.
2. Intrafamilial sexual abuse was significantly correlated with three of the four outcome variables (a higher frequency of adult sexual activities, more frequent sexual contact, and less general well-being).
3. Extrafamilial sexual abuse was significantly correlated with three of the four outcome variables (a higher frequency of adult sexual activities, more frequent sexual contact, and lower general well-being).
4. Completed rapes were significantly correlated with all four of the outcome variables (a higher frequency of adult sexual activities, more frequent sexual contact, lower self-esteem, and lower general well-being).
5. Attempted rapes were significantly associated with one of the outcome variables (higher frequency of adult sexual activities).

Turning next to the correlations among variables for the group scoring low on need to control sexual desires, the following patterns of results were found:

1. Intra- and extrafamilial sexual abuse and completed rapes were all correlated significantly with one another, and all three were not significantly correlated with attempted rapes.
2. Intrafamilial sexual abuse was not significantly correlated with any of the four outcome variables.
3. Extrafamilial sexual abuse was also not significantly correlated with any of the four outcome variables.

Table 15.12 Correlations Between Sexual Abuse and Outcomes With Need to Control Sexual Desire (NCSD) as Moderator Variable

		Intra-familial	Extra-familial	Completed Rapes	Attempted Rapes
			Severity of Sexual Abuse		
Severity of Sexual Abuse					
Extrafamilial	NCSD[a]	.60***	—	—	—
	NCSD[b]	.74***	—	—	—
z-diff		−1.61	—	—	—
Rapes	NCSD[a]	.20*	.41***	—	—
	NCSD[b]	.45***	.25**	—	—
z-diff		−1.76*	1.13	—	—
Attempted rapes	NCSD[a]	−.03	−.01	−.12	—
	NCSD[b]	.09	−.06	−.14	—
z-diff		−.75	.56	.13	—
Outcomes					
Frequency of adult sexual activities	NCSD[a]	.25**	.21*	.25**	.27**
	NCSD[b]	.16	.10	.36***	.09
z-diff		−.59	−.70	−.76	1.17
Frequency of sexual contact	NCSD[a]	.21*	.33**	.20*	.10
	NCSD[b]	.00	−.07	.19*	−.18
z-diff		1.33	2.58**	.06	1.76*
Self-esteem	NCSD[a]	−.15	−.08	−.18*	−.05
	NCSD[b]	−.01	−.01	.09	.10
z-diff		−0.88	−.44	1.70*	−.94
General well-being	NCSD[a]	−.30**	−.43***	−.26**	.03
	NCSD[b]	.02	.11	.12	.03
z-diff		−2.06*	3.56***	−2.41**	0.00

*$p < .05$; **$p < .01$; ***$p < .001$.
[a] NCSD = high need to control sexual desires ($N = 82$).
[b] NCSD = low need to control sexual desires ($N = 80$).

4. Completed rapes were significantly correlated with one of the outcome variables (a higher frequency of adult sexual activities).

5. Attempted rapes were not significantly associated with any of the four outcome variables.

Finally, in regard to z-score differences between correlations, there was one significant z-score among the sexual abuse correlations and six for correlations between sexual abuse and outcome scales. Intrafamilial sexual abuse was correlated significantly lower with completed rapes for the group with high need to control sexual desires (although still positive and significant) than for those who scored low on this moderator variable (who had a higher positive correlation). A significant z-difference was found on correlations between intrafamilial sexual abuse and frequency of adult sexual activities and general well-being. Intrafamilial sexual abuse was positively and significantly correlated with the frequency of adult sexual activities and negatively with general well-being for those scoring high on need to control sexual desires, but these two correlations were not significant for those scoring low on the need to control sexual desires. Significant z-scores were also found for correlations between extrafamilial sexual abuse and the frequency of sexual contact (significantly positive for those with a greater need to control sexual desires) and general well-being (significantly negative for those with high need to control sexual desires). Completed rapes were more significantly and negatively associated with self-esteem and general well-being for those with a high need to control sexual desires compared to those who reported a lower need to control sexual desires. Finally, attempted rapes were negatively correlated with the frequency of sexual contact for those high on need to control sexual desires and negatively for those low on this moderator variable (both correlations were nonsignificant).

16

Discussion of the Moderators of Women's Sexual Abuse Experiences

■ Discussion of Sexual Socialization Moderators

In our discussion of each moderator variable we will follow a sequential format that is determined partially by the strength of the findings' significance and partially by the type of associations that have emerged. Thus we will begin with what we deem to be the strongest and most interesting findings and then proceed to the moderately powerful findings and to the modest results (refer to Tables 15.3 through 15.12 for degree of significance and Table 15.1 for a summary of significant findings). Nevertheless, all of the moderator results we discuss are based on significant interaction effects and are reliable findings.

The following criteria were used to separate the significant moderator effects into the three types. The strongest findings are those that reveal significantly opposite processes in each of the two moderator groups; both correlations were significant and they were also significantly different. These are identified in Table 15.1 by the superscript "b." On the other hand, modest findings are those in which an opposite process occurred in the two moderator groups, but neither correlation was significant. These are noted in column 2 of Table 15.1 by the superscript "a." The bulk of the significant moderator results we discuss are moderate findings. They include significant sign reversal of correlations, where only one of the correlations was significant (column 2 of Table 15.1 with no superscript); effects where one correlation was significant, but the other was essentially zero (column 3 of Table 15.1); and where both correlations were significant in the same direction but differed significantly in magnitude (column 4 of Table 15.1).

■ Parent Endorsement of Body Awareness and Nudity

To review briefly, this variable involved direct verbal communications as well as indirect parental messages about nudity in the home, masturbation, and necking and also included a question as to whether parents had been the first to tell their child about sexual intercourse. In these analyses, we compared two groups of women: Those whose parents were perceived as highly endorsing body awareness and nudity and those whose parents were considered to give very little information or prohibited body awareness and nudity. This moderator had some major effects on the relationship between various outcomes and all of the sexual abuse variables, with the exception of attempted rape. The majority of moderator effects occurred within the context of sexual abuse by a family member.

Strongest Findings

Our most significant findings involved incest. We found that severe intrafamilial abuse was associated with a low need to control sexual desires in adulthood among women who had been exposed to very liberal parental attitudes toward body awareness and nudity in childhood. Evidently, these were parents who were very open about and comfortable with nudity and communication about sexual behavior. These parents would, for example, directly and indirectly convey liberal attitudes about masturbation, necking, or bathing together in the nude. This appearance of openness, however, might have been deceiving because incidents of severe incestuous abuse that were frequent and of long duration also occurred in these families (from the SEM analyses). It becomes obvious that what may appear to be sexually liberal parental attitudes may be coupled with inappropriate transgressions of sexual boundaries on the part of the parents or other family members. Women who grow up in this kind of liberal home environment may seem to internalize healthy sexual standards and be protected from developing negative sexual attitudes and strict needs to control their adult sexual urges. In reality, however, their families' attitudes may buffer the association between incest and lifelong sexual restraint and overrestrictiveness.

Therefore, in some cases, women with parents who endorsed body awareness and nudity were more likely to be abused in the home and to develop little need to control their sexual desires later on. Liberal parental attitudes, in conjunction with incest, may not have promoted the internalization of strict sexual standards and boundaries, resulting in little felt need in adulthood to control sexual desires for these women. This is not to suggest, however, that all families who have liberal attitudes about nudity and body awareness are sexually abusing their daughters. It is important that parents with liberal attitudes about nudity be explicit about when, where, and with whom nudity and masturbation should occur so that children grow up with a strong sense of guidelines about the appropriate expression of liberal attitudes about sex. Children need to be aware that everyone may not share their openness about nudity and masturbation and may misinterpret their behavior as seductive or as encouraging sexual advances. Although liberal attitudes may be the families' preference with regard to sex, children still need to have well established boundaries for their own sexual behavior and the manner in which they want to be approached by others both inside and outside the family.

On the other side of the spectrum, we found that when parents did not endorse body awareness and nudity, severe incestuous abuse was linked to an excessive need in survivors to control their sexuality and sexual urges. This particular scenario may involve the sexually abusive family in which parents espouse highly religious, strict, and repressive moral views with regard to sex and sexuality in general. At the same time, however, these parents or other family members may take advantage of the lack of information conveyed about sex and sexuality and the secrecy maintained about this subject to abuse their own children. Women raised in this kind of family may not have internalized appropriate messages about sexual conduct. Feeling confused because their parents conveyed very restrictive messages about sex, they may blame themselves for the abuse (Finkelhor, 1988), assuming that they must have been sexually provocative. They may internalize the notion that if they had only exercised sufficiently stringent control over their sexual desires, they might have been able to adhere to their parents' espoused moral views and prevent the sexual abuse from occurring. In adulthood, they may indeed join religious or other groups that advocate highly restrictive attitudes about sexual conduct to affirm their own attitudes. This may reflect survivors' attempts to adopt those parental attitudes that appear to be socially sanctioned, as well as an effort to counteract their own confusion and lack of knowledge about sex, sexuality, and the factors contributing to their abuse by rigidly controlling their sexual urges and conduct.

Moderate Findings

The correlations between sexual abuse by a nonfamily member and women's need to control their sexuality and sexual urges in adulthood revealed opposite trends for the two groups of women. Some findings are presented in which only one of the correlations was significant.

For women whose parents highly endorsed body awareness and nudity, severe extrafamilial abuse was significantly correlated with very little need to control their sexual desires. This finding suggests that women who were raised in these families and suffered frequent and prolonged sexual abuse by a nonfamily member, perhaps as a result of having internalized their parents' overly relaxed attitudes toward sex and sexuality, subsequently felt little need to control their sexual desires as adults. It is possible that these parents modeled sexual attitudes that were inappropriately liberal and neglected to provide their children with appropriate guidelines about sexual boundaries. On the other hand, these parents may have acted in ways that allowed their children to experience positive feelings toward their bodies, which may have protected them from developing negative and restrictive sexual attitudes in adulthood, even when they had been sexually abused away from their homes as children.

In summary, given an early environment of accepting sexual messages by parents and experiences of severe sexual abuse by strangers, these women were highly likely to have diminished needs to control their sexual desires later in life. This result may be interpreted in one of two ways. Either women's attitudes toward sex and sexuality were not damaged by the extrafamilial abuse and protected by their parents' positive attitudes toward nudity and the body or survivors did not internalize appropriate sexual standards and boundaries as a result of their abuse experiences and their parents' liberal attitudes toward body awareness and nudity. These differential interpretations hinge on whether one believes that a minimal need to control one's sexual desires reflects positive and healthy attitudes about sexuality or overpermissiveness and a lack of sexual standards and propriety.

Parental endorsement of body awareness and nudity also had a moderating effect on the relationship between incest and the frequency of adulthood sexual behaviors, such as masturbation, intercourse, and oral and anal sex. For women whose parents conveyed very liberal attitudes toward nudity and sexual behaviors, severe abuse by a family member was associated with a high frequency of sexual behaviors in adulthood. It is likely that the latter group of women had parents whose attitudes about nudity and sexual behaviors were either open and accepting or perhaps excessively liberal. Thus, the inappropriate sexualization in these women as a result of being sexually abused may have been compounded by their parents' endorsement of nudity and sexual behaviors, leading to the high frequency of sexual behaviors in adulthood. The latter finding may not only reflect an inappropriate and overstimulating childhood sexualization process, but also could indicate that these women overcame their early victimization experiences and were able to enjoy sexual activities as adults because their parents socialized them to accept their bodies and sexuality.

Women whose parents conveyed very prohibitive attitudes about body awareness and nudity were uniquely vulnerable to developing negative perceptions of themselves and the world as a consequence of having been sexually abused by a family member. For this group of women, severe intrafamilial sexual abuse was associated with a greatly diminished sense of psychological well-being and low self-esteem in adulthood. Apparently, these were women who grew up with parents who outwardly espoused highly moralistic, sexually prohibitive views but at the same time violated their own rules by sexually abusing their children. In addition, these women may have blamed themselves for their parents' transgressions (Wyatt & Newcomb, 1990). When women were not involved in incest with a parent but with another family member, they may not have disclosed their abuse experiences to their parents, fearing that they would be blamed and punished, rather than supported. Given their parents' highly prohibitive stance with regard to nudity and sexual behavior, this kind of fear would certainly be understandable. Nondisclosure of abuse is one of the most damaging of the incident's aftereffects. In the cases of survivors who attempted disclosure, the expectation of nonsupport among parents may have become a reality. The common denominator associated with each of these possible scenarios of incestuous abuse was the survivor's tendency to internalize intense feelings of shame, self-blame, and guilt. This process of internalization may account for survivors' poor self-esteem and their negative perceptions of themselves and others that naturally prevent them from experiencing a true sense of psychological well-being later in life.

As opposed to intrafamilial abuse for which parental endorsement of body awareness and nudity showed opposite processes for our two comparison groups of women, correlations between rape and extrafamilial sexual abuse were in the same direction. In other words, for women whose parents highly endorsed nudity and sexual behaviors, as well as for women whose parents were highly prohibitive, being raped in adulthood was linked to having been sexually abused by a nonfamily member in childhood. This correlation was, however, much smaller (although still significant) for those women whose parents had conveyed liberal attitudes about nudity and sexual behaviors.

These findings suggest that the latter group was less vulnerable to being revictimized in adulthood, whereas women whose parents were more prohibitive were at very high risk of suffering revictimization in the form of rape. It is likely that receiving highly prohibitive messages about body awareness, nudity, and sexual behaviors from parents may have made it extremely difficult for women to deal with being abused by persons outside of the family in childhood. As the discussion of sex may have been forbidden or limited exclusively to prohibitions about sexual behaviors, women may have felt great shame, uncertainty, and a lack of support when they were involved in coercive sexual activities with a nonfamily member. Such feelings may have caused them to remain silent about their abuse experiences and accommodate to more frequent and prolonged molestation (Summit, 1983). Having "learned" to be victims with little or no recourse in childhood, these women may have subsequently become highly vulnerable to being raped in adulthood. Women with parents who were liberal-minded about nudity and sexual behaviors, on the other hand, may have felt greater freedom to talk to their parents or others about their sexual abuse by a nonfamily member. As a result, they may have suffered less frequent and shorter-term abuse and reduced (although not eliminated) their long-term vulnerability to sexual abuse in adulthood.

Modest Findings

Finally, our most modest finding in the context of the parental endorsement of body awareness and nudity moderator revealed significantly different trends between our two comparison groups. Women whose parents had very liberal attitudes toward nudity and communication about sexual behavior were likely to have high self-esteem even in the face of severe sexual abuse by a nonfamily member. On the other hand, women whose parents were prohibitive of body awareness and nudity had low self-esteem when they had experienced severe extrafamilial abuse. These diverging trends again seem to support the great importance that parental attitudes can exert on children and their psychological and sexual development. Prohibitive parental communication with regard to nudity and sexual behaviors may have increased women's vulnerability to abusive sexual activity with a nonfamily member in childhood. In addition, this type of communication may have instilled in the child the feeling that she needed to keep the abuse a secret if she was to avoid punishment. Summit (1983) postulates that by feeling the need to maintain secrecy in and of itself a child will be stigmatized "with a sense of badness and danger" (p. 181). This kind of internal experience is bound to affect the child's self-esteem adversely and increase the likelihood of an unhealthy sense of self.

■ Endorsement of Sexual Intimacy by Socialization Agents

This variable includes direct verbal and more indirect communications about masturbation, petting, premarital intercourse, homosexuality, sexual molestation, and sexual standards by parents and other childhood and adolescent sources of sexual socialization, such as church, temple, or hall, as well as the respondent's age at first awareness of sex and the way in which this awareness occurred. This moderator had a significant impact within the context of two sexual abuse experiences and outcomes associated with them. Again, most of the moderator effects involved intrafamilial sexual abuse; one finding involved attempted rape experiences. There were no results that fit our criteria for modest findings.

Strongest Findings

We found one circumstance under which adult survivors of incest need to control their sexuality and sexual urges differed, depending on the messages about sex and sexuality they received from parents and their childhood religious institutions. A great need to control adult sexual desires was associated with severe intrafamilial abuse for women whose parents and church had conveyed highly endorsing attitudes about sexual behaviors, such as intercourse, petting, or homosexuality. However, for adult survivors whose parents and church had prohibited sexual intimacy, severe intrafamilial abuse was correlated with a greatly diminished need to control sexual urges. Overall, our findings suggest that women were vulnerable to being severely sexually abused by family members whether they were raised in home environments that prohibited or endorsed sexual intimacy (no significant path in the SEM analyses). However, these two groups of women who were incest victims as children appear to have developed opposite and extreme methods of dealing with their sexual desires, one by overcontrolling and the other by undercontrolling them.

These findings provide insight into the impact of different kinds of behaviors modeled and sex-related information conveyed to children before age 18. Previously, sexual socialization in sexually abusive families has been described as ineffectual and inappropriate, leaving the survivor with an impaired ability to solve problems and make decisions concerning sexual issues (Tharinger, 1990). Our findings are more specific, because they describe the type of socialization that occurs in an abusive family climate that facilitates victimization of the most vulnerable family members—the children—and different strategies and sexual attitudes that may be developed.

Moderate Findings

The attitudes parents and other sources of sexual socialization such as the church, temple, or hall, conveyed with respect to sexual intimacy also moderated the relationship between attempted rape experiences and women's need to control their sexual desires. For women who grew up with messages that did not endorse sexual behavior and sexual intimacy, severe rape attempts were significantly associated with an excessive need to exercise control over their sexuality and sexual urges. It appears that women internalized their parents' disapproving attitudes toward sexual intimacy and sexuality. In adulthood, this process of internalization may have manifested itself in a need to exert excessive control over their sexual desires, particularly when they were victims of attempted sexual assault. Constantly stifling their sexual urges, however, may have also heightened women's vulnerability to being sexually victimized (as noted in the SEM analyses). As a consequence, they may have missed important warning signs in dangerous situations and encountered circumstances of attempted rape.

On the opposite side of the spectrum were women raised with highly endorsing messages about sexual behavior and sexual intimacy. In these cases, severe rape attempts tended to be linked to little need to exercise control over sexuality and sexual urges. This relationship did not reach statistical significance, however. Again it appears that women internalized the liberal attitudes of their parents and other sources of sexual socialization toward sexual intimacy and sexuality. This may account for their minimal need to control their sexual desires in adulthood, even when they were subjected to attempted rape.

We found that women whose parents conveyed favorable or even encouraging attitudes about sexual intimacy and were exposed to frequent and prolonged incestuous abuse were uniquely vulnerable to a diminished sense of psychological well-being and low self-esteem. Essentially, this is in contrast to the relationship that emerged for another family context moderator: parents who did not endorse body awareness and nudity.

Incest was specifically associated with lower psychological well-being (both self-esteem and general well-being) when parents did not endorse body awareness and nudity and when all socialization agents, including parents, endorsed sexual intimacy. Therefore, parents who endorse body awareness buffer their daughter from the long-term psychological trauma of incest. On the other hand, parents and other sources of socialization who endorse and perhaps provide sexual intimacy (and maybe without concomitant messages of appropriate boundaries and responsibilities) increase their children's vulnerability to long-term psychological damage associated with incest.

In summary, women whose parents encourage a healthy acceptance of one's body and sexuality while delineating appropriate boundaries and responsible sexual intimacy were affected by incest but not to the extent of having poor self-esteem and a diminished sense of well-being.

We found that severe intrafamilial abuse was correlated with severe extrafamilial abuse for women, regardless of whether parents endorsed or prohibited sexual intimacy. Nevertheless, women whose parents endorsed sexual intimacy were significantly more vulnerable to being abused both in and away from the home as children than were women whose parents were prohibitive. This parallels the previous discussion, suggesting that parents and other socialization agents who do not set clear boundaries and convey sexual responsibility place their daughters at greater risk of childhood sexual abuse in multiple contexts. Apparently, girls do not learn what is appropriate in any particular setting and are therefore vulnerable to sexual abuse across life situations.

■ Parents' Demonstrative Messages About Sexual Expression

Parents' behavioral messages about sex, their direct and indirect communications about nudity in the home, their feelings about their own sex life, and the type and frequency of their demonstrations of physical affection for each are included in this variable. Moderating effects on the relationship between several outcome variables and all sexual abuse experiences, with the exception of attempted rape, were found. Once again, most of the effects occurred within the context of incestuous abuse. There were no results that fit our criteria for strongest findings.

Moderate Findings

When women had parents who were reserved or who avoided sexual expression in their own behavior, severe intrafamilial abuse was correlated with incidents of severe rape experiences. This suggests that these women were uniquely vulnerable to suffering prolonged and frequent abuse by family members in childhood and to being raped in adulthood, whereas women whose parents had conveyed highly demonstrative messages about sexual expression were neither vulnerable to nor protected from experiencing sexual abuse. This finding again confirms the importance of examining direct and indirect parental communications about sex and nudity and the presence or absence of parental demonstrations of affection toward each other. The results indicate that parents who do not model appropriate affection between adults increase their daughters' vulnerability to incidents of rape in adulthood if sexual abuse also occurred in the home.

Growing up in an environment filled with contradictory and confusing messages in which parents avoided behaviors that conveyed messages about their own sexual feelings toward each other on the one hand and were sexually abusing their children on the other hand is bound to have prevented women from understanding that a certain level of affection between adults is appropriate but not between child and adult. This also applies to women who were sexually abused by a family member other than a parent. As explained by Tharinger (1990), sexual socialization in sexually abusive families impairs the survivor's ability to solve problems and make decisions with respect to sexual matters. Because women were unable to internalize appropriate sexual boundaries and standards of sexual conduct, had inadequate methods of protecting themselves from unwanted invasion of their bodies in childhood and adolescence, and did not get the support they needed from their families, they were likely to take inappropriate risks as adults in sexual or potentially sexual situations. It appears that the confusing sexual socialization process that they experienced in childhood increased their vulnerability to revictimization in adulthood.

On the other hand, there was no reliable association between intrafamilial abuse and rape in adulthood when parents' direct and indirect communications to their daughters indicated positive feelings and thoughts about sex, nudity, and their own sex life and when they showed physical affection for each other. This scenario suggests that these parents may have shared a good relationship with each other and may have provided appropriate and positive relationship role models for their children, despite incest by a close family member. Appropriate modeling of this kind usually does not occur in sexually abusive families, who are often characterized by a dysfunctional parental relationship and estrangement among family members (Finkelhor & Baron, 1986). A modicum of healthy sexual expressiveness on the part of parents may neutralize the likelihood of adulthood revictimization among incest survivors.

Women whose parents' communications about sexual expression were reserved or inhibited and who also experienced severe abuse by a family member were uniquely vulnerable to having little need to control their sexual urges in adulthood. No such relationship existed for women whose parents were very open about sexual expression. The fact that women who were raised in an environment in which messages about sexual expression were not allowed and incest occurred showed little need to control their sexual desires as adults once again points to women's difficulty in learning appropriate standards of sexual conduct in a home that exposed them to contradictory messages about sexual expression. Previously, it has been reported that childhood sexual abuse leads to inappropriate sexualization of the survivor, which may manifest itself in preoccupation with sex and sexual acting out (Finkelhor, 1988; Finkelhor & Browne, 1985). Thus incest occurring in a home where parents do not model appropriate affection with each other can be associated with unhealthy sexual patterns later in adulthood.

When parents were inhibited directly and indirectly in their sexual expression and women experienced severe rape experiences as adults, they were extremely vulnerable to a diminished sense of psychological well-being. The comparison group of women whose parents had demonstrated physical affection toward each other did not report a significant association between rape experiences and psychological well-being. This finding provides more support for the notion that parents who do not provide an adequate model for affectionate behaviors that should occur between adults can have a deleterious effect on women even if incest was not occurring. When women are raised in an environment that suppresses sexual expression they may still experience confusion about how and with whom sexuality and affection are to be expressed and about their own expression and sexual desires. Afraid to displease their parents, these women may feel a need to repress their sexual urges. Furthermore, if the sexual information they received from their parents was limited to prohibitive messages about sex, nudity, and demonstrations of physical affection, these women are likely to have been inadequately prepared for interpersonal relationships and, in particular, encounters with partners, especially the opposite sex. In adulthood, they may have finally acted on some of their sexual desires and may in the process have misjudged dangerous situations and suffered psychologically as a result. For these women, severe rape experiences as adults lowered their self-esteem and overall sense of well-being.

When parents were highly demonstrative in their sexual expression or when they communicated highly inhibitory messages to their children, severe incest was significantly correlated with severe abuse outside of the family. Nevertheless, those women whose parents modeled many encouraging demonstrations of sexual expressions were far less susceptible to experiencing both incest and sexual abuse away from the home than those women who were exposed to restrictive expressions of affection and sexuality in their parents' homes. The latter group of women were extremely vulnerable to suffer from one type of sexual abuse if the other one had occurred. In other words, having restrained and nondemonstrative parents almost guaranteed that if the girl experienced sexual abuse in the home, she would also be sexually victimized away from her home by nonfamily members. Parents who did not demonstrate any affection or express sexuality in their relationship may have failed to convey to their daughters the appropriate sexual boundaries between people. Therefore, children inappropriately sexualized by any family member naturally become vulnerable to nonfamily perpetrators.

Modest Findings

Different trends emerged for the two comparison groups with respect to the relationship between rape and self-esteem in adulthood, although neither correlation was significant. Women whose parents were highly demonstrative with respect to sexual expression and who had severe rape experiences as adults retained high self-esteem, whereas adult survivors of severe rape incidents whose parents conveyed restrictive messages about affection and sex and who had not been physically demonstrative suffered low self-esteem. Evidently, parental sexual messages moderated the effects in opposite directions. We had observed similar effects for the moderator variable of parental endorsement of body awareness and nudity. When parents conveyed, directly and indirectly, very positive messages about sex and nudity and when they showed much physical affection toward each other, their daughters' exposure to sexual abuse in childhood (away from the home) and adulthood (completed rapes) was associated with high self-esteem. This kind of sexual socialization may have decreased women's vulnerability to intense feelings of guilt, shame, and self-blame when they were raped or abused by strangers in childhood.

In contrast, the women in the comparison group may have experienced great difficulty reconciling strict inhibitory parental messages about sexual expression with the fact that they were raped. Women in the latter group may have blamed themselves for having been raped and experienced guilt and shame, all of which may have influenced their self-perceptions. Having grown up exclusively with extremely inhibiting messages about sexual expression, they may also have been unaware of when they were encountering potentially dangerous situations that could result in revictimization. In addition, they may have had long-standing sexual feelings and desires as a result of their childhood environment, which may have led them to be less than cautious and somewhat neglectful of their own safety.

17

Discussion of Family Context Moderators

■ Mother's Education

Demographic variables also moderated several relationships between some of the childhood and adulthood abuse experiences. The amount of education that mothers had received was one such moderator variable for women. There were no strong or modest findings for this moderator.

Moderate Findings

For women whose mothers were very well educated, severe sexual abuse by a nonfamily member was correlated with severe rape attempts in adulthood. Having a well-educated mother had mixed effects in the long run, given that higher parent education also reduced the severity of both intra- and extrafamilial sexual abuse. Well-educated mothers may have protected their daughters generally from childhood molestation, but when such traumas occurred they may not have conveyed sufficient information about revictimization, including methods of preventing sexual abuse in the future. As a result of these circumstances, sexually abused daughters of well-educated mothers may have had insufficient knowledge of how to protect themselves and were thus more vulnerable to severe rape attempts in adulthood.

One interesting finding is that severe sexual abuse by nonfamily members was associated with a low severity of rape attempts when women's mothers were poorly educated. This relationship did not reach statistical significance, however. Mothers with low education may be more wise about the dangers of the real world and give their sexually abused child sufficient training to reduce the likelihood of future attempts at sexual victimization. We can speculate that perhaps these survivors grew up in neighborhoods that forced them to learn to protect themselves. Even though they were also subject to extrafamilial sexual abuse as children (as noted in the SEMs), they may have become determined to protect themselves adequately in an adverse environment when they reached adulthood. Ultimately, however, it is unclear why women whose mothers were poorly educated and were abused away from the home did not suffer more severe rape attempts as adults. Yet what is abundantly obvious is that severe abuse crosses all socioeconomic and ethnic boundaries.

We found the opposite of what had emerged for survivors of extrafamilial abuse when we examined sexual abuse by a family member in the context of mother's education. For women whose mothers had received very little education, prolonged and frequent intrafamilial abuse was correlated with severe rape attempts in adulthood. Therefore, having a poorly educated mother significantly increased the likelihood that the daughter would experience incest (as noted in the SEM analyses), as well as the likelihood that the daughter would be sexually victimized in adulthood. On the other hand, there was no such relationship for those women whose mothers were highly educated, suggesting that the latter women were uniquely protected or invulnerable to such repeated abuse experiences.

More than likely, poorly educated mothers lacked the knowledge and power status within the family that would help them to be aware of or prevent the incestuous abuse of their daughters. As a result, these girls probably became deeply traumatized, inappropriately sexualized, internalized a sense of powerlessness, and felt betrayed by the lack of response of their nonoffending parent (Finkelhor & Browne, 1985; Finkelhor, 1988). Having learned inappropriate standards of sexual conduct and feeling powerless vis-à-vis others, survivors of intrafamilial abuse are prone to revictimization, particularly in this scenario in which their mothers had little formal education. Previous research has already established the link between childhood sexual abuse and later sexual assault experiences (Browne & Finkelhor, 1986; Wyatt, Guthrie, & Notgrass, 1992). Our findings appear to lend support to the fact that incestuous abuse frequently has more adverse repercussions for the survivor than do other forms of sexual abuse (Browne & Finkelhor, 1986).

Finally, we discovered that regardless of their mothers' education, women who were subjected to severe sexual abuse by a family member were also abused by a nonfamily member. In essence, being sexually victimized in the home was correlated with more concurrent victimization away from the home. More than likely, these women were first molested by a family member and then exposed to extrafamilial abuse. Given that women learn very poignantly that they are powerless to protect themselves when they are involved in incest and become inappropriately sexualized, their vulnerability to becoming easy targets for extrafamilial abusers increases.

Nevertheless, there was a significant difference in the magnitude of these relationships between intra- and extrafamilial sexual abuse, depending on the level of mother's education. Girls with highly educated mothers were extremely susceptible to being abused away from home if they had experienced incest. This association was still positive and significant but much lower in magnitude for girls with poorly educated mothers. Perhaps highly educated mothers had jobs requiring longer hours away from the home, which made them less accessible and available to their daughters when they were sexually abused either in or away from the home. Thus it appears that educated and possibly career-oriented mothers may have provided inadequate support and assistance to their sexually abused daughters. Even though high parent education is directly related to little or no incest and other childhood sexual abuse (from the SEM analyses), having a mother who is well educated is also associated with increased likelihood of childhood revictimization, if abuse occurs.

On the other hand, having a poorly educated mother directly increased the likelihood that a woman would be sexually abused in childhood, as was found in the SEM analyses (perhaps associated with low SES and neighborhood conditions). However, having a poorly educated mother also slightly reduced the likelihood of childhood revictimization if a woman was sexually abused. We need to examine other characteristics that are associated with mother's education to fully understand the effects on sexual revictimization.

■ Father's Education

Another demographic variable that generated a few significant moderating effects, particularly in the context of incestuous abuse, was the education of women's fathers.

Strongest Findings

For women whose fathers were well educated, prolonged and frequent intrafamilial sexual abuse was linked to a strong need to control their sexual desires in adulthood. The opposite effect emerged for women whose fathers had received very little education. In the latter case, severe incestuous abuse was associated with a low need in adult survivors to control their sexual urges. Previous research has shown that perpetrators of sexual abuse represent all strata of society and vary widely in education and socioeconomic status (Finkelhor, 1979). Our findings support this notion but emphasize a greater likelihood of sexual abuse with poorly educated parents (based on the SEM analyses), although with quite different moderating effects.

Being raised in a home with at least one well-educated parent (fathers in this case) may increase the likelihood that the survivor obtained information and gained awareness of the incest taboo that may not necessarily have been available to girls whose fathers' education was limited. Although women from both types of homes are at risk of childhood revictimization (a high association between intra- and extrafamilial sexual abuse), women whose fathers were poorly educated and who experienced incest may be more vulnerable to engaging in high-risk sexual behaviors and may not exert control over their sexual desires in an appropriate fashion as adults.

Another interpretation of this finding is that women who were abused by their highly educated fathers feel particularly confused about their sexual attitudes because they were betrayed by a presumably well-educated and knowledgeable authority figure. Therefore, they may not wish to exhibit to others any signs or suggestions of sexuality or sexual interest, given that the latter were associated with authority and betrayal. On the other hand, being abused by a poorly educated father conveyed confusing messages about appropriate sexual conduct and did not teach proper sexual boundaries, resulting in little need to control one's sexual desires in adulthood. The survivor may also be able to discount her poorly educated father's transgressions as sexual standards that are too lax and inappropriate. In this case, a diminished need to curb one's sexual urges may also reflect more healthy and accepting attitudes toward sex and sexuality.

Moderate Findings

Father's education also moderated the sense of well-being and self-esteem of adult survivors of incest. When fathers were highly educated, severe intrafamilial sexual abuse was correlated with greatly diminished self-esteem and psychological well-being for their adult daughters. On the other hand, for women whose fathers were poorly educated, prolonged and frequent incestuous abuse was linked to high self-esteem and an enhanced sense of well-being. Once again, these findings imply that although perpetrators come from all walks of life, there was a greater likelihood of childhood sexual abuse in and away from the home among families where the father has minimal education. Furthermore, the results suggest that some aspect of being raised in a home with a well-educated father can adversely affect how survivors will view themselves and the world in adulthood, if they were sexually victimized as children. These women may grow up in an atmosphere that promotes their awareness of the societal incest taboo. Subsequently, their feelings of guilt, shame, and self-blame over having engaged in sexual activity with a family member are increased, which is reflected in diminished psychological well-being in adulthood.

In comparison, other factors may have contributed to the constellation of problems found in families raised by fathers who had received only a minimum of education. It is possible that these women had much less exposure to societal norms of appropriate sexual behavior for female children and subsequently experienced fewer excessive feelings of guilt and self-denigration. Furthermore, it may also be that fathers with limited education experience other psychological problems, including substance abuse, and tend to engage in other adverse family practices, such as the stringent use of corporal punishment—all of which are factors that were not studied here. Finally, when fathers were poorly educated, it is likely that their families' socioeconomic status was relatively low. These women may have grown up in rural areas or inner cities where the family was isolated. Such families may have lacked access to resources easily available to more affluent families with a professional breadwinner. Survivors coming from economically limited backgrounds may have found it somewhat easier to justify to themselves that they were compelled into and subsequently tolerated prolonged and frequent sexual abuse than did their counterparts who grew up under more privileged circumstances. As a result, the former group of women may have been able to emerge from their incest experiences with a comparatively more positive sense of themselves and favorable perceptions of others. They may have become aware of the fact that problems at home contributed to their abuse and were more able to resist blaming themselves for their families' dysfunction.

We found that fathers' education had opposite moderating effects on the relationship between childhood sexual abuse and rape, depending on whether the perpetrator was a family member or not. When fathers were highly educated, there was essentially no relationship between incestuous abuse and rape experiences. Yet when fathers were poorly educated and women were sexually abused by a family member, they were uniquely vulnerable to being raped in adulthood. In light of the previous findings, women who were sexually abused in their homes as children and had poorly educated fathers may have developed comparatively adequate self-esteem and well-being but were nevertheless ill prepared for the possibility of revictimization as adults. Therefore, they may have been at increased risk of being raped in adulthood when they had been abused as girls. In other words, women whose self-esteem and well-being were not necessarily low may still not have learned the skills necessary to avoid revictimization.

On the other hand, women whose fathers were highly educated and who suffered extrafamilial sexual abuse were particularly vulnerable to being raped in adulthood. Perhaps highly educated fathers were unavailable and inaccessible to their daughters merely as a result of increased work demands away from home. When their daughters were abused outside of home, the fathers may not have responded appropriately or at all, particularly if they were not informed. In this study, few parents were told that the abuse had occurred. Consequently, daughters may have felt little support and received inadequate responses from their fathers, as well as mixed messages about their trauma, which increased the likelihood that they would be sexually victimized as adults. In essence, their fathers' responses to childhood abuse may have minimized survivors' ability to cope adaptively to avoid molestation in adulthood (Wyatt & Mickey, 1988).

It appears that having fathers on either side of the educational scale predisposed women to being revictimized in adulthood, although in quite different ways, depending on the type of childhood sexual abuse. It has been previously noted in many studies that women who were sexually abused as children tend to be revictimized later in life (for example, Finkelhor & Browne, 1985; Wyatt, Guthrie, & Notgrass, 1992). This finding has been confirmed in this study, but with greater specificity. We found that survivors of extrafamilial sexual abuse were at high risk of being raped and thus revictimized, particularly when their fathers' educational level was high. Women who were abused in the home were highly vulnerable to revictimization in the form of severe completed rapes in adulthood when the father's education was low and the perpetrator was a family member.

■ Good Parental Relationship

Other family variables, such as the nature of the parents' relationship, also influenced the association between sexual abuse experiences and various outcome variables. Our two most significant and interesting findings involved incestuous abuse and self-esteem, as well as extrafamilial abuse and psychological well-being, which includes self-esteem. No results that met our modest findings' criteria were apparent here.

Strongest Findings

For women whose parents had a very close relationship to each other, severe intrafamilial abuse was correlated with high self-esteem, whereas for women whose parents had not been close, prolonged and frequent abuse by a family member was associated with low self-esteem. To a lesser extent, these relationships remained true not only for women's self-esteem, but also for their overall sense of well-being. This indicates that the nature of the parental relationship had a great impact on women's development of self even in the face of incest.

Previous research has established a link between low self-esteem in adult women and perceived unhappiness in their parents' relationship (Long, 1986).

This was confirmed by the SEM analyses. Growing up in a family in which a good parental relationship exists or where two adults model compatibility in their relationship apparently counteracts many of the overall negative effects of sexual abuse on survivors' self-esteem (see for example, Browne & Finkelhor, 1986), creating more resilience among survivors to internalizing low self-esteem. It is also possible that these are families in which the survivor is not abused by a parent, but by another family member. Parents or parenting figures who have a good marital relationship are less likely to sexually abuse their children than parents who are estranged from each other, as evidenced in our SEM results and corroborated in other research (Finkelhor & Baron, 1986).

At great risk of developing low self-esteem are child incest survivors who grow up in families where there is a considerable degree of marital or relationship discord and little or no harmony. Women who suffer from impaired self-esteem as adults may be more vulnerable to engaging in risky sexual behaviors simply because their feelings of worthlessness reinforce their need to comply with the demands of others in order to elicit from external sources the love and esteem that they have not been able to internalize for themselves. However, our SEM results did not confirm this speculation. Nevertheless, intrafamilial abuse in families where adults had a poor relationship certainly increased the likelihood that women developed a poor overall sense of themselves in adulthood.

We also found that the quality of family life significantly moderated effects between extrafamilial sexual abuse and general well-being. Severe sexual abuse in childhood by a nonfamily member was correlated with a high degree of general well-being in adulthood for women who recalled that their parents had a very close relationship. On the other hand, for women whose parents had shared little or no closeness or whose parents may have been openly hostile or antagonistic toward each other, a high severity of extrafamilial abuse was associated with a greatly diminished sense of general well-being in adulthood. This finding further supports the notion that parental closeness has the potential to attenuate certain deleterious effects of severe extrafamilial sexual abuse on survivors.

Parents or responsible adults who modeled a close relationship make it possible for their children to internalize a positive perception of themselves. Consequently, children may be more likely to turn to these adults when they are sexually violated away from their home and thus decrease their own trauma and increase their health and well-being as adults. When parenting figures are distant from each other, however, children lack a good parental model of how people relate to each other in a mutually satisfactory intimate relationship. In this case, the adults may have been unavailable or inaccessible when their daughters suffered severe extrafamilial sexual abuse, subsequently contributing to the development of a poor sense of well-being in their adult children. Daughters who face both sexual exploitation by a non-family member and parental figures who are estranged from each other are particularly susceptible to low levels of well-being as adults. These survivors are at extremely high risk of developing negative perceptions of the world, which interferes with their enjoyment, fulfillment, and happiness in life.

Moderate Findings

A good parental or provider relationship also had a significant impact on the association between intra- and extrafamilial sexual abuse. When parents were perceived as very close to each other, women were uniquely protected from multiple abuse by family and nonfamily members. For instance, if the girl experienced extrafamilial sexual abuse, a good parent relationship reduced the typically high likelihood that she would also be abused in the home. Yet when the parent or adult caretaker relationship was extremely poor, women were at very high risk of suffering prolonged and frequent intrafamilial abuse if extrafamilial sexual abuse had occurred. The opposite was also true: Girls experienced a greater vulnerability to extrafamilial abuse when they were abused in the home. This finding demonstrates the crucial moderating influence exerted by a good relationship between parenting adults. Closeness in the parental or adult caretaker relationship apparently prevents the simultaneous occurrence of incestuous and extrafamilial abuse, possibly because this type of parent interaction improves the overall quality of the family life and provides a more open and supportive environment. Sexual abuse can be more easily reported and appropriately responded to, which reduces childhood revictimization in other contexts. Parents who are satisfied with each other and model that they meet each other's needs for closeness will be less likely to act on urges to abuse their children in an effort to satisfy their own needs (as evident in the SEM analysis). They are also more responsive and supportive if sexual abuse occurs, be it with other families members or away from the home.

On the other hand, parents or parenting figures who are incapable or unwilling to meet each other's needs for closeness are much more likely to transgress on their children, as it became evident in the SEM analyses. Such parents are often unavailable and unresponsive, as well as unsupportive should their child encounter sexual abuse in the family or outside of the home. This tragic nonresponse by parenting figures increases children's vulnerability to repeated abuse in diverse contexts. As a result, child incest survivors are at high risk for being revictimized and also tend to suffer prolonged and frequent extrafamilial abuse.

■ Family Closeness

Family closeness refers to the overall degree of closeness that the members of the respondent's family of origin shared. This is another moderator that had considerable impact, especially within the context of intra- and extrafamilial sexual abuse in childhood. Six of the findings merit our attention; none of these outcomes were among the strongest findings.

Moderate Findings

For women who reported that family members had been very close, severe sexual abuse by a nonfamily member was correlated with a strong sense of general well-being in adulthood. The opposite trend was found for women who reported that members of their immediate family were estranged from each other. In the latter case, prolonged and frequent sexual abuse by a nonfamily member was linked to a greatly diminished sense of general well-being in adulthood. Family closeness had similar moderating effects as a close parental or adult provider relationship on the association between extrafamilial abuse and adult general well-being. Of interest, however, is that the effects were more pronounced when a close parental or adult relationship was reported by the survivor than when she had perceived her family to be close overall. Once again, this finding reiterates the importance of parental or adult modeling of relationship closeness for the child. By the same token, feeling close to one's family may counteract adverse experiences with nonfamily members to some extent. When a girl feels close to the other members of her family or feels emotionally supported and has a sense of belonging to a cohesive group, she is more able to develop positive perceptions of her world despite having been sexually abused by a person who is a nonfamily member.

We also found that women who experienced minimal closeness in their family of origin and had been abused by a nonfamily member in childhood were uniquely at risk of engaging in intercourse at a high frequency with several or many different partners in adulthood. This relationship between extrafamilial sexual abuse and a high frequency of sexual contact was not found for women who reported that their family of origin was very close. A girl who did not experience closeness in her family of origin was at increased risk of being abused by a nonfamily perpetrator, as noted in our SEM analyses. She was likely to feel emotionally deprived and unsupported by the people who were responsible for her care. As a consequence, she may have endured prolonged and frequent sexual abuse by a nonfamily member and also received little attention and acceptance in her home. That survivors of such dismal childhood circumstances engaged in adult sexual contact very frequently and are at risk for the transmission of disease may reflect the inappropriate sexualization process they experienced in childhood (Finkelhor, 1988). Through frequent sexual contact, adult survivors may have tried to gain the love and affection they did not receive in childhood, except through sexual means. Consistent with this trend in our findings, previous research has reported that sexual abuse survivors are at much higher risk of becoming prostitutes, changing sexual partners frequently, and engaging in sexual activities with casual acquaintances than are cohorts who do not report histories of sexual abuse (Zierler et al., 1991). Our results extend these findings by demonstrating that these circumstances and outcomes occur primarily in families that are not close and may even be hostile and antagonistic.

Similarly, for women who experienced minimal closeness in their families of origin, a significant relationship was found between prolonged and frequent sexual abuse by a family member and adult survivors' tendency to engage frequently in intercourse, oral and anal sex, and masturbation. No such association emerged for the comparison group of women who had felt very close to their family in childhood. Emotional estrangement in the families apparently increased the risk of intrafamilial abuse (noted in the SEM analyses) and increased these women's vulnerability to extensive sexual activities as adults. Again, being sexually abused may have been the only attention received by survivors, in particular in an estranged family environment. Therefore, survivors may seek fulfillment through sexual means as adults, probably with little satisfaction. In other words, the inappropriate sexualization by a family member, in the context of a family environment fairly devoid of support and help, and the subsequent process of internalizing an inappropriate method of emotional need fulfillment seems to have resulted in greatly increased sexual activity for the adult survivor. A previous study found sexual abuse survivors to be 40% more likely to report a history of sex with someone they did not know and two times more likely to have multiple sexual partners on an average yearly basis than those people reporting no sexual abuse (Zierler et al., 1991). Clearly, survivors are at high risk of disease transmission through sexual contact, especially when the quality of family of origin life was poor.

Women who had experienced both estrangement among members of their family and severe incestuous abuse in childhood were very vulnerable to a greatly diminished sense of psychological well-being in adulthood. Among the comparison group of women who reported that their family was very close, however, this correlation was not found. Previous studies have indicated that a poor quality of family life may constitute a risk factor for sexual abuse (Bagley & Ramsay, 1985; Briere, 1988a; Brunold, 1980; Finkelhor, 1984; Finkelhor et al., 1990; Fromuth, 1983; Kaufman, Peck, & Tagiuri, 1954; Lustig, Dresser, Spellman, & Murray, 1966). Our SEM analyses confirm these results. Specifically, little closeness between fathers and daughters has been associated with both intra- and extrafamilial sexual abuse (Fromuth, 1983). Previously established links between incestuous abuse and adulthood psychological adjustment (for example, Browne & Finkelhor, 1986) have also been corroborated by our results. In addition to confirming existing research evidence, however, these findings stress the critical importance of the emotional family climate, of family closeness, in moderating this relationship. Girls from close families had no reliable association between incest and later diminished general well-being, whereas this association occurred when there was little family closeness. Strong positive relationships were found between intra- and extrafamilial sexual abuse for both moderator groups of family closeness. However, the magnitude of these associations differed significantly. For women who had experienced little family closeness, as well as for those who felt that their family of origin had been extremely close, prolonged and frequent incestuous abuse was associated with prolonged and frequent sexual abuse by a nonfamily member. This relationship was significantly stronger for girls raised in families that were not close. Our SEM analyses revealed that intra- and extrafamilial sexual abuse were significantly related. Analyses of this moderator showed that this vulnerability to childhood sexual abuse across contexts was enhanced by little family closeness and reduced by high family closeness. Families described as estranged and distant may reflect family environments where it is extremely difficult to meet one's emotional needs. The sexual transgressions on the part of adult family members are likely to constitute an utterly misguided striving toward need fulfillment at the expense of the female children. It is not surprising that incest survivors who are raised with blurred sexual boundaries between themselves and others as a result of constant intrusions into their physical space and bodily territory are at high risk of also being sexually victimized by a nonfamily member. On the other hand, children who have been sexually abused and have difficulty internalizing a healthy sense of boundaries but are part of a close family home are less likely to become victims of sexual abuse.

Significant positive relationships were also found both for women who had experienced very little family closeness and those who reported that their families of origin were extremely close. For both groups, severe incidents of completed rape in adulthood were correlated with a very high frequency of sexual activity in adulthood. This association was significantly higher for women from close families who were also less likely to experience any type of childhood sexual abuse. Thus women who came from estranged families and who were more vulnerable to childhood abuse may have been less likely to assess risk factors of adulthood victimization as a result of their early trauma. Women from supportive and nonincestuous families may have been less traumatized and freely engaged in sexual activities, but they also may not have learned to take adequate precautions in a dangerous world. Consequently, they may have been ill prepared to cope with sexual assault in adulthood. Their high frequency of sexual activity may reflect sexual acting out following a rape experience.

Modest Findings

Finally, women from close families who were also abused by a family member had higher self-esteem later in life (perhaps because of the protection of a supportive and responsive family). On the other hand, women from homes with little or no closeness in which they experienced incest suffered from lower self-esteem, possibly resulting from the lack of family support and responsiveness when they were sexually abused by a family member.

■ Who Women Felt Closest to in Family

Whether a woman had felt closest to a member of her immediate family, such as her mother, father, sister, or brother, or had felt closest to other relatives in the extended family had several significant effects on the relationship between abuse and outcome variables. Sexual abuse experiences in childhood and adulthood were subject to moderating effects involving the family member to whom the girl felt closest as a child.

Strongest Findings

Our strongest and most significant findings involved rape, although similar moderate and modest effects were noted for incest and extrafamilial abuse, respectively. When women had felt very close to one immediate family member in childhood, severe rape incidents in adulthood were associated with little need to control sexual desires. Yet when women had not felt close to anyone in their immediate family, severe rape incidents were correlated with an excessive need to control their sexual urges. It is likely that women who grew up feeling very close to an immediate family member were able to internalize standards of sexual conduct that reflected a very high degree of openness and trust in others in intimate relationships. These values may, however, have remained intact when these women were abused as adults. It cannot be established which direction of effect exists between rape experiences and sexual attitudes: Women's open attitude may have increased their vulnerability to rape or the trauma of being raped may not have resulted in negative attitudes about sex because of the already existing close childhood connection with a close family member.

On the other hand, women who had not experienced a close relationship with an immediate family member may have responded with an excessive need to control their sexual desires if they had been subject to severe rape as adults. They may have developed a protective shell around themselves, which may have led to problems in interpersonal relationships. Consequently, the experience of rape for those women who had not felt close to anyone in their family of origin contributed to an excessive need to control their sexual urges, reinforcing and exacerbating their early problems in relating to others. It is possible, on the other hand, that because they had no one with whom they could identify closely and from whom they could learn healthy sexual attitudes as children, these women were overly cautious and inhibited in responding to their sexual desires. This may have somehow increased their vulnerability to victimization by rape.

Moderate Findings

Similar to our results with respect to rape, we found two associations with opposite directions between both incestuous and extrafamilial abuse and the need to control one's sexual desires. There were some differences, however, in the strength of the statistical relationships. Extrafamilial abuse and the need to control one's sexual desires were only trends and not significant on their own; they were modest findings by our criteria. On the other hand, the link between intrafamilial abuse and the need to control one's sexual desires was statistically significant and positive for women who did not feel close to immediate family members. The fact that severe incest was correlated with an excessive need to control one's sexual urges in adulthood for survivors who as children had not felt close to any family member is likely to reflect these women's inability to internalize appropriate standards of sexual conduct. In addition, needing to exert stringent control over one's sexuality probably also arises from feelings of guilt, shame, and self-blame that often derive from the sexual abuse experience and are exacerbated by having no close connection to an immediate family member.

The opposite trend was found for women who felt closest to one or several immediate members of their family. Severe incestuous abuse tended to be related to little need to control sexual urges as an adult. It appears that feeling closest to a family member and being sexually victimized by a family member, not necessarily the same person, is associated with an internalization of less rigid sexual boundaries and a reduced fear of sexual urges. The confusing messages the survivor receives in the incest scenario with regard to closeness and sexuality may result in excessive openness to intimate sexual relationships. It is also possible that being close to an immediate family member may have made it difficult for the incest survivor to develop appropriate boundaries over her adult sexual desires.

Women who reported that they had not felt close to any member of their immediate family in childhood and who were sexually abused as children were at particularly high risk of suffering from a greatly diminished sense of psychological well-being, including poor self-esteem and little general well-being. The sexual victimization experiences involved either incest or extrafamilial abuse and incest survivors were especially vulnerable. For the comparison group of women who reported having felt close to at least one immediate family member in childhood, no relationship was found between sexual abuse experiences and women's self-perceptions and sense of well-being in the world as adults. It is likely that women who did not feel close to members of their family grew up in families whose members felt alienated from one another. The fact that family estrangement may be a risk factor for sexual abuse has already been discussed and demonstrated in the SEM analyses. Women from these home environments are likely to have unfulfilled emotional needs that may in turn facilitate prolonged and frequent intra- or extrafamilial sexual abuse, given that the molestation may have been the only type of attention received. In other words, feeling very close to an immediate family member as a child protected women from long-term negative effects on psychological well-being if they were also abused as children. Not feeling close to any close family member exacerbated the psychological damage to their well-being in adulthood that occurred as a result of being sexually abused in childhood.

One interesting finding is that women who did not feel close to anyone in their immediate family and were subject to severe rape attempts tended to have high self-esteem in adulthood. No relationship between rape attempts and self-esteem emerged, however, for the comparison group of women who had felt close to at least one family member in childhood. Attempted rape survivors may have been able to report high self-esteem because their sexual assaults were not completed. If they were able to resist the assault, they may have felt more able to take care of themselves in a dangerous situation. They may also have emerged from childhood feeling more independent, and self-reliant because they did not have the experience of closeness and support from family members.

Apparently, it is significantly more traumatizing to have been subjected to completed, prolonged, and frequent intra- or extrafamilial sexual abuse in childhood. Childhood abuse survivors are at higher risk of internalizing a sense of powerlessness and subsequently a low self-esteem than are survivors of rape attempts in adulthood, even when the latter did not feel close to anyone in their immediate family as children.

Women who reported having felt close to one or several members of their immediate family and experienced severe rape incidents as adults were uniquely vulnerable to engaging in a high frequency of sexual contact as adults. However, no such correlation was found for women who had not felt close to any immediate family member in childhood. This finding suggests that women who are at high risk of being raped and having sexual contact very often in adulthood may have been involved in excessively close emotional relationships with family members in childhood but without incestuous sexual abuse. It seems plausible that women involved in potentially enmeshed family relationships internalized diffuse boundaries between themselves and others. They may also have been overprotected and isolated from contact with others outside of the family. As a result of this constellation of factors, these women may have developed little ability to detect warning signs in dangerous situations. They may have been prone to seek excessive emotional closeness with members of the opposite sex, trusting them too readily. In dating situations, for example, in which the other person was more or less a stranger or merely an acquaintance, this striving for emotional closeness may have been misinterpreted as a sexual invitation, at times leading to unwanted sexual assaults. Furthermore, these women may have been unable to protect themselves adequately when facing the threat of unwanted sexual advances on the part of a partner. Given that this group of women may have internalized diffuse self-other boundaries, however, it is also possible that they actually attempted to achieve a measure of closeness by engaging in frequent sexual contact. Finally, another interpretation of the fact that these women who had experienced excessively close relationships with family members in childhood engaged in frequent intercourse with partners in multiple relationships is that their severe rape experiences resulted in unhealthy sexual acting out.

We also found that regardless of how women perceived closeness to a family member, a significant association emerged between severe intra- and severe extrafamilial sexual abuse. This effect, however, was significantly stronger for those women who were closest to an immediate family member. We have discussed this moderating effect when we examined the impact of women's perceptions of overall family closeness. The difference is the reversal in the findings' magnitudes. Encountering this moderating effect again in the current context further confirms the profound effect that relationships with family members can have on children. As mentioned earlier, both estrangement and enmeshment with individual family members may result in unfulfilled emotional needs. Being emotionally needy and confused about appropriate self-other boundaries, children in such home environments are at risk for prolonged and frequent intrafamilial as well as extrafamilial sexual abuse.

In the present instance, those women who felt closest to an immediate family member were at higher risk of being abused both in and away from the home compared to those who did not feel close to an immediate family member. The latter group of women were slightly more protected from this type of multiple victimization in diverse contexts. In the case of the higher-risk group, the close contact with immediate family members may reflect enmeshment, diffuse boundaries, and inadequate communication, all of which heightened women's vulnerability to being sexually abused.

18

Discussion of Women's Behavior and Attitude Moderators

■ Voluntary Adolescent Sexual Behavior

A few moderator effects for this variable emerged in the context of intra- and extrafamilial sexual abuse and attempted and completed rape in adulthood. All significant moderator effects were moderate findings, and none met our criteria for either strongest or modest findings.

Moderate Findings

Women who engaged in frequent adolescent sexual activity—such as masturbation, an early onset of first intercourse, and brief relationships with multiple partners before age 18—were found to be uniquely vulnerable to both prolonged and frequent intra- and extrafamilial sexual abuse. In other words, if they experienced one type of childhood sexual abuse, they were at very high risk of becoming victims of the other type of childhood sexual abuse. For the comparison group of women who engaged in very little voluntary adolescent sexual behavior, no relationship emerged for the likelihood of experiencing the two types of childhood sexual abuse.

Sexualized behavior in children and adolescents (Finkelhor, 1988; Finkelhor & Browne, 1985) and a tendency to change sex partners frequently in adulthood (Zierler et al., 1991) have previously been associated with childhood sexual abuse. Our finding of increased adolescent sexual behavior among survivors who have a very high association between severe intra- and extrafamilial sexual abuse lends support to the existing research evidence. It is likely that severe childhood sexual abuse occurring in multiple contexts results in confusion and internalization of inappropriate standards of sexual behavior, which may manifest themselves in sexual acting out in adolescence. The strong relationship we found between intra- and extrafamilial abuse for women who engaged in a high rate of sexual activity in adolescence is not surprising. When children first suffer sexual abuse at the hands of a parent or other family member, they learn inappropriate standards of sexual conduct that are likely to become deeply ingrained, given that they are "taught" by perpetrators who are entrusted with their care. As a result, survivors are highly vulnerable to being revictimized by a nonfamily member.

High rates of voluntary childhood and adolescent sexual behavior are associated with a much higher risk of experiencing one type of abuse, should the other one occur. This reflects a highly sexualized childhood and adolescence that combines coerced sexual contact in diverse contexts and voluntary sexual activity. A low level of voluntary teenage sexual activity was associated with no increased likelihood of one type of abuse, given that another type was is experienced. This pattern represents a childhood and adolescence that was much less sexualized.

It is conceivable that women who engaged in a high rate of voluntary sexual behaviors as adolescents were perceived as seductive by potential perpetrators, both within or outside of the family. This provides an alternative explanation for the strong association between intra- and extrafamilial sexual abuse among women with high levels of voluntary teenage sexual behavior. We also found that women who had engaged in very low rates of voluntary adolescent sexual behavior and experienced severe rape attempts were highly vulnerable to engaging in masturbation, oral and anal sex, and intercourse on a frequent basis in adulthood. This type of association between severe rape attempts and a high frequency of adulthood sexual activity was not found for the comparison group of women who had engaged in high rates of voluntary adolescent sexual behavior. Women who had little experience with sexual relationships as teenagers may have had difficulty accurately judging potentially dangerous sexual situations. These women may have neglected necessary caution and misread situations in which they were at risk of being raped. After having been sexually assaulted, they may have begun to act out sexually. On the other hand, it is possible that these women were also very sexually active as adults in an attempt to overcompensate for their lack of sexual experience in adolescence. If they engaged in sexual activity very frequently, men who attempted to rape them may have found them attractive because of their frequent sexual contact and relative inexperience. However, these women may not have been able to avoid such men or to heed warning signs of an impending attack. Our findings also revealed that women who engaged in frequent masturbation, as well as early intercourse with multiple partners in brief relationships during their adolescence, and suffered severe rape attempts in adulthood demonstrated a strong need to control their adult sexual desires. No link was found between rape attempts and the need to control sexual urges for those women who had engaged in low rates of adolescent sexual behavior.

The women who scored high on voluntary adolescent sexual behavior may have impulsively and freely acted on their sexual desires in adolescence without being able to establish appropriate internal controls over these urges. As a result, these women may have overcompensated by reversing their interest in and openness to sexual behavior after having suffered severe attempted rape incidents. They may have blamed themselves for having been sexually active and for being vulnerable to rape attempts. Perhaps they felt that they had increased their vulnerability to rape attempts themselves and therefore concluded that they needed to exercise stringent control over their sexual urges to prevent further sexual victimization experiences.

Finally, we found strong correlations between prolonged and frequent sexual abuse by a nonfamily member and severe rape incidents in adulthood for women both high and low on voluntary adolescent sexual behavior. This association was significantly smaller for those women who had engaged in a high degree of voluntary adolescent sexual behavior compared to those women whose adolescent sexual activity had been very limited. Women who were only minimally sexually active in adolescence and had been sexually victimized as a child away from their home were highly vulnerable to being raped in adulthood, perhaps as a result of naivete with regard to sex and sexual situations. Even though sexualized behavior in survivors often is a consequence of childhood sexual abuse (as noted in our SEM correlations), avoidance of sexual intimacy by some women may be another reaction to the victimization experience (see Finkelhor, 1988). Should this occur, the survivor may still be at high risk for rape in adulthood because she has had little experience with developing more effective sexual decision-making skills and has difficulty accurately judging potentially dangerous situations.

■ A Need to Control Sexual Desires

This variable refers primarily to the respondent's perceptions of herself in her relationship with her partner, including initiation, satisfaction, and feelings about sexual activity. There were no strong findings as defined by our criteria for this moderator variable. The variable was related as a potential moderator, even though it was assessed in adulthood. We expect, however, that the attitudes toward sexuality that are discussed here were established early in life and remain relatively stable throughout life.

Moderate Findings

For women who reported a strong need to control their sexual desires, we found significant correlations between several types of sexual abuse experiences and diminished psychological well-being in adulthood, including reduced general well-being and self-esteem. When women acknowledged the need to exercise stringent control over their sexual desires and had experienced either severe extrafamilial abuse or severe rape incidents, they reported decreased general well-being (negative perceptions of others and the world), as well as poor self-esteem for those who were raped. On the other hand, when women felt only a minimal need to control their sexual desires, prolonged and frequent sexual abuse by a nonfamily member and severe rape incidents were associated with a greater sense of psychological well-being. Apparently, women in the latter group were better able to maintain a positive image of themselves and others, despite sexual abuse experiences in childhood or adulthood. It is possible that these women grew up in families in which very liberal attitudes toward sexuality were espoused. Thus they may have internalized highly liberal standards of sexual conduct and may not have experienced long-lasting feelings of guilt, shame, and self-blame over having been sexually involved with a nonfamily member as a child or over having been raped as an adult. In addition, they may have found their families of origin to be supportive, rather than condemning, if and when they disclosed the abuse experiences.

A strong need to control their adult sexual desires, as well as a greatly diminished sense of psychological well-being, was reported by women who were sexually abused as children or as adults. The fact that women needed to curb their adult sexual urges greatly may have its origin in a more sexually restrictive socialization process in childhood. Being sexually abused by a nonfamily member or being raped later in life may have increased existing feelings of sex guilt and shame and therefore the need to control one's sexuality even more.

We found that women who had a strong need to control their sexual desires and experienced prolonged and frequent extrafamilial sexual abuse as children also tended to have frequent sexual contact in adulthood. No such relationship emerged, however, between abuse by a nonfamily member and frequency of sexual contact for those women who reported only a minimal need to control their sexual desires. Women who reported a great need to control their sexual desires and who suffered severe extrafamilial sexual abuse engaged in intercourse with multiple partners after age 18. It is likely that these women were prematurely and inappropriately sexualized and learned to distrust others as a result of having been sexually victimized (Finkelhor & Browne, 1985; Finkelhor, 1988). In adulthood, this learning process may subsequently have manifested itself in a tendency to have sex frequently with multiple partners in short-term relationships characterized by an emotional distance that may have ultimately led to the relationship's termination. This was detected in our SEM analyses. At the same time, these women may also be struggling with feelings of guilt, again as an outgrowth of their early abuse experiences, which is likely to account for their excessive need to control their sexual desires (also found in the SEM analyses). In summary, women who have internalized overly restrictive needs to control their sexual urges and were molested away from the home are extremely vulnerable to engaging in frequent sexual contact with different people as adults. This places them at great risk for sexual disease transmission and little opportunity to develop their sexual decision making.

One interesting note is that regardless of women's level of concern about their sexual urges, prolonged and frequent intrafamilial sexual abuse was significantly associated with severe rape incidents in adulthood. Nevertheless, this relationship was more than twice as strong for women who had a minimal need to control their sexual desires. Both groups of women may have internalized inappropriate boundaries and standards of sexual conduct as a result of their sexual abuse experiences at the hands of a parent or other relative. The fact that child sexual abuse survivors are vulnerable to being revictimized has previously been reported (for example, Browne & Finkelhor, 1986), and our SEM analyses clearly support this conclusion. However, having a strong need to control their sexual urges may have resulted in women being slightly less vulnerable to being revictimized, even though it did not prevent sexual assault in adulthood. A minimal need to control one's sexual desires seemed to further enhance the risk of revictimization.

Modest Findings

Finally, we found some interesting trends within the context of the moderator variable of the need to control one's sexual desires. These associations were statistically nonsignificant. Only the difference between the correlations in the two comparison groups of women reached statistical significance.

When women's need to control their sexual urges was strong and they were exposed to severe rape attempts, there was an increased likelihood that women had engaged in intercourse with multiple sexual partners since age 18. However, for women who reported a minimal need to control their sexual desires and experienced severe attempted rape incidents, there was a low frequency of adult sexual contact. We speculate that the first group of women who had a strong need to control their sexual desires but nevertheless had sexual contact very frequently in adulthood was at an increased risk of being targeted for rape because of the contradiction between their attitudes and behavior. They may have conveyed mixed messages or placed themselves in dangerous situations as a result of their conflict and confusion about sex and sexuality. Having a strong need to control one's sexual urges does not necessarily mean that actual sexual activity will be infrequent or controlled to the extent a woman feels the need to do so. Thus women may have had a strong need to control their sexual desires to begin with but nevertheless engaged in intercourse with multiple partners, thus becoming more likely to be victimized in severe rape attempts. These are women who often appear to be disinterested in sex but have difficulty extricating themselves from these situations.

On the other hand, women in the second group who felt little need to control their sexual desires and engaged in frequent sexual contact were less vulnerable to becoming victims of attempted rape, perhaps because of the congruity of their attitudes and sexual behavior. In this case, it appears that few inner conflicts that might distort their perceptions of dangerous situations interfered; as a consequence, their vulnerability to being targets for severe rape attempts decreased.

19

Implications for Prevention and Intervention

■ Methodological Issues and Implications

Before discussing the implications of these findings, we need to place some of the methodological and sampling issues discussed in these chapters into the perspective of what we know to be state-of-the-art research on consensual and nonconsensual sexual experiences. The decisions made about how the study was conducted influence what we found. The reader needs to review and understand how we came to report the findings before the implications are discussed.

There are numerous advantages and innovations in this methodological and statistical approach, as well as several limitations. We have much to learn about optimal methodologies to use with general populations in human sexuality research, overall, but attention has recently been given to methodological issues in the study of sexual abuse. Many of the critical issues that Briere (1992) has raised apply to the *first wave* of preliminary research into the proximal and distal psychosocial consequences of childhood sexual abuse (Briere, 1988b). Although several of these criticisms are applicable to our present effort, many of them have been addressed in our methodological approach and statistical treatment of the data. Therefore, we hope this book not only will help the transition of the research field on child sexual abuse into the *second wave* of more sophisticated and appropriate research, but also will demonstrate the importance of broadening research on sexual abuse to fit within the context of human sexual and psychological functioning.

Design of the Study

As Briere (1992) correctly points out, the best study design for examining the initial and lasting effects of childhood sexual abuse is a multiwave prospec-

198

tive approach. This is the optimal design, because an experimental study is definitely unethical and illegal (Newcomb, 1990); we certainly cannot randomly assign children to abuse and nonabuse conditions and measure the effects. Therefore, the prospective study of naturally occurring and emerging life events is the most suitable available method.

This study does not meet this qualification, but it may be the next best thing until such prospective data become available. Such a study, however, may require at least 10 to 20 years to complete. Even so, there will always be survivors of sexual abuse who do not disclose their trauma or who receive adequate treatment for its effects. Consequently, it is still useful to understand the interaction of consensual and nonconsensual sexual experiences and their effects on adult survivors and their attempts to achieve some level of sexual and psychological health. A reasonable compromise to the issue of how to collect data on the effects of consensual and nonconsensual sexual experiences was a carefully constructed retrospective study within a developmental perspective. Each period in the woman's life was meticulously reviewed in chronological order by skilled interviewers trained to enhance memory recall, facilitate open disclosure, pursue subtle cues, and confront contradictions and ambiguities. This approach is far superior to simple retrospective questionnaires, because it incorporates the interpersonal contact and rapport developed between the interviewer and the woman. The approach used here also differs from studies based on reported cases of abuse, because those are usually the more severe cases that come to the attention of legal authorities, child welfare agencies, hospitals, or rape crisis centers. This study incorporated all incidents of abuse that women could recall, reported or not, and assessed their effects on selected outcome variables. Although all retrospective methods are subject to recall bias and distortion (e.g., Briere, 1992), the safeguards and interview techniques help minimize the deleterious impact of these recall difficulties.

Until prospective data become available, the retrospective interview procedure seems an optimal method. Future prospective data can be used to verify and cross-validate many of the results and conclusions we have reached in our less than ideal design.

The Nature of the Sample

Virtually all of the research cited in Chapters 2 through 10 involves either clinical samples or college students. Those respondents recruited from clinical or treatment populations, by definition are experiencing difficulties and trouble in their lives. To infer etiological or causal outcomes from such samples is erroneous and a clear example of the ecological fallacy. This serious inferential problem is only somewhat mitigated by appropriate control or comparison groups (e.g., Briere, 1992). Typically, women seeking treatment who have been sexually abused as children have also experienced many other difficulties and traumas throughout their lives, and it is impossible to determine which outcomes are related specifically to sexual problems including sexual abuse and which are outgrowths of other problems during their lives. It may well be a combination of these, but such designs and studies rarely, if ever, have the capability to separate and categorize the numerous influences that coalesce into some psychosocial dysfunction that motivates women to seek treatment.

Using college students is definitely an improvement over clinical samples, because the respondents have not self-selected into a treatment intervention. Nevertheless, college students are still a very highly select group. All have completed high school and somehow have acquired the motivation to seek higher education. They do not, however, represent the variety of ethnic, racial, and cultural groups that make up the diversity of the United States or the range of life- and age-related experiences of the general population. College students who matriculate in educational institutions may be more resilient to life's traumas and clearly have achieved some success in their lives. For instance, some women may have been so damaged and wounded by severe incidents of sexual abuse at any point in their lives, unintended pregnancies, or other sexual health problems that they could not complete high school and therefore never attend college. These women would never be represented in studies of college students.

Obviously, the best sample is one that is least subject to biasing selection effects. This is a randomly selected sample from the general community. Our research makes it possible to generalize some of the findings and is not biased because of treatment-seeking or educational advantage. Of course, it remains biased toward those women who are willing to discuss details of their sexual life and development. However, this is a bias that may never be eliminated, and we believe this sample is one of the best yet gathered to study the influences on and outcomes of consensual and nonconsensual sexual experiences over the life course.

Variables Considered

No single study can examine all potentially interesting or theoretically relevant variables. But previous research on childhood sexual abuse has been restricted to studying only select variables related to abuse and a few outcome variables. Mediating, moderating, and confounding variables in this type of research have been largely ignored (e.g., Briere, 1992). The same can be said of studies of sexual experiences (Wyatt, 1991a).

This study included numerous family quality, characteristics, and sexual socialization variables that may covary with childhood sexual experiences and contribute to long-term developmental outcomes. Briere (1988a) has considered the possible confounds resulting from family variables and criticized techniques to control for this potential spuriousness. However, no one has yet included the range of possible family and socialization variables that are examined here. Therefore, the results are based on consideration of various possible family-context influences. Nevertheless, several other potentially important variables were not included in this protocol. For instance, we did not assess the presence or extent of childhood physical or major psychological abuse that may have similar or different life consequences as childhood sexual abuse years later (e.g., Briere & Runtz, 1990). Future investigations should regularly assess other forms of childhood abuse and maltreatment and the full range of effects, including those manifested in major mental illness.

There is also a growing awareness that childhood sexual abuse is not the same for all girls and, in fact, differs in regard to numerous circumstances of abuse (e.g., Wyatt & Newcomb, 1990). We also attempted to assess psychological well-being, which is a measure of health and adequate coping styles, in an attempt to identify those women whose consensual and nonconsensual experiences ranged from no effects to more severe effects. Most previous research has simply considered the presence or absence of sexual abuse and did not delineate the particular characteristics of the abuse. Similarly, many women, as noted in the data, experience multiple incidents of sexual abuse both within and outside the home. Such details are often glossed over in studies. Although we did not have the luxury to include all circumstances of abuse in this model or in the analyses (because of the sheer size of the model), we did incorporate the frequency, duration, severity, and degree of force associated with one or more incidents of four types of sexual abuse: intra- and extrafamilial childhood sexual abuse and severity of adult attempted and completed incidents of rape. Next we hypothesized that many of the consequences of early sexual abuse may be mediated by other aspects and expediences of sexual development. Therefore, we included various measures of child, adolescent, and adult voluntary sexual behavior. This allows a much richer and complex context within which to study the correlates and consequences of sexual abuse.

Finally, we included various psychosocial, sexual activity, and sexual practices outcomes in adulthood. The Wyatt Sex History Questionnaire was developed for this study, and other established measures of well-being, self-esteem, and sex guilt (the need to control sexual desires) were also used. However, it is important to emphasize that women in this study may have suffered from other psychological problems not adequately assessed by the choice of health-related instruments. For example, Peters (1988) found a significant number of women with sexual abuse histories in a subset of this sample who reported depressive symptoms that resulted in hospitalization. Needless to say, we do not infer from these results that other psychological problems may not have been present in this sample. They simply were not the central focus of this study.

Briere and Runtz (1989) rightly believe that specific instruments should be constructed that are most sensitive to determining the outcomes of childhood sexual abuse. However, it is unclear whether such measures as the Trauma Symptom Checklist (Briere & Runtz, 1989) can differentiate childhood sexual abuse from other consensual childhood sexual experiences that may also be distressing during the formative years of life, and separate incidents of abuse that occurred in childhood from sexual abuse in adulthood. Because the discriminative utility of abuse-specific measures is still being examined in research, it seems most prudent at this time to include both established scales and potentially trauma specific instruments in studies. A measure that identifies and assesses trauma in both childhood and adulthood is needed to examine developmental and cumulative effects on psychological functioning.

Processes Examined

Most previous research has examined univariate descriptive statistics or bivariate associations between sexual abuse in childhood or adulthood, or high risk sexual practices and other risk factors or outcomes. Rarely are consensual and abusive experiences reported over the life course included in one study. In other words, at best these findings demonstrate a reliable statistical association that directly links sexual abuse or consensual sexual practices and some other variable (or uncovers a significant difference between abused and nonabused groups). These analyses can examine only the direct relationship between abuse and other variables.

Many processes in the behavioral and social sciences cannot be adequately described or explained by such direct effects. While considering such effects, we also tested for both mediating and moderating effects to help understand associations between childhood and adulthood sexual abuse, consensual sexual experiences and various predictors and outcomes. Such potential mediators and moderators are particularly important processes to study in social-psychological behavior and phenomena (Baron & Kenny, 1986).

Testing such processes has been a fruitful and valuable approach in the present work and should be considered and pursued in future research on understanding child and adult sexual abuse and consensual sexual behavior predictors and outcomes. These mechanisms help to specify and explain the potential causal relations between variables. Child and adult sexual abuse along with consensual sexual experiences are complex and multifaceted phenomena that must be examined with methods and mechanisms that can appreciate and establish these processes.

Analytic Approach

Our analytic approach incorporated two specific methods: (a) SEMs to establish the correlates, direct, and mediating processes among consensual and nonconsensual sexual experiences and various predisposing, confounding, and outcome factors; and (b) interaction tests to identify potential moderators that account for differential associations between consensual sexual experiences, the four types of sexual abuse, and adult outcome measures over the life course. In the SEM analyses, a mixed latent and measured variable path model was developed that also included nonstandard effects (e.g., Newcomb, 1990; Newcomb & Bentler, 1988b,c). This innovative procedure, never before used to study consensual and nonconsensual sexual experiences, allowed a very rich and differentiated elucidation of the direct, correlated, and mediated relationships among sexual abuse, consensual sex, and various predictors and adult consequences. The moderator effects identify those factors that increase women's vulnerability or resistance to adverse consequences related to overall sexual functioning and the four types of sexual abuse.

Briere (1992) suggested that such multivariate path models are necessary to study the multiple forces and influences associated with sexual abuse. Ours is the first study to present a comprehensive application of such approaches, although smaller applications of path analyses have been made to child sexual abuse (Wyatt & Newcomb, 1990) and adult rape experiences (Wyatt & Mickey, 1988; Wyatt et al., 1990).

The Utility of Current Theories to These Findings

The review of current theories and conceptual frameworks in Chapter 1 illustrated that normal sexual development appears to follow social learning theory: Direct and indirect learning from socialization sources and personal experience form the basis for internalizing attitudes and behaviors that are either maintained over the life course or extinguished (Bandura, 1969; Powell, 1975). However, social learning theory does not adequately address the cognitive and affective processes involved in consensual and particularly nonconsensual sexual experiences. Likewise, while several conceptualizations describe the effects of child sexual abuse (Finkelhor & Browne, 1985; Lindberg & Distad, 1985; Summit, 1983), none addresses the cumulative impact of multiple incidents or considers some of the developmental issues when abuse occurs at certain ages. Similarly, theories of rape do not consider other forms of sexual coercion or abuse and the cumulative impact of these experiences on rape trauma. Furthermore, discussions of cognitive appraisals of rape do not explain how decisions about one's consensual sexual practices and overall sexual health become compromised as a result of sexual victimization.

To move toward the development of a conceptual framework that would incorporate the multifaceted dimensions of sexual experiences over the life course as well as the cognitive and affective components, one of the major issues that still requires more study is the concept of consent. As discussed briefly in Chapter 1, if individuals are allowed to learn about sex through their socialization sources and from experience, they develop a pattern that is usually consistent with those teachings. It is when sexual experiences are either forced on them or introduced to them before they can cognitively, emotionally, and sometimes physically incorporate these experiences that the deleterious effects begin to accumulate and influence the development of both the self- and the sexual self-image. If these premature and often traumatic experiences occur within the context of a culture or family where such behaviors are given an explanation or justification (e.g., as a ritual), the effects or even the interpretation of effects can mediate some of the outcomes. If these experiences are labeled as inappropriate and unacceptable, as they are by the majority of our society, the effects appear to impact more directly emotional and sometimes physical development, as well as cognitive evaluations of the events.

At best, this is an initial attempt to incorporate a range of sexual experiences and their effects into the cultural context of how sexual development is to occur in the United States. Much more research and thinking needs to be devoted to conceptualizations that can better help us understand the many issues in sexual development and expression. Hopefully, these findings will stimulate such thinking by presenting a more comprehensive picture of the effects of sexual abuse on a range of sexual and psychological outcomes.

Limitations

Ours is clearly not an ideal study, and various limitations and cautions must be appreciated when interpreting the results. Most of these have been alluded to in the preceding discussion.

Several other cautions must also be raised. First, even though our sample is moderately large for a community survey of sexual abuse, the large number of variables in our SEMs may make some of the parameters unstable. Our findings must be retested in a larger sample. Second, in both the SEMs and moderator tests, many tests of significance were made without adjusting the probability levels for these multiple simultaneous comparisons. Therefore, some of the smaller effects may reflect chance findings and again must be examined in research that cross-validates these results. We chose not to adjust probability levels to accommodate these multiple comparisons, because this is really the first research of this extent and kind, and we wanted all possible associations to be identified. Obviously, those effects with a smaller significance level should be given greater weight than those with higher, though significant, probability levels. Finally, even though the sample is a random selection of only two ethnic groups of Los Angeles County residents, this location and population may be atypical in various regards. Therefore, other populations must also be studied to verify the results for this particular sample. In the future, we also need to address male sexuality and the influence of sexual abuse on high risk behaviors with these research methods. With this effort to include these types of studies of males and females, we will obtain a more comprehensive picture of the components of sexual health in the United States.

■ Sexual Health: The Expression of Women's Sexuality Without Sexual Abuse

In this section, we will discuss the implications of findings that reflect dimensions of sexual health. The suggestions offered to clinicians and educators are based on our expertise as sex educators and clinicians.

One of the most powerful messages these data convey is that the quality of family relationships and closeness, as well as the messages that are communicated about sex, are important predictors of early and later sexual experiences. Two distinct types of family socialization styles emerged from this study that were associated with women's recollections of permissive and conservative attitudes and sexual practices later in life.

■ Permissive and Conservative Sexual Socialization

Permissive messages about sex can influence both the type and frequency of sexual context over the life course. Parental messages to engage in and enjoy nudity and sexual arousal tended to encourage sexual exploration and early sexual activity, as well as a diverse sexual pattern among these women. Similarly, more conservative parents who conveyed either prohibitions or no information about sex and sexuality that were reinforced by religious sources tended to influence childhood sexuality and to lead to an overall pattern of less frequent sexual contact and effective contraceptive use throughout life. Indeed, whatever was learned and practiced in childhood was a strong predictor of how a woman would express her sexuality throughout life. However, during adolescence and adulthood, women who were taught little about sexual socialization as children also became influenced by others, including friends and lovers, and less by parents and religious sources. This information provides a perspective to the review of sexual practices reported in Chapters 2 through 4. Although we know something about what to expect of sexual development, we have not fully understood how to interpret patterns of early or later onset of sexual behaviors. These findings can be extrapolated to address what parents need to know to be able to positively influence a daughter's sexual patterns. If parents wish to reinforce a more moderate, reasoned approach to sexual health, they need to avoid conveying permissive messages as well as teach the following about sexual decision making:

- guidelines for developing a healthy sense of self first and sexual self second, with boundaries given for appropriate sexual behavior—where, with whom, and under what circumstance;
- the importance of developing nonsexual friendships and ways of developing them; and
- how to assess relationships that may eventually involve sexual expression for their degree of trust, respect, and open communication about sexual histories and preferences for contraceptive use.

The acceptance of this task of discussing sexuality and decision making with children requires an ongoing dialogue that may include others. Professionals and trusted family members should be identified as resources as the child matures and develops a need to discuss these personal issues with persons other than her parents. Parents cannot and should not be the sole educators of their children on any topic, including sexual decision making. However, the recognition that their children need this information can form the impetus to involve or make available other professionals or responsible persons from whom their children will seek information.

On the other hand, parents also need to relinquish the myth that teaching children and youth about sex or having conversations about sex in the home gives them permission to engage in sex before marriage and that sex-related information is best obtained in adulthood. This is the rationale that highly conservative and uninformed parents often cite when they are asked if they teach their children about human sexuality or are asked to give permission to include them in sex education classes at school. Parents who prohibit or are nonverbal about any appropriate form of sexual expression simply increase the likelihood that their female children will emulate the same pattern of not discussing sex with their friends, their sexual partners, and even with their physicians. Consequently, these children often impose standards of sexual conduct on themselves or others, some of which are too rigid or inconsistent, and do not allow for an opportunity to develop a sexual self-image that is distinct and separate from their role as sexual partners in a relationship. The development of the sexual self is built on knowledge and acceptance of the self and forms the basis for how individuals will express themselves sexually. Parents need to understand that to say nothing about sexuality in the home and to discourage any form of self-expression leaves children to develop their own guidelines and practices, many of which are impractical, naive, and too poorly conceived to withstand a sexual encounter initiated by a family or nonfamily member. Parents who do not educate their children and establish a dialogue with them about sex are, by their silence, making a statement that they are not willing to share aspects of their child's sexual maturation and experience, including sexual abuse.

■ Suggestions for Prevention of High-Risk Sexual Practices

To enhance sexual health by expressing sexuality and avoiding risks of disease and unintended pregnancy, it might be most effective to teach females to:

1. know and understand their own bodies and ultimately their own sexual needs;
2. develop friendly, warm, trustful, and nonexploitative relationships with both males and females regardless of whether they are related to them or not; and
3. understand the degree of physical and psychological risks that they will encounter when they do not consider the consequences of their sexual behaviors.

In other words, if parents want to convey that sex is a wonderful, natural way of expressing one's most intimate emotions, it is important to have specific information about how and why sex can be wonderful and natural and under what circumstances. Parents, however, are often reluctant to enter into a conversation with their children that requires these kinds of details. They often believe that children can have a healthy attitude about sex if they simply tell them that sex is not dirty. Similarly, some parents erroneously assume that they can limit their children's curiosity about sex by describing it in negative, fear-inducing terms. Children are as concrete in learning about sex as they are about learning spelling or math. They need to be taught how to develop positive and responsible attitudes about sex. These attitudes do not necessarily have to come from a sexual experience: They can come from getting to know oneself and learning how to select and maintain mutually respectful friendships in childhood. That may be the greatest lesson that children before age 12 need to learn about developing a healthy attitude about sex, aside from proper anatomical names, and human growth and development.

The knowledge gained and lessons learned must be developmentally appropriate for the child and should include building relationships and developing the self-confidence necessary to make decisions in one's own best interest.

Research indicates that American parents are not educating their children about human sexuality much more than they were 40 years ago when Kinsey and associates first gathered information about sexual socialization (Wyatt et al., 1988a,b). Thus, it is often the therapist or counselor who will need to explain to parents the importance of identifying what they want to convey to children and adolescents about sexuality in accordance with family, cultural, and religious values. It may also be the professional who works with the parents, the family, or the child in constructing the specific life experiences that are needed to develop sexual decision making. Our data dramatize the importance of educating parents about the effect they can have on their children's emerging sexuality by being too permissive in an attempt to be "liberal" or too prohibitive in an attempt to impose standards of sexual conduct.

Parent Education Classes

Parent education classes need to stress that facilitating the delay of a female child's sexual activity requires several considerations:

1. Parents need to work on the quality of their relationship and the family closeness. Harmony in the home is a basic ingredient to a healthy self-concept and sexual self-image.

2. Parents need to provide education about sexuality and decide on sexual boundaries for their children that will be respected by them (e.g., privacy, the appropriateness of sex play, and body touching). A similar set of boundaries needs to be established for children relating to other children and to adults. In other words, the sexual taboo needs to be taught. It is fairly obvious now that not everyone understands how to live with children and to respect their emerging sexuality. Curiosity about sex should be anticipated, but addressed by open discussions within the family. Educational information about anatomical differences between genders or sexual behaviors should be available in the home for family discussions and for children to refer to as needed.

3. The absence of school (academic and social) and peer problems among children and other family-related problems such as violence, substance abuse, or criminal activity, as well as an emphasis on academic achievement and no history of sexual abuse, will ensure that the age of first intercourse will be delayed.

■ Increasing Sexual Health When Sexual Abuse Has Occurred

The following are some of the characteristics of sexual abuse or family socialization patterns that increase or compromise women's sexual and psychological well-being.

Moderate Patterns of Sexual Activity and Extrafamilial Abuse

Some of the most critical health-related information for women to receive early in their development concerns the effective use of contraception to prevent unintended pregnancy versus methods that prevent the transmission of disease. These findings indicated that women who reported less sexual contact, engaged in fewer sexual practices, and were older at their first sexual experience, usually limiting themselves to vaginal penile penetration, were more likely to use effective methods of birth control, even if they were severely sexually abused by someone outside the family before age 18. This more *moderate* pattern of sexual activity, even with a history of severe extrafamilial abuse, should be identified in women's sexual histories. Health professionals can better inform women about the level of intervention needed to minimize high-risk sexual practices when issues of contraceptive use are discussed in therapy, counseling, or the professional-patient relationship. The likelihood that women with incest histories and a more *extreme* pattern of sexual activity will be effective contraceptors is fairly remote without counseling. These survivors may need a great deal of therapeutic intervention that addresses their their decision-making processes as well as educational information designed to minimize the compulsive sexual patterns that incest survivors often develop.

■ Distinguishing Sexual Risk-Taking Patterns

Different Reasons for High-Level Sexual Activity

There is no question, according to these data, that early sexual activity reinforced the frequency of sexual contact in adulthood and the likelihood that women would initiate sexual activity with others. This pattern, however, was also noted among incest survivors. Consequently, females who exhibit high levels of sexual activity may be incest survivors, but they may also be highly sexualized individuals who have lifetime histories of early and frequent sexual contact and who do not report sexual abuse. The latter group of women are sometimes suspected to be abuse survivors, even though they may deny such a history. In fact, when clinicians identify a highly sexualized pattern of behavior among women, they often refuse to believe that no abuse has occurred and attribute nondisclosure to dissociation or repression of the incident. These data are important in illustrating the *similarity* in the sexual patterns of highly sexualized women and women with incest histories. The critical predictor that may differentiate women who are sexualized and are also incest survivors from those who can be characterized solely as highly sexual may be a history of unplanned pregnancies and nonuse of contraception. The latter are risk factors for incest survivors.

These data also offer a different perspective to understanding women with histories of frequent unintended pregnancies. Assumptions have been made in the past that these were possibly:

- welfare mothers receiving income by having children, many of them African-American;
- irresponsible women who were too lazy to use birth control;
- manipulative women who became pregnant to keep a man; or
- women who loved babies, but who were often ill equipped to raise or afford them.

Rarely has research attempted to identify the antecedents of unintended pregnancies other than women's ethnic or racial group identification or economic status. The strongest predictor for such pregnancies was sexual abuse. We found that incest survivors may be unable to identify their sexual needs and to anticipate when and with whom they would have sex. They may also have aversions to touching their own or their partner's bodies, a factor that can complicate contraceptive and especially condom use. They are also often likely to be reported by their partners, or to report their partners, as sexually dysfunctional because they often do not enjoy the sexual encounters they agree to have. Indeed, these are women who often complain of no interest in sex or low sexual desire and request therapy for anxiety or depression or sex therapy for themselves or their partners (Maltz, 1988; Westerlund, 1992). They may also be identified as clients in marital or divorce counseling or eating-disorder, weight-reduction, or STD-treatment clinics. A careful sexual history taken by a health professional that includes consensual and nonconsensual sexual experiences can help to identify these women who are in need of counseling far beyond the issue of family planning.

■ The Threat of Revictimization

Survivors of sexual abuse who are counseled need to understand their risk for revictimization and the reasons why they may again encounter situations in which they feel powerless and unable to say "no" to someone who initiates a sexual advance, to identify their sexual feelings, or to control their sexual behaviors (Wyatt, Guthrie, & Notgrass, 1992). Research indicates that the severity of incidents, with incest being the most severe, and repeated incidents with multiple perpetrators increase the risk of revictimization (Wyatt, Guthrie, & Notgrass, 1992). For example, to whom the survivor should tell about sexual advances from a potential perpetrator and what to say and do to prevent a reoccurrence can be role-played in therapy. It is also important to discuss the lethality of any potential situation so that survivors can role-play their reactions to threats of force or harm.

■ Patterns of Intrafamilial Abuse: The Ruse of Sexually Healthy Families

Permissive, Incestuous Families

These findings are unique in identifying parents who may appear to be very liberal and comfortable not only about their own sexuality, but also about the sexuality of their children, while at the same time being involved in a long-term incestuous relationship with them. These parents may be difficult for supportive organizations such as child-protection agencies, mental health, as well as legal and law-enforcement professionals to recognize and to suspect as being at high risk for sexual abuse. Many professionals are trained to expect highly punitive and more obviously dysfunctional parents who may be poor and more easily identified in the public sector for health and family services. The kind of families who may espouse liberal sexual attitudes with their children while incest is occurring may be middle-class, highly visible, and respectable families who may never be suspected of such heinous offenses. Disclosure from survivors or prosecution of perpetrators may be more difficult in incidents of abuse in such a family because of its social and economic characteristics and credibility. In contrast to outward appearances, however, children growing up in these families may encounter a high degree of estrangement and isolation from their parents and be ill equipped to develop their own internal standards of sexual conduct.

These findings confirm the longitudinal research of William Friedrich (1990): Highly sexualized children have a poor sense of self and lack the emotional and physical boundaries needed for healthy psychological and social development and decision making. According to these data, the most damaging sex-related experience in which to involve children was incest. It had major ramifications that influenced subsequent sexual and interpersonal growth and development that lasted a lifetime if therapeutic intervention did not take place. Unfortunately, few of these women received professional help for their victimization experiences.

People who engage in high-risk behaviors such as nonuse of condoms or other barrier methods of contraception, have high-risk partners, or engage in sexual practices such as unprotected anal, vaginal, or oral intercourse also need to be assessed for histories of sexual victimization (Laszlo, Burgess, & Grant, 1991). Far too often, these individuals are condemned for their irresponsibility, such as women who have too many pregnancies, abortions, or children. Without understanding the context of their prior sexual socialization and sexual histories, it is far too simplistic to expect that they will change behaviors that they have yet to identify as being under their control. It is also overly simplistic to assume that if they have histories of sexual abuse, they are survivors. They may still be victims in the sense that they survived abuse but succumb to sexually transmitted and often deadly diseases.

Conservative, Incestuous Families

We also identified another group whose vulnerability was increased by its sexual socialization: Women from highly religious and strict families were more often characterized as most likely to use external standards of conduct, as opposed to their own, as guidelines for sexuality. Women growing up in these restrictive families require a great deal of education about sexuality, because they are unlikely to receive any. More critically, therapists or counselors need to convey that it is appropriate to engage in healthy sexual practices so that women can develop their own values about sex within the context of what feels right for them.

Regardless of whether women developed few internalized standards because they were socialized to assume that standards, codes, or values were not under their control or were not necessary, or whether they used rigid guidelines set by others, the process of identifying their own limits can be best accomplished in therapy.

■ Parents Who Endorsed Nudity and Body Awareness

Women who grew up in permissive homes where incest occurred also need to reexamine the range of sexual behaviors in which they may be engaging; some of them are high risk for STDs. Certain sexual behaviors may reflect an obsessive reenactment of past abuse incidents. Other behaviors may stem from a lack of identification of what women may prefer and may reflect what they think their partner prefers in a sexual encounter. In other words, these women need to learn that they can have a preference for certain behaviors and that they have a choice about when and with whom they engage in a specific behavior.

These survivors need to practice communication about sexual issues in therapy or with a partner who understands how important it is for a survivor to select sexual behaviors she prefers and to control the expression of these behaviors.

Similar outcomes resulting from a marginal development of sexual guidelines for what is appropriate can also be identified for rape survivors. Women whose parents were more prohibitive and conveyed negative messages about sexuality will also need to become aware of their risk for revictimization. These women are least likely to disclose abuse, probably because conversations about sex were not considered appropriate in their homes. As these individuals mature into adulthood, they often lack the ability to have conversations about sex and sexuality.

The dynamics of revictimization appear to rest partly on the detachment or dissociation of survivors from abuse incidents because of guilt, shame, or feelings of powerlessness over the pain of sexual abuse (Finkelhor & Browne, 1985). Consequently, it is important to help survivors recognize warning signs that place them at risk for revictimization. Examples of such warning signs could be meeting attractive people who make them feel that they need to do whatever the potential partner wishes. Optimally, survivors need to develop a more consistent system of monitoring their behavior in relationships and their safety in the world.

Once abuse is disclosed and discussed, the process of helping survivors develop their own standards of sexual conduct requires a great deal of patience on the part of the client and the therapist. The implementation of these standards is best accomplished through real-life encounters as survivors attempt to develop relationships. As they confront their unsuccessful efforts to avoid recreating the perpetrator-victim dyad, they tend to gain insight into their abilities to establish more equitable relationships and more confidence in their ability to advocate for themselves.

■ Parents Who Endorsed Sexual Intimacy With Others

Women who grew up in families that endorsed sexual practices that would involve other people, such as intercourse and other sexual behaviors including same-gender sexual experiences, and who also reported incest were likely to develop a need to control their sexual desires with people outside of the family. For these survivors, sex within the family appears to be perceived differently and often more saliently than sex with persons outside of the family. Issues of intimacy and trust become especially important in therapy, because some of the demonstrative behaviors and feelings of trust and comfort may be more easily expressed with family members. These are individuals who sometimes interact poorly with others and appear to be withdrawn socially. Helping them establish trusting relationships with nonfamily members and develop appropriate social skills becomes the major focus of therapy.

In contrast, incest survivors raised by adults who were highly prohibitive in regard to sexual contact involving others reported a diminished need for sexual standards. These women were most vulnerable to being abused and manipulated by both family and nonfamily members. An optimal plan for intervention would again be to help them understand how the power imbalance between themselves and the perpetrators of sexual abuse has to be corrected through awareness and development of their own needs and values about sexual expression.

■ The Importance of Parental Demonstrative Behavior

When parents failed to be affectionate in front of their children, they tended to create a vacuum in terms of their daughters' understanding of appropriate expression of affection between adults. If incest also occurred, these women were at risk of revictimization later in life, perhaps because they lacked adequate role models for the establishment of appropriately affectionate relationships.

The socialization process that occurred when parents were extremely prohibitive about sexuality and did not demonstrate hugging, kissing, or other appropriate forms of intimacy in front of their children was most likely to increase the daughters' vulnerability to developing their own internalized sexual attitudes and values, as well as lower self-esteem and psychological well-being. These children may develop internalized sexual standards without the proper information on which to base such standards.

Parents who are extremely conservative, religious, or perhaps have themselves been raised in families that did not discuss, encourage, or perceive sexuality as positive need to understand how they increase the risk that their daughters will overcome the negative effects of incest by remaining silent on these matters. Parents' comfort with and appropriate expression of intimacy forms the basis for the best model that children can have. This information has particular value for clinicians working to reconstitute families who separated after abuse was uncovered. Family therapy needs to include information about the kind of affectionate environment that parents should model for their children as they continue to recover from incest.

■ Family Demographic Variables

Other dimensions of the family structure can also influence sexual health when abuse has occurred. The financial resources that usually come with being educated, as these data indicate, do not necessarily diminish the likelihood of abuse. However, poorly educated mothers tended to increase their daughters' vulnerability to being victimized within the family and again by nonfamily members. The same was true for women whose fathers had little education. These findings are consistent with what we know of risk factors for other forms of child maltreatment (Helfer, 1991).

In addition, women whose fathers were poorly educated were also more at risk of suffering increased psychological effects of sexual abuse.

Parents who are poor, have limited educational resources, and may have other psychological problems need to be identified for programs that decrease the chances that sexual abuse will occur. For this group, the importance of parenting classes that emphasize the prevention of sexual abuse should be stressed. An adequate amount of research has already underscored the importance of early intervention among families at risk for child maltreatment (Helfer, 1991). These data confirm the need for such efforts.

■ The Psychological Environment

Research has established the significance of the parent-child relationship (Cole & Putnam, 1992). This study highlighted the importance of the parental relationship or the relationship between two adults who parent in developing a climate of sexual health and in mediating the effects of sexual abuse. The development and maintenance of women's self-esteem and psychological well-being was influenced by their recollection of warmth, compatibility, and a good relationship between the adults who raised them. The quality of the adult relationship in the home can also decrease the likelihood that abuse will occur. Consequently, the parental relationship is not only a risk factor to assess, but also, in terms of prevention, a dimension of parenting in which adults responsible for the care of children should strive to attain health.

Similarly, family closeness has been identified in this study, as well as others, as one of the most salient risk factors for abuse (Friedrich, Beilke, & Urquiza, 1987). In this study, the likelihood of women engaging in a variety of high-risk sexual behaviors was increased by family estrangement. Women apparently engaged in such sexual behaviors to obtain the closeness, nurturance, and intimacy that was unavailable in the family. The patterns established by lack of family closeness are probably one of the most resistant to therapeutic intervention. The reason for its intransigence may be that survivors of abuse tend to express a variety of unfulfilled needs that sometimes seem insatiable. Consequently, failed attempts to develop intimacy skills often reinforce low self-esteem and poor psychological well-being. However, these women are often good candidates for psychotherapy groups in addition to or instead of individual long-term therapy, depending on the availability of services and the client's financial status. They often face daily challenges when they attempt to develop and maintain abilities to cope with their needs, and group therapy tends to augment an adequate and nurturant support system.

■ Ethnicity

What are the implications of these findings for African-American and European-American women?

These analyses do not examine each group separately because we found that the influence of sexual abuse on women's sexual and psychological well-being as assessed in this study was similar overall. The degree of influence might differ because one group may not have engaged in a behavior pattern to the same extent as the other (e.g., African-American women reported less-frequent patterns of masturbation and oral and anal sex). However, the relationships between variables and the effects on subsequent sexual patterns or psychological functioning was similar for both ethnic groups of women. Does this mean that both groups exhibited exactly the same sexual patterns to the same extent? No. Does this mean that we should not include ethnicity as a grouping variable in sex research in light of these findings? No. These analyses indicate, for example, that when an African-American or European-American family with very marginal economic resources has very restrictive and conservative attitudes about teaching or even mentioning human sexuality to its children, then the information conveyed is essentially the same. The manner in which the information is conveyed occurs within a cultural context. Financial resources and religious beliefs that can influence what may be appropriate suggestions need to be considered. Furthermore, if an African-American family reports that its members are very close and if incest has occurred, clinicians may need to assess the issue of enmeshment of family members based on these findings. Enmeshment may prohibit individuation, self-esteem, and independence among children. However, other factors that contribute to enmeshment also need to be assessed, such as the degree of racial and social isolation that the family experiences in its community, involvement in activities out of the home, other incidents of trauma experienced by all members, perceived personal safety to move about in the community, relationships with others, and availability of extended family members. A host of factors may contribute to enmeshment that may have developed because of social, economic, and structural issues that impinge on African-American families. Overlooking the need to address all of these issues suggests that the clinician may be unaware of or insensitive to the reality of the ethnic family in need of help with a variety of issues, one of which is sexual abuse.

■ Conclusions

These data emphasize the importance of the family in establishing early attitudes about sex—how and with whom sex is to be discussed, if at all, the appropriate types of affection to be shown with family members, and the need to internalize one's own standards for sexual behaviors. Furthermore, the family's emotional closeness as well as the quality of the relationship between adults who served as parents influenced and often mediated psychological well-being and self-esteem, even when abuse both within and outside of the family occurred.

One of the most important buffers to negative sexual and psychological outcomes in this study was family closeness and endorsement of body awareness and nudity. Some of the factors that increased women's vulnerability to negative outcomes were families who did not discuss sexuality with their children and who were estranged. Indeed, the ability to connect with and to maintain satisfactory feelings about oneself and relationships with others is facilitated by the psychological functioning of the survivor's family of origin, as well as her immediate family or support system, depending on her age. If the supportive people in the abuse survivor's life are psychologically healthy, better educated, and have financial resources, they are more likely to be able to help in the recovery process. They do not, however, have to be biological parents, married, of opposite gender, or limited to two persons. It is also not essential that they have financial resources. They must, however, support the survivor's efforts to develop a system of decision making about her sexual and psychological functioning that enhances her quality of life.

While education and financial resources can increase the likelihood that abuse survivors will experience lesser effects of abuse, the more valuable contribution to their healing is gaining the understanding that sexuality is not a forbidden topic but a lifelong human experience, as the introductory chapters indicate.

The findings highlight the need to develop a national agenda for and commitment to human-sexuality programs for parents and children that include discussions of consensual and nonconsensual sexual experiences and their effects. To better inform families about how to develop a climate of sexual health in the home, such information needs to become available to the general and professional community. Similarly, professionals need to be trained to assess a wide range of sexual experiences along with psychological status to understand the interaction of immediate and later effects on sexual health. Each person has the ability and the right to choose his or her preference of self-expression. As professionals, it is our task to ensure that women and children, abused or not, learn how to make these decisions on their own behalf. Hopefully, these data will help us better understand the sources of behaviors that compromise and enhance sexual health and to advocate for the rights of those who cannot yet advocate for themselves.

References

Abramson, P. R., & Imai-Marquez, Y. (1982). The Japanese-American: A cross-cultural, cross-sectional study of sex guilt. *Journal of Research in Personality, 16*, 227-237.

Abramson, P. R., & Mosher, D. L. (1975). Development of a measure of negative attitudes toward masturbation. *Journal of Consulting and Clinical Psychology, 43*, 485-490.

Abramson, P. R., Mosher, D. L., Abramson, L. M., & Woychowski, B. (1977). Personality correlates of the Mosher Guilt Scales. *Journal of Personality Assessment, 41*, 375-382.

Adams-Tucker, C. (1982). Proximate effects of sexual abuse in childhood: A report on 28 children. *American Journal of Psychiatry, 139*, 1252-1256.

Adler, N. E., David, H. P., Major, B. N., Roth, S. H., Russo, N. F., & Wyatt, G. E. (1991). Psychological responses to abortion. *Science, 248*, 41-43.

Alan Guttmacher Institute. (1981). *Factbook on teenage pregnancy*. New York: Author.

Aldous, J. (1983). Birth control socialization: How to avoid discussing the subject. *Population and Environment, 6*(1), 27-38.

Alter-Reid, K., Gibbs, M. S., Lachenmeyer, J. R., Sigal, J., & Massoth, N. A. (1986). Sexual abuse of children: A review of the empirical findings. *Clinical Psychology Review, 6*, 249-266.

Aral, S. O., & Cates, W., Jr. (1989). The multiple dimensions of sexual behavior as a risk factor for sexually transmitted diseases: The sexually experienced are not necessarily sexually active. *Sexually Transmitted Diseases, 16*, 173-177.

Athanasiou, R., Shaver, P., & Tavris, C. (1970, July). Sex. *Psychology Today*, pp. 39-52.

Bachrach, C. A., & Horn, M. C. (1988). Sexual activity among U.S. women of reproductive age. *American Journal of Public Health, 78*(3), 320-321.

Bagley, C., & McDonald, M. (1984). Adult mental health sequels of child sexual abuse, physical abuse and neglect in maternally separated children. *Canadian Journal of Community Mental Health, 3*, 15-26.

Bagley, C., & Ramsay, R. (1985). Psychosocial correlates of suicidal behaviors in an urban population. *Crisis, 6*, 63-77.

Bagley, C., & Ramsay, R. (1986). Sexual abuse in childhood: Psychosocial outcomes and implications for social work practice. *Journal of Social Work and Human Sexuality, 4*(1-2), 33-47.

Bakwin, H. (1974). Erotic feelings in infants and young children. *Medical Aspects of Human Sexuality, 8*(10), 200-215.

Bandura, A. (1969). *Principles of behavior modification*. New York: Holt, Rinehart & Winston.

Bandura, A. (1977). *Social learning theory*. Englewood Cliffs, NJ: Prentice-Hall.

Bard, M., & Sangrey, D. (1980). Things fall apart: Victims in crisis. *Evaluation and Change*, special issue, pp. 28-35.

Baron, R. M., & Kenny, D. A. (1986). The moderator-mediator variable distinction in social psychological research: Conceptual, strategic, and statistical considerations. *Journal of Personality and Social Psychology, 51*, 1173-1181.

Barrett, F. M. (1980). Sexual experience, birth control usage, and sex education of unmarried Canadian university students: Changes between 1968 and 1978. *Archives of Sexual Behavior, 9*(5), 367-390.

Becker, J. V. (1989). Impact of sexual abuse on sexual functioning. In S. Leiblum & R. Rosen (Eds.), *Principles and practice of sex therapy* (pp. 298-318). New York: Guilford.

Becker, J. V., Abel, G. G., Bruce, K., & Howell, J. (1978). *Follow-up and comparison of victims of attempted rape and rape one year following a sexual assault.* Unpublished manuscript, University of Tennessee.

Becker, J. V., & Kaplan, M. S. (1991). Rape victims: Issues, theories, and treatment. In J. Bancroft (Ed.), *Annual review of sex research* (pp. 267-291). Lake Mills, IA: Society for the Scientific Study of Sex.

Becker, J. V., Skinner, L. J., & Abel, G. G. (1983). Sequelae of sexual assault: The survivor's perspective. In I. R. Stuart & J. G. Greer (Eds.), *Sexual aggression: Current perspectives in treatment.* New York: Van Nostrand Reinhold.

Becker, J. V., Skinner, L. J., Abel, G. G., Axelrod, R., & Cichon, J. (1984). Sexual problems of sexual assault survivors. *Women and Health, 9*(4), 5-20.

Becker, J. V., Skinner, L. J., Abel, G. G., & Cichon, J. (1986). Level of post-assault sexual functioning in rape and incest victims. *Archives of Sexual Behavior, 15*, 37-49.

Becker, J. V., Skinner, L.J., Abel, G. G., Howell, J., & Bruce, K. (1982). The effects of sexual assault on rape and attempted rape victims. *Victimology: An International Journal, 7*(1-4), 106-113.

Bentler, P. M. (1980). Multivariate analysis with latent variables: Causal modeling. *Annual Review of Psychology, 31*, 419-345.

Bentler, P. M. (1989). *EQS structural equations program manual.* Los Angeles: BMDP Statistical Software.

Bentler, P. M. (1990). Comparative fit indexes in structural models. *Psychological Bulletin, 107*, 238-246.

Bentler, P. M., & Bonett, D. G. (1980). Significance tests and goodness of fit in the analysis of covariance structures. *Psychological Bulletin, 88*, 588-606.

Bentler, P. M., & Newcomb, M. D. (1986). Personality, sexual behavior, and drug use revealed through latent variable methods. *Clinical Psychology Review, 6*, 363-385.

Bjork, D., & Yutrzenka, B. (1991, August). *Long-term effects of childhood sexual abuse: A comparative group study.* Paper presented at American Psychological Association meeting, San Francisco, CA.

Blum, R. W. (1989). *The state of adolescent health in Minnesota, February, 1989.* Minneapolis: University of Minnesota, Department of Pediatrics, Adolescent Health Program.

Blumstein, P., & Schwartz, P. W. (1983). *American couples.* New York: Morrow.

Bolling, D. R. (1977). Prevalence, goals, and complications of heterosexual anal intercourse. *The Journal of Reproductive Medicine, 19*, 120-124.

Bolling, D. R. (1987). *Heterosexual anal intercourse: A common entity, perceived rarity, neglected patients, and ostrich syndrome.* Paper presented at the 1987 Kinsey Institute conference, Bloomington, IN, December 5-8.

Bradburn, N. M., & Davis, C. (1984). Potential contributions of cognitive sciences to survey questionnaire design. In J. Tanur (Ed.), *Cognitive aspects of survey methodology: Building a bridge between disciplines* (pp. 15-25). Washington, DC: National Academy Press.

Brecher, E. M. (1984). *Love, sex, and aging* (Consumers Union Report). Boston, MA: Little, Brown.

Briere, J. (1984a). *The effects of childhood sexual abuse on later psychological functioning: Defining a "post-sexual syndrome."* Paper presented at Third National Conference on Sexual Victimization of Children, Washington, DC.

Briere, J. (1984b). *The long-term effects on childhood sexual abuse: Defining a post-sexual syndrome.* Paper presented at the 92nd Annual Convention of American Psychological Association, Toronto, Canada.

Briere, J. (1988a). Controlling for family variables in abuse effects research: A critique of the "partialling" approach. *Journal of Interpersonal Violence, 3,* 80-89.

Briere, J. (1988b). The long-term clinical correlates of childhood sexual victimization. *Annals of the New York Academy of Sciences, 528,* 327-335.

Briere, J. (1991). Adult survivors: Treatment for the long-term effects of child abuse. *The Advisor, 4*(2), 3-4.

Briere, J. (1992). Methodological issues in the study of sexual abuse effects. *Journal of Consulting and Clinical Psychology, 60,* 196-203.

Briere, J., & Runtz, M. (1988a). Symptomatology associated with childhood sexual victimization in a non-clinical adult sample. *Child Abuse & Neglect, 12,* 51-59.

Briere, J., & Runtz, M. (1988b). Post sexual abuse trauma. In G. E. Wyatt & J. J. Powell (Eds.), *The lasting effects of child sexual abuse* (pp. 85-99). Newbury Park, CA: Sage.

Briere, J., & Runtz, M. (1989). The Trauma Symptom Checklist (TSC-33): Early data on a new scale. *Journal of Interpersonal Violence, 4,* 151-163.

Briere, J., & Runtz, M. (1990). Differential adult symptomatology associated with three types of child abuse histories. *Child Abuse & Neglect, 14,* 357-364.

Briere, J., & Zaidi, L. Y. (1989). Sexual abuse histories and sequelae in female psychiatric emergency room patients. *American Journal of Psychiatry, 146,* 1602-1606.

Browne, A., & Finkelhor, D. (1986). Impact of child sexual abuse: A review of the research. *Psychological Bulletin, 99*(1), 66-77.

Brownmiller, S. (1975). *Against our own will: Men, women, and rape.* New York: Bantam.

Brunold, H. (1980). Observations after sexual traumata suffered in childhood. In L. G. Schultz (Ed.), *The sexual victimology of youth.* Springfield, IL: Charles C Thomas.

Bureau of the Census. (1980). *Statistical abstract of the United States.* Washington, DC: U.S. Department of Commerce.

Bureau of the Census. (1990). *Statistical abstract of the United States.* Washington, DC: U.S. Department of Commerce.

Burgess, A. W. (1983). Rape trauma syndrome. *Behavioral Sciences and the Law, 1*(3), 97-113.

Burgess, A. W., Groth, N,. & McCausland, M. S. (1981). Child sex initiation rings. *American Journal of Orthopsychiatry, 51*(1), 110-119.

Burgess, A. W., Hartman, C. R., McCausland, M. S., & Powers, P. (1984). Response patterns in children and adolescents exploited through sex rings and pornography. *American Journal of Psychiatry, 141*(5), 656-662.

Burgess, A. W., Hartman, C. R., & McCormick, A. (1987). Abused to abuser: Antecedents of socially deviant behaviors. *American Journal of Psychiatry, 144*(11), 1431-1436.

Burgess, A. W., & Holmstrom, L. L. (1979a). *Rape and crisis recovery.* Bowie, MD: Brady.

Burgess, A. W., & Holmstrom, L. L. (1979b). Rape: Sexual disruption and recovery. *American Journal of Orthopsychiatry, 49,* 648-657.

Burnett, R. C., Templer, D. I., & Barker, P. C. (1985). Personality variables and circumstances of sexual assault predictive of a woman's resistance. *Archives of Sexual Behavior, 14*(2), 183-188.

Burt, M. R. (1980). Cultural myths and supports for rape. *Journal of Personality and Social Psychology, 38,* 217-230.

Burt, M. R., & Estep, R. E. (1981). Who is a victim? Definitional problems in sexual victimiza-
    tion. *Victimology, 6*, 15-28.
Cado, S., & Leitenberg, H. (1990). Guilt reactions to sexual fantasies during intercourse.
    Archives of Sexual Behavior, 19(1), 49-63.
Calderone, M. S. (1978). Is sex education preventive? In C. B. Qualls, J. P., Wincze, & D. H.
    Barlow (Eds.), *The prevention of sexual disorders* (pp. 139-155). New York: Plenum.
Cash, W. S., & Moss, A. J. (1972). Optimum recall period for reporting persons injured in motor
    vehicle accidents. *Vital and Health Statistics, 50*, 1-33.
Centers for Disease Control. (1990, October). National overview of sexual transmitted disease,
    1989. In *Sexually transmitted disease control surveillance, 1989*. Atlanta, GA: Author.
Centers for Disease Control. (1991). *National overview of sexual transmitted disease*. Atlanta,
    GA: Author.
Centers for Disease Control. (1992, January). *Morbidity and Mortality Weekly Report, 40*(51 &
    52). Atlanta, GA: Author.
Centers for Disease Control. (1993, May). *HIV/AIDS surveillance*. Atlanta, GA: Author.
Chou, C. P., & Bentler, P. M. (1990). Model modification in covariance structure modeling: A
    comparison among likelihood ratio, Lagrange multiplier, and Wald tests. *Multivariate
    Behavioral Research, 25*, 115-136.
Cicchetti, D., & Howes, P.W. (1991). Developmental psychopathology in the context of the
    family: Illustrations from the study of child maltreatment. *Canadian Journal of Behavioral
    Science, 23*, 257-281.
Cimons, M. (1990, November 30). AIDS cases up 29% for U.S. women. *Los Angeles Times*, pp.
    A1, A40.
Cohen, J. A., & Mannarino, A. P. (1988). Psychological symptoms in sexually abused girls. *Child
    Abuse & Neglect, 12*, 571-577.
Cohen, L. J. (1988). Providing treatment and support for partners of sexual-assault survivors.
    Psychotherapy, 25, 94-98.
Cohen, L. J., & Roth, S. (1987). The psychological aftermath of rape: Long-term effects and
    individual differences in recovery. *Journal of Social and Clinical Psychology, 5*(4), 525-534.
Cohen, S., & Wills, T. A. (1985). Stress, social support, and the buffering hypothesis. *Psychological
    Bulletin, 98*, 310-357.
Cole, B. P. (1978). *Race and self-esteem: A comparative study of black and white adults.*
    Unpublished doctoral dissertation, University of California, Los Angeles.
Cole, P. M., & Putnam, F. W. (1992). The effect of incest on self and social functioning: A
    developmental psychopathology perspective. *Journal of Consulting and Clinical Psychol-
    ogy, 60*, 174-184.
Conte, J. R., & Schuerman, J. R. (1988). The effects of sexual abuse on children: A multidimen-
    sional view. In G. E. Wyatt & G. J. Powell (Eds.), *Lasting effects of child sexual abuse*
    (pp. 157-170). Newbury Park, CA: Sage.
Couchman, I. (1970). The self-concept of low-income blacks: A descriptive evaluation. *Disser-
    tation Abstracts International, 31*(3), 1400A-1401A.
Courtois, C. A. (1979). The incest experience and its aftermath. *Victimology: An International
    Journal, 4*(4), 337-347.
Cronbach, L. J. (1987). Statistical tests for moderator variables: Flaws in analyses recently
    proposed. *Psychological Bulletin, 102*, 414-417.
Darling, C. A., & Davidson, J. K. (1986). Coitally active university students: Sexual behaviors,
    concerns, and challenges. *Adolescence, 11*, 403-419.
D'Augelli, J. F., & Cross, H. J. (1975). Relationship of sex guilt and moral reasoning to premarital
    sex in college women and in couples. *Journal of Consulting and Clinical Psychology, 43*,
    40-47.

Dawson, D. A. (1986). The effects of sex education on adolescent behavior. *Family Planning Perspectives, 18*(4), 162-170.

DeJong, A. R., Emmett, G. A., & Hervada, A. R. (1982). Sexual abuse of children. *American Journal of Diseases of Children, 136*, 129-134.

DeJong, A. R., Hervada, A. R., & Emmett, G. A. (1983). Epidemiologic variations in childhood sexual abuse. *Abuse & Neglect, 7*, 155-162.

Dickinson, G. E. (1978). Adolescent sex information sources: 1964-1974. *Adolescence, 13*(52), 653-658.

DiClemente, R. J. (1990). The emergence of adolescents as a risk group for human immunodeficiency virus infection. *Journal of Adolescent Research, 5*(1), 7-17.

Diepold, J., Jr., & Young, R. D. (1979). Empirical studies of adolescent sexual behavior: A critical review. *Adolescence, 14*, 45-64.

Dregar, R., & Miller, K. S. (1960). Comparative psychological studies of Negroes and Whites in the United States. *Psychological Bulletin, 57*(5), 361-402.

Dregar, R., & Miller, K. S. (1968). Comparative psychological studies of Negroes and Whites in the United States, 1959-65. *Psychological Bulletin, 70*(3), 1-58.

Dube, R., & Hebert, M. (1988). Sexual abuse of children under 12 years of age: A review of 511 cases. *Child Abuse and Neglect, 12*, 321-330.

Dunlap, W. P., & Kemery, E. R. (1987). Failure to detect moderating effects: Is multicollinearity the problem? *Psychological Bulletin, 102*, 418-420.

Dunn, K. M. (1986). *Sex guilt and religiousness in relation to ethnicity, socioeconomic status, age, marital status, and sexual satisfaction.* Unpublished doctoral dissertation, Fuller Theological Seminary, Los Angeles.

Edwards, J. J., & Alexander, P. C. (1992). The contributions of family background to the long-term adjustment of women sexually abused as children. *Journal of Interpersonal Violence, 7*(3), 306-320.

Ehrhardt, A. A., Yingling, S., & Warne, P. A. (1991). Sexual behavior in the era of AIDS: What has changed in the United States? In J. Bancroft (Ed.), *Annual review of sex* (pp. 25-47). Lake Mills, IA: Society for the Scientific Study of Sex.

Elias, J. E. (1978, March-April). Adolescents and sex. *Humanist*, pp. 29-31.

Ellis, E. M., Atkeson, B. M., & Calhoun, K. S. (1982). Short report: An examination of differences between multiple- and single-incident victims of sexual assault. *Journal of Abnormal Psychology, 91*(3), 221-224.

Ellis, E. M., Calhoun, K. S., & Atkeson, B. M. (1980). Sexual dysfunctions in victims of rape: Victims may experience a loss of sexual arousal and frightening flashbacks even one year after the assault. *Women and Health, 5*, 39-47.

Feldman-Summers, S., Gordon, P., & Meagher, J. (1979). The impact of rape on sexual satisfaction. *Journal of Abnormal Psychology, 88*, 101-105.

Finkelhor, D. (1979). *Sexually victimized children.* New York: Free Press.

Finkelhor, D. (1984). *Child sexual abuse: New theory and research.* New York: Free Press.

Finkelhor, D. (1988). The trauma of child sexual abuse: Two models. In G. E. Wyatt & G. J. Powell (Eds.), *The lasting effects of child sexual abuse* (pp. 61-82). Newbury Park, CA: Sage.

Finkelhor, D. (1990). Early and long-term effects of child sexual abuse: An update. *Professional Psychology, 21*(5), 325-330.

Finkelhor, D., & Baron, L. (1986). High risk children. In D. Finkelhor and associates (Eds.), *Sourcebook on child sexual abuse* (pp. 60-88). Newbury Park, CA: Sage.

Finkelhor, D., & Browne, L. (1985). The traumatic impact of child sexual abuse: A conceptualization. *Journal of Orthopsychiatry, 55*, 530-541.

Finkelhor, D., Hotaling, G., Lewis, I. A., & Smith, C. (1990). Sexual abuse in a national survey of adult men and women: Prevalence, characteristics, and risk factors. *Child Abuse & Neglect, 14,* 19-28.

Fisher, S. (1973). *The female orgasm.* New York: Basic Books.

Fisher, S. (1980). Personality correlates of sexual behavior in black women. *Archives of Sexual Behavior, 9*(1), 27-35.

Flora, J. A., & Thorensen, C. E. (1988). Reducing the risk of AIDS in adolescents. *American Psychologist, 43*(11), 965-970.

Forrest, J. D. (1987). Unintended pregnancy among American women. *Family Planning Perspectives, 19,* 76-77.

Forrest, J. D., & Fordyce, R. R. (1989). U.S. women's contraceptive attitudes and practice: How have they changed in the 1980s? *Family Planning Perspectives, 21,* 112-118.

Fox, F. L. (1979). The family's influence on adolescent sexual behavior. *Child Today, 8,* 21-36.

Frank, E., Turner, S. M., & Duffy, B. (1979). Depressive symptoms in rape victims. *Journal of Affective Disorders, 1,* 269-277.

Frank, E., Turner, S. M., & Stewart, B. D. (1980). Initial response to rape: The impact of factors within the rape situation. *Journal of Behavioral Assessment, 2*(1), 39-53.

Friedrich, W. N. (1988). Behavior problems in sexually abused children: An adaptational perspective. In G. E. Wyatt & G. J. Powell (Eds.), *Lasting effects of child sexual abuse* (pp. 171-191). Newbury Park, CA: Sage.

Friedrich, W. N. (1990). *Psychotherapy of sexually abused children and their families.* New York: Norton.

Friedrich, W. N., Beilke, R., & Urquiza, A. J. (1987). Children from sexually abusive families: A behavioral comparison. *Journal of Interpersonal Violence, 2,* 391-402.

Friedrich, W. N., Grambsch, P., Broughton, D., Kuiper, J., & Beilke, R. L. (1991). Normative sexual behavior in children. *Pediatrics, 88*(3), 456-464.

Friedrich, W. N., Urquiza, A. J., & Beilke, R. L. (1986). Behavior problems in sexually abused young children. *Journal of Pediatric Psychology, 11*(1), 47-57.

Fromuth, M. E. (1983). *The long-term psychological impact of childhood sexual abuse.* Unpublished doctoral dissertation, Auburn University, Alabama.

Fromuth, M. E. (1986). The relationship of childhood sexual abuse with later psychological and sexual adjustment in a sample of college women. *Child Abuse & Neglect, 10,* 5-15.

Furstenberg, F. F., Jr., Moore, K. A., & Peterson, J. L. (1985). Sex education and sexual experience among adolescents. *American Journal of Public Health, 75,* 1331-1332.

Galbraith, G. (1964). *Variation in sexual behavior to word association stimuli under conditions of sexual arousal, guilt, and situational expectancies of censure.* Unpublished doctoral dissertation, Ohio State University, Columbus, OH.

Games, P. A. (1978). A four-factor structure for parametric tests on independent groups. *Psychological Bulletin, 85,* 661-672.

Gebhard, P. H. (1977). The acquisition of basic sex information. *Journal of Sex Research, 13*(3), 148-169.

Gebhard, P. H., & Johnson, A. B. (1979). *The Kinsey data: Marginal tabulations of the 1938-1963 interviews conducted by the Institute for Sex Research.* Philadelphia: W. B. Saunders.

George, L. K., Winfield, I., & Blazer, D. G. (1992). Socio-cultural factors in sexual assault: Comparison of two representative samples of women. *Journal of Social Issues, 48*(1), 105-125.

Gerrard, M. (1982). Sex, sex guilt, and contraceptive use. *Journal of Personality and Social Psychology, 42*(1), 153-158.

Gerrard, M. (1987). Sex, sex guilt, and contraceptive use revisited: The 1980s. *Journal of Personality and Social Psychology, 52*(95), 975-980.

Gerrard, M., & Gibbons, F. X. (1982). Sexual experience, sex guilt, and sexual moral reasoning. *Journal of Personality, 50*(3), 345-359.

Girelli, S. A., Resick, P. A., Marhoefer-Dvorak, S., & Hutter, C. K. (1986). Subjective distress and violence during rape: Their effects on long-term fear. *Victims and Violence, 1*(1), 35-46.

Goffman, E. (1967). *Interaction ritual.* Garden City, NY: Doubleday.

Gordon, S., Scales, P. & Everly, K. (1979). *The sexual adolescent* (2nd ed.). North Scituate, MA: Duxbury.

Greenwald, E., & Leitenberg, H. (1990). Posttraumatic stress disorder in a nonclinical and nonstudent sample of adult women sexually abused as children. *Journal of Interpersonal Violence, 5,* 217-228.

Gundersen, B. H., Melas, P. S., & Skar, J. E. (1981). Sexual behavior of preschool children: Teachers' observations. In L. L. Constantine & F. M. Martinson (Eds.), *Children and sex* (pp. 45-62). Boston: Little, Brown.

Guinan, M. E., & Hardy, A. (1987). Epidemiology of AIDS in women in the United States: 1981 through 1986. *Journal of the American Medical Association, 257,* 2039-2042.

Guinan, M. E., Wolinsky, S. M., & Reichman, R. C. (1985). Epidemiology of genital herpes simplex infection. *Epidemiologic Reviews, 7,* 127-146.

Harlow, L. L., & Newcomb, M. D. (1990). Towards a general hierarchical model of meaning and satisfaction in life. *Multivariate Behavioral Research, 25,* 387-405.

Heiman, J. R., Gladue, B. A., Roberts, C. W. & LoPiccolo, J. (1986). Historical and current factors discriminating sexually functional from sexually dysfunctional married couples. *Journal of Marital and Family Therapy, 12*(2), 163-174.

Helfer, R. E. (1991, October). Child abuse and neglect: Assessment, treatment, and prevention. *Child Abuse & Neglect, 15,* 5-15.

Henshaw, S. K., & Silverman, J. (1988). The characteristics and prior contraceptive use of U.S. abortion patients. *Family Planning Perspectives, 20*(4), 158-168.

Herman, J. L. (1981). *Father-daughter incest.* Cambridge, MA: Harvard University Press.

Herman, J., Russell, D., & Trocki, K. (1986). Long-term effects of incestuous abuse in childhood. *American Journal of Psychiatry, 143,* 1293-1296.

Hicks, D. R., Voeller, B., Resnick, L., Silva, S., Weeks, C. & Cassity, C. L. (1990). Chemical inactivation of human immunodeficiency virus type 1 (HIV-1 isolates HTLV-III and HB2) by spermicides, and other common chemical compounds. In B. Voeller, J. M. Reinisch, & M. Gottlieb (Eds.), *AIDS and sex: An integrated biomedical and biobehavioral approach* (pp. 365-370). New York: Oxford University Press.

Hofferth, S. L. (1990). Trends in adolescent sexual activity, contraception, and pregnancy in the United States. In J. Bankcroft & J. M. Reinisch (Eds.), *Adolescence and puberty* (pp. 217-233). New York: Oxford University Press.

Hofferth, S. L., Kahn, J. R., & Baldwin, W. (1987). Premarital sexual activity among U.S. teenage women over the past three decades. *Family Planning Perspectives, 19*(2), 46-53.

Holmbeck, G. N., & Hill, J. P. (1986). A path-analytic approach to the relations between parental traits and acceptance and adolescent adjustment. *Sex Roles, 14*(5-6), 315-334.

Holmes, M., & St. Lawrence, J. (1983). Treatment of rape-induced trauma: Proposed behavioral conceptualization and review of the literature. *Clinical Psychology Review, 3,* 417-433.

Holroyd, K. A., & Lazarus, R. S. (1982). Stress, coping, and somatic adaptation. In L. Goldberger & S. Breznitz (Eds.), *Handbook of stress: Theoretical and clinical aspects* (pp. 21-35). New York: Free Press.

Housley, K., Martin, S., McCoy, H., Greenhouse, P., Stigger, F., & Chopin, L. (1987). Self-esteem of adolescent females as related to race, economic status, and area of residence. *Perceptual and Motor Skills, 64*, 559-566.

Husaini, B. A., & Neff, J. A. (1980, October). *Mental health in rural Tennessee: Final report of an epidemiological study of mental health needs of rural counties in Tennessee.* Nashville: Tennessee State University, Health Research Projects.

Inazu, J. K., & Fox, G. L. (1980). Maternal influence on the sexual behavior of teen-age daughters. *Journal of Family Issues, 1*(1), 81-102.

Jackson, J. L., Calhoun, K. S., Amick, A. E., Maddever, H. M., & Habif, V. L. (1990). Young adult women who report childhood intrafamilial sexual abuse: Subsequent adjustment. *Archives of Sexual Behavior, 19*, 211-221.

Jacques, J. (1976). Self-esteem among Southeastern black American couples. *Journal of Black Studies, 7*(1), 11-28.

Jaffe, L. R., Seehaus, M., Wagner, C., & Leadbeater, B. J. (1988). Anal intercourse and knowledge of acquired immunodeficiency syndrome among minority-group female adolescents. *Journal of Pediatrics, 12*, 1005-1007.

Jobes, P. C. (1986). The relationship between traditional and innovative sex-role adaptations and sexual satisfaction among a homogeneous sample of middle-aged Caucasian women. *Journal of Sex and Marital Therapy, 12*(2), 146-156.

Jöreskog, K. G., & Sörbom, D. G. (1988). *LISREL 7: A guide to the program and applications.* Chicago: SPSS.

Kaats, G., & Davis, K. (1970). The dynamics of sexual behavior of college students. *Journal of Marriage and the Family, 32*, 390-400.

Kantrowitz, B., Hager, M., Cowley, G., Beachy, L., Rossi, M., Craffey, B., Annin, P., & Crandall, R. (1992, August). Teenagers and AIDS. *Newsweek*, pp. 44-49.

Kaufman, I., Peck, A., & Tagiuri, C. K. (1954). The family constellation and overt incestuous relations between father and daughter. *American Journal of Orthopsychiatry, 24*, 266-279.

Kelley, K. (1979). Socialization factors in contraceptive attitudes: Roles of affective responses, parental attitudes, and sexual experience. *The Journal of Sex Research, 15*(1), 6-20.

Kenney, A. M., Guardad, S., & Brown, L. (1989). Sex education and AIDS education in the schools. *Family Planning Perspectives, 21*, 56-64.

Kilpatrick, A. C. (1986). Some correlates of women's childhood sexual experiences: A retrospective study. *The Journal of Sex Research, 22*, 221-242.

Kilpatrick, A. C. (1987). Childhood sexual experiences: Problems and issues in studying long-range effects. *The Journal of Sex Research, 2*, 173-196.

Kilpatrick, D. G., Best, C. L., Amick-McMullen, A., Saunders, B. E., Sturgis, E., Resick, H., & Veronen, L. (1989). *Criminal victimization, post-traumatic stress disorder and substance abuse: A prospective study.* Washington, DC: Association for Advancement of Behavior Therapy.

Kilpatrick, D. G., Best, C. L., Veronen, L. J., Amick, A. E., Villeponteau, L. A., & Ruff, G. A. (1985). Mental health correlates of criminal victimization: A random community survey. *Journal of Consulting and Clinical Psychology, 53*, 866-873.

Kilpatrick, D. C., Veronen, L. J., & Resick, P. A. (1982). Psychological sequelae to rape: Assessment and treatment strategies. In D. M. Doleys, R. L. P. Meredith, & A. R. Ciminero (Eds.), *Behavioral medicine: Assessment and treatment strategies* (pp. 473-497). New York: Plenum.

Kinsey, A. C., Pomeroy, W. B., Martin, C. E., & Gebhard, P. H. (1953). *Sexual behavior in the human female.* Philadelphia: W. B. Saunders.

Kleeman, J. A. (1975). Genital self-stimulation in infant and toddler girls. In I. M. Marcus & J. J. Francis (Eds.), *Masturbation: From infancy to senescence* (pp. 77-106). New York: International Universities Press.

Kluft, R. P. (1984). Multiple personality in children. *Psychiatric Clinic of North America, 7*, 121-143.

Koblinsky, S. A., & Palmeter, J. G. (1984). Sex-role orientation, mother's expression of affection toward spouse, and college women's attitudes toward sexual behaviors. *The Journal of Sex Research, 20*(1), 32-43.

Kohn, M. L. (1969). *Class and conformity: A study in values.* Homewood, IL: Dorsey.

Kolodny, R. C. (1980, November). *Adolescent sexuality.* Paper presented at the Annual Convention of the Michigan Personnel and Guidance Association, Detroit, Michigan.

Koss, M. (1985). The hidden rape victim: Personality, attitudinal, and situational characteristics. *Psychology of Women Quarterly, 9*, 193-212.

Koss, M., & Burkhart, B. (1989). A conceptual analysis of rape victimization. *Psychology of Women Quarterly, 13*, 27-40.

Koss, M., Dinero, T., Seibel, C., & Cox, S. (1988). Stranger and acquaintance rape: Are there differences in the victim's experience? *Psychology of Women Quarterly, 12*, 1-24.

Koss, M. P., & Gidycz, C. A. (1985). Sexual experiences survey: Reliability and validity. *Journal of Consulting and Clinical Psychology, 42*, 162-170.

Kramer, T. L., & Green, B. L. (1991). Posttraumatic stress disorder as an early response to sexual assault. *Journal of Interpersonal Violence, 6*(2), 160-173.

Kutner, S. J. (1971). Sex guilt and the sexual behavior sequence. *The Journal of Sex Research, 7*, 107-115.

Lamb, C. (1963). *Personality correlates of humorous behavior following motivational arousal.* Unpublished master's thesis, Ohio State University, Columbus, OH.

Landis, J. (1956). Experiences of 500 children with adult sexual deviants. *Psychiatric Quarterly Supplement, 30*, 91-109.

Langfeldt, T. (1979). Child sexuality: Development and problems. In J. M. Samson (Ed.), *Childhood and sexuality: Proceedings of the International Symposium* (pp. 105-109). Montreal: Editions Etudes Vivantes.

Langfeldt, T. (1981). Processes in sexual development. In L. L. Constantine & F. M. Martinson (Eds.), *Children and sex* (pp. 37-44). Boston: Little, Brown.

Langmade, C. J. (1983). The impact of pre- and postpubertal onset of incest experiences in adult women as measured by sex anxiety, sex guilt, sexual satisfaction, and sexual behavior. *Dissertation Abstracts International, 44*, 917B.

Langston, R. D. (1973). Sex guilt and sex behavior in college students. *Journal of Personality Assessment, 37*, 467-472.

Laszlo, A. T., Burgess, A. W., & Grant, C. A. (1991). HIV counseling issues and victims of sexual assault. In A. W. Burgess (Ed.), *Rape and sexual assault* (3rd ed.) (pp. 221-232). New York: Garland.

Leitenberg, H., Greenwald, E., & Tarran, M. J. (1989). The relation between sexual activity among children during preadolescence and/or early adolescence and sexual behavior and sexual adjustment in young adulthood. *Archives of Sexual Behavior, 18*(4), 299-313.

Lewin, B. (1982). The adolescent boy and girl: First and other early experiences with intercourse from a representative sample of Swedish school adolescents. *Archives of Sexual Behavior, 11*, 417-428.

Lewis, R. A. (1973). Parents and peers: Socialization agents in the coital behavior of young adults. *Journal of Sex Research, 9*(2), 156-170.

Lewis, R. J., & Janda, L. H. (1988). The relationship between adult sexual adjustment and childhood experiences regarding exposure to nudity, sleeping in the parental bed, and parental attitudes toward sexuality. *Archives of Sexual Behavior, 17,* 349-362.

Libby, R. W., Gray, L., & White, M. (1978). A test and reformulation of reference group and role correlates of premarital sexual permissiveness theory. *Journal of Marriage and the Family, 40,* 79-92.

Lindberg, F. H., & Distad, L. J. (1985). Post-traumatic stress disorders in women who experienced childhood incest. *Child Abuse & Neglect, 9,* 329-334.

Long, B. H. (1986). Parental discord vs. family structure: Effects of divorce on the self-esteem of daughters. *Journal of Youth and Adolescence, 15*(1), 19-27.

Long, P. J., & Jackson, J. L. (1991). Children sexually abused by multiple perpetrators: Familial risk factors and abuse characteristics. *Journal of Interpersonal Violence, 6*(2), 147-159.

Love, R. E., Sloan, L. R., & Schmidt, M. J. (1976). Viewing pornography and sex guilt: The priggish, the prudent, and the profligate. *Journal of Consulting and Clinical Psychology, 44*(4), 624-629.

Lusk, R., & Waterman, J. (1986). Effects of sexual abuse on children. In K. MacFarlane & J. Waterman (Eds.), *Sexual abuse of young children: Evaluation and treatment* (pp. 101-118). New York: Guilford.

Lustig, N., Dresser, J. W., Spellman, S. W., & Murray, T. B. (1966). Incest: A family group survival pattern. *Archives of General Psychiatry, 14,* 31-40.

MacCallum, R. C. (1986). Specification searches in covariance structure modeling. *Psychological Bulletin, 100,* 107-120.

MacCallum, R. C., Roznowski, M., & Necowitz, L. B. (1992). Model modifications in covariance structure analysis: The problem of capitalization on chance. *Psychological Bulletin, 111,* 490-504.

MacDonald, N. E., Wells, G. A., Fisher, W. A., Warren, W. K., King, M. A., Doherty, J. A., & Bowie, W. R. (1990). High-risk STD/HIV behavior among college students. *Journal of the American Medical Association, 263*(23), 3155-3159.

Mackey, T. F., Hacker, S. S., Weissfeld, L. A., Ambrose, N. C., Fisher, M. G., & Zobel, D. L. (1991). Comparative effects of sexual assault on sexual functioning of child sexual abuse survivors and others. *Issues in Mental Health Nursing, 12,* 89-112.

Maltz, W. (1988). Identifying and treating the sexual repercussions of incest: A couples therapy approach. *Journal of Sex and Marital Therapy, 14*(2), 142-170.

Marhoefer-Dvorak, S., Resick, P. A., Hutter, C. K., & Girelli, S. A. (1988). Single- versus multiple-incident rape victims. *Journal of Interpersonal Violence, 3*(2), 145-160.

Marsiglio, W., & Mott, F. L. (1986). The impact of sex education on sexual activity, contraceptive use and premarital pregnancy among American teenagers. *Family Planning Perspectives, 18,* 151-162.

Martinson, F. M. (1977). Eroticism in childhood: A sociological perspective. In E. K. Oremland & J. D. Oremland (Eds.), *The sexual and gender development of young children: The role of the educator* (pp. 73-82). Cambridge, MA: Ballinger.

Martinson, F. M. (1980). Child sexuality: Trend and consequences. In J. M. Samson (Ed.), *Childhood and sexuality: Proceedings of the international symposium* (pp. 41-55). Montreal: Editions Etudes Vivants.

Masters, W. H., & Johnson, V. E. (1966). *Human sexual response.* Boston, MA: Little, Brown.

Masters, W. H., & Johnson, V. E. (1970). *Human sexual inadequacy.* Boston, MA: Little, Brown.

Masters, W. H., & Johnson, V. E. (1979). *Homosexuality in perspective.* Boston, MA: Little, Brown.

Masters, W. H., Johnson, V. E., & Kolodny, R. C. (1992). *Human sexuality* (4th ed.). New York: Harper-Collins.

McCahill, T., Meyer, L., & Fischman, A. (1979). *The aftermath of rape.* Lexington, MA: D. C. Heath.

McCarthy, J. (1981). Social consequences of childbearing during adolescence. *Birth Defects, 17,* 107-122.

McCormick, N. B. (1979). Come ons and put offs. Unmarried students' strategies for having and avoiding sexual intercourse. *Psychology of Women Quarterly, 4,* 194-211.

McCormick, N., Izzo, A., & Folcik, J. (1985). Adolescents' values, sexuality, and contraception in a rural New York county. *Adolescence, 20,* 385-395.

McGee, L., & Newcomb, M. D. (1992). General deviance syndrome: Expanded hierarchical evaluations at four ages from early adolescence to adulthood. *Journal of Consulting & Clinical Psychology, 60,* 766-776.

McNab, W. (1976). Sexual attitude development in children and the parents' role. *Journal of School Health, 46*(9), 537-542.

Meiselman, K. (1978). *Incest: A psychological study of causes and effects with treatment recommendations.* San Francisco: Jossey-Bass.

Mendelsohn, M. J., & Mosher, D. L. (1979). Effects of sex guilt and premarital sexual permissiveness on role-played sex education and moral attitudes. *The Journal of Sex Research, 15*(3), 174-183.

Meyer, B., & Taylor, S. (1986). Adjustment to rape. *Journal of Personality and Social Psychology, 50,* 1226-1243.

MIRA (1987). Proceedings: U.S. minorities and the Third International Conference on AIDS. Atlanta, GA, Summer.

Mirande, A. M. (1968). Reference group theory and adolescent sexual behavior. *Journal of Marriage and the Family, 30,* 572-578.

Money, J. (1976). Childhood: The last frontier in sex research. *Sciences, 16*(6), 12-15.

Money, J., & Ehrhardt, A. A. (1972). *Man and woman: Boy and girl: The differentiation and dimorphism of gender identity from conception to maturity.* Baltimore, MD: The John Hopkins University Press.

Mooijaart, A., & Bentler, P. M. (1991). Robustness of normal theory statistics in structural equation models. *Statistic Neerlandica, 45,* 159-171.

Morokoff, P. J. (1986). Volunteer bias in the psychophysiological study of female sexuality. *The Journal of Sex Research, 22*(1), 35-51.

Morrison, D. M. (1985). Adolescent contraceptive behavior: A review. *Psychological Bulletin, 8,* 538-568.

Mosher, D. L. (1968). Measurement of guilt in females by self-report inventories. *Journal of Consulting and Clinical Psychology, 32*(6), 690-695.

Mosher, D. L. (1973). Sex differences, sex experience, sex guilt, and explicitly sexual films. *Journal of Social Issues, 29*(3), 95-112.

Mosher, D. L. (1979). Sex guilt and sex myths in college men and women. *The Journal of Sex Research, 15*(3), 224-234.

Mosher, D. L., & Cross, H. J. (1971). Sex guilt and premarital sexual experiences of college students. *Journal of Consulting and Clinical Psychology, 36*(1), 27-32.

Mosher, D. L., & Vonderheide, S. G. (1985). Contributions of sex guilt and masturbation guilt to women's contraceptive attitudes and use. *The Journal of Sex Research, 21*(1), 24-39.

Mott, F. L. (1984). *The patterning of female teenage sex behaviors and attitudes.* Revision of paper presented at the annual meeting of the American Public Health Association, Anaheim, CA.

Murphy, G. (1947). *Personality: A biosocial approach to origin and structure.* New York: Harper & Row.

Murphy, S. M., Kilpatrick, D. G., Amick-McMullan, A., Veronen, L. J., Paduhovich, J., Best, C. L., Villeponteaux, L. A., & Saunders, B. E. (1988). Current psychological functioning of child sexual assault survivors: A community study. *Journal of Interpersonal Violence*, *3*(1), 55-79.

Murstein, B. I., Chalpin, M. J., Heard, K. V., & Vyse, S. A. (1989). Sexual behavior, drugs, and relationship patterns on a college campus over thirteen years. *Adolescence*, *24*, 125-139.

Murstein, B. I., & Holden, C. C. (1979). Sexual behavior and correlates among college students. *Adolescence*, *14*, 625-639.

Muthén, B. (1984). A general structural equation model with dichotomous, ordered categorical, and continuous latent variable indicators. *Psychometrika*, *49*, 115-130.

Muthén, B. (1987). LISCOMP: Analysis of linear structural relations using a comprehensive measurement model. Mooresville, IN: Scientific Software.

National Academy of Science (1986). *Confronting AIDS: Directions for public health, health care, and research.* Washington, DC: National Academy Press.

Neff, J. A., & Husaini, B. (1980). Race, socioeconomic status, and psychiatric impairment: A research note. *Journal of Community Psychology*, *8*, 16-19.

Newcomb, M. D. (1984). Sexual behavior, responsiveness, and attitudes among women: A test of two theories. *Journal of Sex & Marital Therapy*, *10*(4), 272-286.

Newcomb, M. D. (1985). Sexual experience among men and women: Associations within three independent samples. *Psychological Reports*, *56*, 603-614.

Newcomb, M. D. (1986). Sexual behavior of cohabitors: A comparison of three independent samples. *The Journal of Sex Research*, *22*(4), 492-513.

Newcomb, M. D. (1990). What structural modeling techniques can tell us about social support. In I. G. Sarason, B. R. Sarason, and G. R. Pierce (Eds.), *Social support: An interactional view* (pp. 26-63). New York: John Wiley.

Newcomb, M. D. (1992). Understanding the multidimensional nature of drug use and abuse: The role of consumption, risk factors, and protective factors. In M. D. Glantz and R. Pickens (Eds.), *Vulnerability to drug abuse* (pp. 255-298). Washington, DC: American Psychological Association.

Newcomb, M. D. (in press). Families, peers, and adolescent alcohol abuse: A paradigm to study multiple causes, mechanisms, and outcomes. In R. Zucker, G. Boyd, & J. Howard (Eds.), *Development of alcohol problems: Exploring the biopsychosocial matrix of risk.* Rockville, MD: NIAAA.

Newcomb, M. D., & Bentler, P. M. (1983). Dimensions of subjective female orgasmic responsiveness. *Journal of Personality and Social Psychology*, *44*, 862-873.

Newcomb, M. D., & Bentler, P. M. (1988a). The impact of family context, deviant attitudes, and emotional distress on adolescent drug use: Longitudinal latent variable analyses of mothers and their children. *Journal of Research in Personality*, *22*, 154-176.

Newcomb, M. D., & Bentler, P. M. (1988b). *Consequences of adolescent drug use: Impact on the lives of young adults.* Newbury Park, CA: Sage.

Newcomb, M. D., & Bentler, P. M. (1988c). Impact of adolescent drug use and social support on problems of young adults: A longitudinal study. *Journal of Abnormal Psychology*, *97*, 54-75.

Newcomb, M. D., & Felix-Ortiz, M. (in press). Multiple protective and risk factors for drug use and abuse: Cross-sectional and prospective findings. *Journal of Personality and Social Psychology*.

Newcomb, M. D., Huba, G. J., & Bentler, P. M. (1983, April). *Patterns of adolescent sexual behavior, competence, attitudes and desire.* Paper presented at meeting of the Western Psychological Association, San Francisco, CA.

Newcomb, M. D., Huba, G. J. & Bentler, P. M. (1986). Determinants of sexual and dating behavior among adolescents. *Journal of Personality and Social Psychology*, *44*, 862-873.

Newcomb, M. D., & McGee, L. (1991). The influence of sensation seeking on general and specific problem behaviors from adolescence to young adulthood. *Journal of Personality and Social Psychology, 61*, 614-628.

Newson, J., & Newson, E. (1968). *Four years old in an urban community.* London: Allen & Unwin.

Oppenheimer, R., Howells, K., Palmer, R. L., & Chaloner, D. A. (1985). Adverse sexual experience in childhood and clinical eating disorder: A preliminary description. *Journal of Psychiatric Research, 19*, 357-361.

Orlando, J. A., & Koss, M. P. (1983). The effect of sexual victimization on sexual satisfaction: A study of the negative-association hypothesis. *Journal of Abnormal Psychology, 92*(1), 104-106.

Orr, D. P., & Downes, M. C. (1985). Self-concept of adolescent sexual abuse victims. *Journal of Youth and Adolescence, 14*(5), 401-409.

Orr, M. T. (1982). Sex education and contraceptive education in U.S. public high schools. *Family Planning Perspectives, 14*, 304-313.

Ostrov, E., Offer, D., Howard, K. I., Kaufman, B., & Meyer, H. (1985). Adolescent sexual behavior. *Medical Aspects of Human Sexuality, 19*, 28-36.

Padian, N., Marquis, L., Francis, D. P., Anderson, R. E., Rutherford, G. W., O'Malley, P. M., & Winkelstein, W. (1987). Male-to-female transmission of human immunodeficiency virus. *Journal of American Medical Association, 258*, 788-790.

Panzarine, S., & Santelli, J. (1987). Risk factors in early sexual activity and early unplanned pregnancy. *Maryland Medical Journal, 36*(11), 927-931.

Peters, J. (1977). The Philadelphia victim project. In D. Chapell, R. Geis, & G. Geis (Eds.), *Forcible rape: The crime, the victim, and the offender* (pp. 339-355). New York: Columbia University Press.

Peters, S. D. (1984). *The relationship between childhood sexual victimization and adult depression among Afro-American and white American women.* Unpublished doctoral dissertation, University of California, Los Angeles.

Peters, S. D. (1988). Child sexual abuse and later psychological problems. In G. E. Wyatt & G. J. Powell (Eds.), *Lasting effects of child sexual abuse* (pp. 101-117). Newbury Park, CA: Sage.

Pinney, E. M., Gerrard, M., & Denney, N. W. (1987). The Pinney Sexual Satisfaction Inventory. *The Journal of Sex Research, 23*, 233-251.

Planned Parenthood Federation of America. (1986). *American teens speak: Sex, myths, TV, and birth control* (The Planned Parenthood Poll, Project No. 864012). New York: Louis Harris and Associates.

Porter, F. C., Blick, L. C., & Sgroi, S. M. (1982). Treatment of the sexually abused child. In S. M. Sgroi (Ed.), *Handbook of clinical intervention in child sexual abuse* (pp. 109-145). Lexington, MA: Lexington Books.

Powell, G. J. (1975). *Social and emotional problems of minority-group children.* Handbook for Los Angeles School District, Los Angeles, CA.

Putnam, F. (1985). Dissociation as a response to extreme trauma. In R. P. Kluft (Ed.), *Childhood antecedents of multiple personality* (pp. 66-97). Washington, DC: American Psychiatric Press.

Putnam, F. (1989). *Diagnosis and treatment of multiple personality disorder.* New York: Guilford.

Putnam, F. W., Guroff, J. J., Silberman, E. K., Barban, L., & Post, R. M. (1986). The clinical phenomenology of multiple personality disorder: Review of 100 recent cases. *Journal of Clinical Psychology, 47*, 285-292.

Queen's Bench Foundation. (1975). *Rape victimization study.* San Francisco: Queen's Bench Foundation.

Reinisch, J. M., Hill, C. A., Sanders, S. A., & Ziemba-Davis, M. (1990). Sexual behavior among heterosexual college students. *Focus, 5*(4), 3.

Reinisch, J. M., Sanders, S. A., & Ziemba-Davis, M. (1988). The study of sexual behavior in relation to the transmission of human immunodeficiency virus: Caveats and recommendations. *American Psychologist, 43*(11), 921-927.

Reinisch, J. M., Sanders, S. A., & Ziemba-Davis, M. (in press). Self-labeled lesbianism, sexual behavior, and knowledge of AIDS: Implications for biomedical research and education programs. In S. J. Blumenthal, A. Eichler, & G. Weissman (Eds.), *Women and AIDS: Promoting healthy behaviors*. Proceedings of workshop held by the National Institute of Mental Health and National Institute of Drug Abuse.

Reiss, I. L. (1967). *The social context of premarital sexual permissiveness*. New York: Holt, Rinehart & Winston.

Resick, P. (1983). The rape reaction: Research findings and implications for intervention. *The Behavior Therapist, 6*, 129-132.

Rew, L. (1989). Long-term effects of childhood sexual exploitation. *Issues in Mental Health Nursing, 10*, 229-244.

Rimsza, M. E., Berg, R. A., & Locke, C. (1988). Sexual abuse: Somatic and emotional reactions. *Child Abuse and Neglect, 12*, 201-208.

Rosenberg, M. (1979). *Concerning the self*. New York: Basic Books.

Rosenberg, M., & Simmons, R. G. (1971). *Black and white self-esteem: The urban school child*. Washington, DC: American Psychological Association.

Rubenstein, C., & Tavris, C. (1987, September). Special survey results. *Redbook*, pp. 147-149, 214-215.

Ruch, L. O., & Chandler, S. (1983). Sexual assault trauma during the acute phase: An exploratory model and multivariate analysis. *Journal of Health and Social Behavior, 24*, 174-185.

Ruch, L. O., & Leon, J. J. (1983). Sexual assault trauma and trauma change. *Women and Health, 8*(4), 5-21.

Russell, D. E. H. (1983). The incidence and prevalence of intrafamilial and extrafamilial sexual abuse of female children. *Child Abuse & Neglect, 7*, 133-146.

Russell, D. E. H. (1986). *The secret trauma: Incest in the lives of girls and women*. New York: Basic Books.

Russell, D. E. H., Schurman, R. A., & Trocki, K. (1988). The long-term effects of incestuous abuse: A comparison of Afro-American and white American victims. In G. E. Wyatt & G. J. Powell (Eds.), *Lasting effects of child sexual abuse* (pp. 119-134). Newbury Park, CA: Sage.

Rutter, M. (1971). Normal psychosexual development. *Journal of Child Psychology and Psychiatry, 11*, 259-283.

Sack, A. R., Keller, J. F., & Hinkle, D. E. (1984). Premarital sexual intercourse: A test of the effects of peer group, religiosity, and sexual guilt. *The Journal of Sex Research, 20*(2), 168-185.

Sales, E., Baum, M., & Shore, B. (1984). Victim readjustment following assault. *Journal of Social Issues, 40*(1), 117-136.

Satorra, A., & Bentler, P. M. (1990). Model conditions for asymptotic robustness in the analysis of linear relations. *Computational Statistics and Data Analysis, 10*, 235-249.

Saucier, J. F., & Ambert, A. M. (1986). Adolescents' perception of self and of immediate environment by parental marital status: A controlled study. *Canadian Journal of Psychiatry, 31*, 505-512.

Scheier, L. M., & Newcomb, M. D. (in press). Multiple dimensions of affective and cognitive disturbance: Latent variable models in a community sample. *Psychological Assessment: A Journal of Consulting and Clinical Psychology*.

Sedney, M. A., & Brooks, B. (1984). Brief communication: Factors associated with a history of childhood sexual experience in a nonclinical female population. *Journal of the American Academy of Child Psychiatry, 23*(2), 215-218.

Seidner, A. L., & Calhoun, K. S. (1984, August). *Child sexual abuse: Factors related to differential adult adjustment*. Paper presented at Second National Conference for Family Violence Researchers, Durham, NH.

Shelley, S. I. (1981). Adolescent attitudes as related to perception of parents and sex education. *Journal of Sex Research, 17*(4), 350-367.

Siegel, J. M., Golding, J. M., Stein, J. A., Burnam, M. A., & Sorenson, S. B. (1990). Reactions to sexual assault: A community study. *Journal of Interpersonal Violence, 5*(2), 229-246.

Siegel, J. M., Sorenson, S. B., Golding, J. M., Burnam, M. A., & Stein, J. A. (1987). The prevalence of childhood sexual assault: The Los Angeles epidemiologic catchment area project. *American Journal of Epidemiology, 126*, 1141-1153.

Silverman, J., Torres, A., & Forrest, J. D. (1987). Barriers to contraceptive services. *Family Planning Perspectives, 3*, 94-102.

Simon, W., Berger, A. S., & Gagnon, J. H. (1972). Beyond anxiety and fantasy: The coital experiences of college youth. *Journal of Youth and Adolescence, 1*, 203-222.

Slane, S., & Morrow, L. (1981). Race differences in feminism and guilt. *Psychological Reports, 49*, 45-46.

Sorensen, R. C. (1973). *Adolescent sexuality in contemporary America*. New York: World Publishing.

Sorenson, S. B, Stein, J. A., Siegel, J. M., Golding, J. M., & Burnam, M. A. (1987). The prevalence of adult sexual assault: The Los Angeles epidemiologic catchment area project. *American Journal of Epidemiology, 126*, 1154-1164.

Spanier, G. B. (1977). Sources of sex info and premarital sex behavior. *Journal of Sex Research, 13*(2), 73-88.

Stacy, A. W., Newcomb, M. D., & Bentler, P. M. (in press). Interactive and higher-order effects of social influences on drug use. *Journal of Health and Social Behavior.*

Strasburger, V. C. (1985). Sex, drugs, rock 'n' roll: Are solutions possible? — A commentary. *Pediatrics* (supplement), pp. 704-712.

Summit, R. C. (1983). The child sexual abuse accommodation syndrome. *Child Abuse & Neglect, 7*, 177-193.

Summit, R. C. (1988). Hidden victims, hidden pain: Societal avoidance of child sexual abuse. In G. E. Wyatt & G. J. Powell (Eds.), *Lasting effects of child sexual abuse* (pp. 39-60). Newbury Park, CA: Sage.

Tanaka, J. (1987). How big is big enough: The sample size issue in structural equation models with latent variables. *Child Development, 58*, 134-146.

Taylor, A. (1992). AIDS in communities of color: We won't let the center burn! *Minority Health News, 3*(3), 1-2.

Tharinger, D. (1990). Impact of child sexual abuse on developing sexuality. *Professional Psychology: Research and Practice, 21*(5), 331-337.

Thornton, A., & Camburn, D. (1987). The influence of the family on premarital sexual attitudes and behavior. *Demography, 24*(3), 323-340.

Tietze, C., Forrest, J. D., & Henshaw, S. K. (1988). United States of America. In P. Sachdev (Ed.), *International handbook on abortion* (pp. 474-483). Westport, CT: Greenwood.

Tormes, Y. (1968). *Child victims of incest*. Denver: American Humane Association.

Tsai, M., Feldman-Summers, S., & Edgar, M. (1979). Childhood molestation: Variables related to differential impacts on psychosexual functioning in adult women. *Journal of Abnormal Psychology, 88*(4), 407-417.

Tsai, M., & Wagner, N. N. (1978). Therapy groups for women sexually molested as children. *Archives of Sexual Behavior, 7*, 417-427.

Tufts New England Medical Center. (1984). Sexually exploited children: Service and research project. *Final report for the Office of Juvenile Justice and Delinquency Prevention.* Washington, DC: Division of Child Psychiatry.

Upchurch, M. L. (1978). Sex guilt and contraceptive use. *Journal of Sex Education and Therapy, 4*, 27-31.

Veronen, L., & Kilpatrick, D. (1980). Self-reported fears of rape victims: A preliminary investigation. *Behavior Modification, 4*, 383-396.

Voeller, B. (1988, December). *Heterosexual anorectal intercourse: An AIDS risk factor* (Mariposa Occasional Paper No. 10). Topanga, CA: Mariposa Education and Research Foundation.

Voeller, B. (1991). AIDS and heterosexual anal intercourse. *Archives of Sexual Behavior, 20*, 233-276.

Ware, J. E., Davies-Avery, A., Brook, R. H., & Johnston, S. A. (1978). *Associations among psychological well-being and other health constructs.* Unpublished manuscript.

Weinstein, M., & Thornton, A. (1989). Mother-child relations and adolescent sexual attitudes and behavior. *Demography, 26*, 563-578.

Weis, D. L. (1983). Affective reactions of women to their initial experience of coitus. *The Journal of Sex Research, 19*(3), 209-237.

Westerlund, E. (1992). *Women's sexuality after childhood incest.* New York: Norton.

Wheeler, R. J., & Berliner, L. (1988). Treating the effects of sexual abuse on children. In G. E. Wyatt & G. J. Powell (Eds.), *Lasting effects of child sexual abuse* (pp. 227-247). Newbury Park, CA: Sage.

Woody, J. (1973). Contemporary sex education: Attitudes and implications for childbearing. *Journal of School Health, 43*(4), 241-246.

Wyatt, G. E. (1982). The sexual experience of Afro-American women: A middle income sample. In M. Kirkpatrick (Ed.), *Women's sexual experience: Explorations of the dark continent* (pp. 17-39). New York: Plenum.

Wyatt, G. E. (1985). The sexual abuse of Afro-American and white American women in childhood. *Child Abuse and Neglect: The International Journal, 9*, 507-519.

Wyatt, G. E. (1988a). The relationship between child sexual abuse and adolescent sexual functioning in Afro-American and white American women. *Annals of the New York Academy of Sciences, 528*, 111-122.

Wyatt, G. E. (1988b). The relationship between the cumulative impact of a range of child sexual abuse experiences and women's psychological well-being. *Victimology: An International Journal, 11*(4).

Wyatt, G. E. (1989). Re-examining factors predicting Afro-American and white American women's age of first coitus. *Archives of Sexual Behavior, 18*, 271-298.

Wyatt, G. E. (1990a). Maximizing appropriate populations and responses for sex research. In B. Voeller, J. M. Reinisch, & M. Gottlieb (Eds.), *AIDS and sex: An integrated biomedical and biobehavioral approach* (pp. 81-96). New York: Oxford University Press.

Wyatt, G. E. (1990b). The aftermath of child sexual abuse of African American and white American women: The victim's experience. *Journal of Family Violence, 5*(1), 61-81.

Wyatt, G. E. (1990c). Sexual abuse of ethnic minority children: Identifying dimensions of victimization. *Professional Psychology, 21*, 338-343.

Wyatt, G. E. (1990d). Changing influences on adolescent sexuality over the past forty years. In J. Bancroft & J. M. Reinisch (Eds.), *Adolescence and Puberty* (pp. 182-206). New York: Oxford University Press.

Wyatt, G. E. (1991a). Ethnic and cultural differences in women's sexual behavior. In S. Blumenthal, A. Eichler, & G. Weissman (Eds.), *Women and AIDS: Promoting healthy behavior.* Washington, DC: Department of Health and Human Services.

Wyatt, G. E. (1991b). Examining ethnicity versus race in AIDS-related sex research. *Social Science Medicine, 33*(1), 37-45.

Wyatt, G. E. (1992). The sociocultural context of African American and white American women's rape. *Journal of Social Issues, 48*(1), 77-91.

Wyatt, G. E., & Dunn, K. M. (1991). Examining predictors of sex guilt in multiethnic samples of women. *Archives of Sexual Behavior, 20*, 471-485.

Wyatt, G. E., Guthrie, D., & Notgrass, C. M. (1992). Differential effects of women's child sexual abuse and subsequent sexual revictimization. *Journal of Consulting and Clinical Psychology, 60*, 1-7.

Wyatt, G. E., Lawrence, J., Vodounon, A., & Mickey, M. R. (1992). The Wyatt Sex History Questionnaire: A structured interview for female sexual history taking. *Journal of Child Sexual Abuse 1*(4), 51-68.

Wyatt, G. E., & Lyons-Rowe, S. (1990). Afro-American women's sexual satisfaction as a dimension of their sex roles. *Sex Roles, 22*, 509-524.

Wyatt, G. E., & Mickey, R. M. (1988). Ameliorating effects of child sexual abuse: An exploratory study of support by parents and others. *The Journal of Interpersonal Violence, 2*, 403-414.

Wyatt, G. E., & Newcomb, M. (1990). Internal and external mediators of women's sexual abuse in childhood. *Journal of Consulting and Clinical Psychology, 58*, 758-767.

Wyatt, G. E., Newcomb, M., & Notgrass, C. M. (1990). Internal and external mediators of women's rape experiences. *Psychology of Women Quarterly, 14*, 153-176.

Wyatt, G. E., Newcomb, M., & Skidmore, S. (1992). *Long-term effects of incest on self-esteem: Mediating and moderating factors.* Unpublished manuscript.

Wyatt, G. E., Notgrass, C., & Gordon, G. (in press). The effects of African American women's sexual victimization: Strategies for prevention. *Prevention in Human Services.*

Wyatt, G. E., & Peters, S. D. (1986a). Methodological considerations in research on the prevalence of child sexual abuse. *Child Abuse and Neglect: The International Journal, 10*, 241-251.

Wyatt, G. E., & Peters, S. D. (1986b). Issues in the definition of child sexual abuse in prevalence research. *Child Abuse and Neglect, 10*, 231-240.

Wyatt, G. E., Peters, S. D., & Guthrie, D. (1988a). Kinsey revisited, Part I: Comparisons of the sexual socialization and sexual behavior of white women over 33 years. *Archives of Sexual Behavior, 17*, 201-239.

Wyatt, G. E., Peters, S. D., & Guthrie, D. (1988b). Kinsey revisited, Part II: Comparisons of the sexual socialization and sexual behavior of black women over 33 years. *Archives of Sexual Behavior, 17*, 289-332.

Yamaguchi, K., & Kandel, D. (1985). On the resolution of role incompatibility: A life event history analysis of family roles and marijuana use. *American Journal of Sociology, 90*, 1284-1325.

Yancey, W. L., Rigsby, L., & McCarthy, J. D. (1972). Social position and self-evaluation: The relative importance of race. *American Journal of Sociology, 78*, 338-359.

Yarber, W. L. & Greer, J. M. (1986). The relationship between the sexual attitudes of parents and their college daughters' or sons' sexual attitudes and sexual behavior. *Journal of School Health, 56*(2) 68-72.

Zabin, L. S., Hirsch, M. B., Smith, E. A., Streett, R., & Hardy, J. B. (1986). Evaluation of a pregnancy prevention program for urban teenagers. *Family Planning Perspectives, 18*(3), 119-126.

Zelnik, M. (1979). Sex education and knowledge of pregnancy risk among U.S. teenage women. *Family Planning Perspectives, 11*, 355-357.

Zelnik, M. (1983). Sexual activity among adolescents: Perspective of a decade. In E. R. McAnarney (Ed.), *Premature adolescent pregnancy and parenthood* (pp. 21-33). New York: Grune & Stratton.

Zelnik, M., & Kantner, J. F. (1972). Sexuality, contraception, and pregnancy among young unwed females in the United States. In F. Westoff & Parke, Jr. (Eds.), *Research reports* (Vol. 1). U.S. Commission on Population Growth and the American Future. Washington, DC: Government Printing Office.

Zelnik, M., & Kantner, J. F. (1979). Reasons for non-use of contraception by sexually active women aged 15-19. *Family Planning Perspectives, 11*, 289-296.

Zelnik, M., & Kantner, J. F. (1980). Sexual activity, contraception use and pregnancy among metropolitan-area teenagers: 1971-1979. *Family Planning Perspectives, 12*, 230-238.

Zelnik, M., Kantner, J. F., & Ford, K. (1981). *Sex and pregnancy in adolescence.* Beverly Hills, CA: Sage.

Zelnik, M., & Kim, Y. J. (1982). Sex education and its association with teenage sexual activity, pregnancy, and contraceptive use. *Family Planning Perspectives, 14*, 117-126.

Zierler, S., Feingold, L., Laufer, D., Velentgas, P., Kantrowitz-Gordon, I., & Mayer, K. (1991). Adult survivors of childhood sexual abuse and subsequent risk of HIV infection. *Public Health, 81*, 572-575.

Author Index

Author Index

Subject Index

About the Authors

Gail Elizabeth Wyatt (Ph.D.) is a licensed Clinical Psychologist and Professor in the Department of Psychiatry and Biobehavioral Sciences at the University of California at Los Angeles (UCLA) and a Research Scientist for the National Institute of Mental Health. She also is a sex educator, certified sex therapist, diplomate and Founding Clinical Fellow of the American Academy of Clinical Sexologists, and a Fellow of the American Psychological Association. She is principal investigator of research projects examining AIDS-related sexual decision making in Jamaica among men and women and among African-American, Latina, and European-American women in Los Angeles County. Her numerous scientific publications and books involve ethnic and cultural considerations and methodological issues in research and the effects of sexual victimization on women. Her interests are in broadening understanding of human sexuality and decision making within a cultural context.

Michael D. Newcomb (Ph.D.) is a licensed Clinical Psychologist, Professor and Chair of the Division of Counseling and Educational Psychology at the University of Southern California, and a Research Psychologist in the Psychology Department at UCLA. He is principal investigator on several grants from the National Institute on Drug Abuse. He has published more than 100 papers and chapters and written two books on drug problems: *Consequences of Adolescent Drug Use* (with P. M. Bentler; Sage) and *Drug Use in the Workplace*. His interests include etiology and consequences of adolescent drug abuse; structural equation modeling, methodology, and multivariate analysis; human sexuality; health psychology; attitudes and affect related to nuclear war; and cohabitation, marriage, and divorce. He has served on several national review and advisory committees for such groups as the National Academy of Science, National Institute on Drug Abuse, Office of Substance Abuse Prevention, and various research centers.

Monika H. Riederle (M.A.) is a Research Associate at the Neuropsychiatric Institute, UCLA, who has coauthored several articles on sexual abuse, sexual harassment, and abortion. She is in clinical practice as a psychological assistant and is currently conducting her dissertation research on father-daughter incest and intimacy. Her major interests are in the areas of childhood sexual abuse, intimacy in relationships, psychodynamic theory, and multiple personality disorder.

Cindy M. Notgrass is a former Research Associate at the Neuropsychiatric Institute at UCLA. She holds a master's degree in clinical psychology and is interested in the sexual experiences of women. She has coauthored several papers in the areas of child sexual abuse, rape, sexual revictimization, and sexual harassment among multiethnic samples of women. She is currently working as a Research Associate in the Department of Psychiatry at Vanderbilt University, investigating the effects of sexual revictimization of life attitudes.

Jennifer Lawrence received the M.P.H. and M.D. degrees from UCLA. She is currently a Family Practice resident in Santa Rosa, California.

Family Context

Childhood

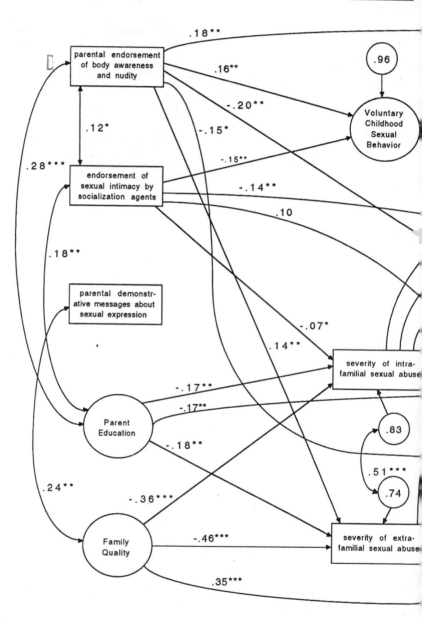